CEO LEADERSHIP

CEO LEADERSHIP

Navigating the New Era in
Corporate Governance

THOMAS A. COLE

THE UNIVERSITY OF CHICAGO PRESS

CHICAGO AND LONDON

The University of Chicago Press, Chicago 60637
The University of Chicago Press, Ltd., London
© 2019 by Thomas A. Cole
Published 2019
Printed in the United States of America

28 27 26 25 24 23 22 21 20 19   1 2 3 4 5

ISBN-13: 978-0-226-66516-0 (cloth)
ISBN-13: 978-0-226-66533-7 (e-book)
DOI: https://doi.org/10.7208/chicago/978022665337.001.0001

Library of Congress Cataloging-in-Publication Data

Names: Cole, Thomas A. (Lawyer), author.
Title: CEO leadership : navigating the new era in corporate governance / Thomas A. Cole.
Description: Chicago ; London : The University of Chicago Press, 2019. | Includes index.
Identifiers: LCCN 2019021378 | ISBN 9780226665160 (cloth) |
    ISBN 9780226665337 (ebook)
Subjects: LCSH: Corporate governance.
Classification: LCC HD2741 .C6233 2019 | DDC 658.4/22—dc23
LC record available at https://lccn.loc.gov/2019021378

♾ This paper meets the requirements of ANSI/NISO Z39.48-1992
(Permanence of Paper).

For Connie

Contents

Introduction

A swinging pendulum is an appropriate metaphor for the history of many developments. In describing the leadership of a public corporation, there was a time when the chief executive officer was all-powerful—imperial and, in some instances, imperious. In the past thirty years or so, developments have caused that pendulum to swing quite far in the other direction. That is certainly not all bad, but there are now circumstances and trends that make it fair to ask, Who's in charge of the U.S. public company?

For any public company to operate well, it is imperative that critical business decision making be centered in an unambiguous leader who, while certainly not all-powerful, is appropriately empowered. Who but the CEO is the proper answer to the question, Who's in charge? The CEO "lives" the company 24/7. All of the employees, and especially the rest of the C-suite, take their lead from the CEO—either literally or by watching his or her behavior. Who but the CEO should be the decision maker on whose desk "the buck stops" and the person who takes responsibility when things go wrong, no matter how deeply into the organization mistakes are made? Who but the CEO is in the best position to motivate the rest of the team to be creative and innovative, to work hard and to behave ethically and with integrity?

There are, of course, important subjects for which decision making is centered in the board and not the CEO. The board should be the centerpiece of corporate governance. First and foremost, the board must take the lead on who is to be the CEO. For this decision, it is imperative that the board focus on leadership qualities. Other governance decisions include how to compensate and incentivize the executive team, who should be on the board, and how the board organizes its efforts. The board is where the big issues must be finally decided (benefiting from the CEO's input). Those big issues include, Do we sell the company? Do we make a material acquisition? and What should our capital structure be? The board also must oversee the activities of management on important subjects such as financial reporting, compliance, and risk management. The board should iterate with the CEO on strategy. All of this is part of the appropriate role of the board and, done right, does not erode the authority of the CEO as the leader of the enterprise.

The corporate world now lives in what we can call the New Era in Corporate Governance. This is a time when corporate governance and process seem to receive as much attention as strategy, finance, and operations. Interest in the subject of corporate governance has been around for a long time, although it has not necessarily been known by that designation. It is unclear when this "new era" began, but it was probably sometime in the early 1990s. Key events around then included the 1992 Cadbury Report in the United Kingdom, the 1992 publication of the proposed final draft of *Principles of Corporate Governance* by the American Law Institute (a project initiated in 1978), the first NACD Blue Ribbon Commission Report in 1993, the 1994 issuance of the GM Governance Guidelines, the 1996 Delaware Chancery Court decision in *Caremark*, the establishment of directors' colleges and governance conferences at various elite graduate business schools, and institutional ownership of common stock surpassing household ownership (see the figure in chapter 3). Those events were a signal that the subject "had legs," even though at the time some observers thought it would eventually play itself out. The trend certainly got a boost with Enron and Sarbanes-Oxley. Indeed, there is now so much focus on the subject that it was referenced in a *Wall Street Journal* review about a new car model—"Dieselgate [at VW] was a massive failure of corporate governance."[1] Whenever the new era did start, it is now pretty clear that it will never end.

As we sit here today, we have "a system that no one would have designed from scratch,"[2] and one that keeps evolving.

The New Era in Corporate Governance has introduced many positive practices to the corporate world. For example, when more is expected about the quality of board decision making on the big issues, managements are required to provide boards with a higher quality of analysis to stand behind their recommendations for board action. The exercise that management goes through in developing and vetting that analysis can lead to a more thoughtful decision by management about whether to even raise a subject with the board. Similarly, the iterative process by which strategy is developed—management to board to management to board—creates a more disciplined approach to a corporation's most significant decisions.

Nevertheless, the new era has produced the potential for inappropriate board encroachment on the leadership role of the CEO. The list of subjects for board oversight keeps growing, and it is easy for oversight to drift across the line into management. It is easy, for example, for the definition of a "big issue" to evolve from the truly material and strategic to the operational and tactical, which leads in turn to a risk of micromanaging. If reacting to a CEO's recommendation goes beyond a diligent "critical eye" to unnecessary or inappropriate negativity in front of the CEO's team, it may make it more difficult for a CEO to lead. The CEO may be demotivated, and in a time of shorter CEO tenures, the rest of the team may wonder about how long he or she will be at the helm. Boards should not confuse being supportive with being "captured."[3] Boards should include "helping the CEO succeed" in their job description. There is an element of self-interest in this; if a CEO fails, the company may falter, and the board will share the blame with the CEO. Boards should want their CEOs to be leaders, not just operational managers, and certainly not just caretakers.

The potential for impeding the leadership role of the CEO is amplified by another aspect of the New Era in Corporate Governance— shareholder activism. Financially oriented activists have replaced the hostile takeover as the principal means of disciplining Corporate America. They sometimes have good ideas, and their presence can play a useful role.[4] But if the board does not resist activists' bad ideas, or ideas that are good only for the short term but bad for the long term, then the ability of the CEO to lead for the long term can be severely damaged.

If nothing else, in this new era, CEOs must now give significant time and attention to governance matters involving both the board and shareholders. If those matters are excessive or simply not useful, that is time and attention inappropriately taken away from minding the business of the company and leading the team.

Enabling CEOs to provide strong business leadership in U.S. public companies *really* matters. Those companies play a vital role in our economy. They are a significant source of innovation and jobs in every industry sector. When they care about diversity and inclusion, public companies (through hiring, training, and pipeline programs) can help address inequalities that have plagued our society. Their executives can serve as civic leaders in their ambassadorial roles. The companies themselves, and their executives and major shareholders who experience wealth creation, provide substantial financial and in-kind philanthropic support to our universities, hospitals, the arts, and other not-for-profits. Companies that embrace corporate social responsibility as part of their strategy for the advancement of shareholder interests make other contributions to societal well-being. When success is reflected in market value, retirement funds are enhanced. In all of these ways, well-run public companies contribute to our standard of living.

The leadership position of the CEO, as well as the company's performance, will be enhanced if both the CEO and the members of the board have a clear understanding of four subjects that are at the heart of corporate governance in the new era:

- their obligations to shareholders and other stakeholders of the company, and the various forces that continue to shape our system of governance (the subject of Part I of this book)
- the attributes, requirements, and practices of a well-functioning board (Part II)
- how shareholder activism works, what its positive aspects are, and how and why to resist the negative influences (Part III)
- what is required of a CEO to be an effective leader focused on the long term and the role of the board in helping the CEO succeed (Part IV)

This book is directed principally at CEOs and directors and to the general counsel and others who advise them. (In particular, Parts II and III could stand alone as something of a how-to manual for directors and officers.) The book is also designed to be useful to business and law school professors who are educating the future occupants of those positions. It is those professors and their students who may make the most use of the extensive endnotes. (Notes that may be of particular interest to CEOs and directors are called out parenthetically in the text.) Finally, this book may even be of interest to other members of the general public, including journalists and politicians who are not otherwise involved in Corporate America but nevertheless want to know what all this stuff called corporate governance is really about.

The perspectives presented in this book are informed by decades of a law practice involved in advising and observing CEOs and boards. To illustrate the substantive points made in the text (and perhaps some entertainment value), there are sidebars containing vignettes collected over those decades. And those were not just any decades. The past 30-plus years have been the most consequential in history for corporate governance.

Glossary of Acronyms

ADA	Americans with Disabilities Act of 1990
ADEA	Age Discrimination in Employment Act of 1967
AFSCME	American Federation of State, County, and Municipal Employees
BJR	Business Judgment Rule
BSP	Board Service Provider
CalPERS	California Public Employees Retirement System
CFO	Chief Financial Officer
CII	Council of Institutional Shareholders
CPSA	Consumer Product Safety Act
CSR	Corporate Social Responsibility
DCF	Discounted Cash Flow
D&O	Director and Officer
EEOC	Equal Employment Opportunity Commission, agency created by the Civil Rights Act of 1964
ERISA	Employee Retirement Income Act of 1974
ESG	Environmental, Social and Governance
ETF	Exchange-Traded Fund
FCPA	Foreign Corrupt Practices Act of 1977
FDA	Food and Drug Administration, agency created by the Federal Food and Drugs Act
FLSA	Fair Labor Standards Act
HR	Human Resources
HSR	Hart-Scott-Rodino Antitrust Improvements Act of 1976
ISS	Institutional Shareholder Services
LBO	Leveraged Buyout
LID	Lead Independent Director

M&A	Mergers and Acquisitions
MD&A	Management's Discussion and Analysis [of Financial Condition and Results of Operations], a centerpiece of public company reporting under the securities laws
MOE	Merger of Equals
NACD	National Association of Corporate Directors
NEPA	National Environmental Policy Act of 1969, one of the statutes administered by the Environmental Protection Agency
NLRA	National Labor Relations Act
OSHA	Occupational Safety and Health Act
RFA	Request for Activism
SCOTUS	Supreme Court of the United States
SEC	Securities and Exchange Commission
SOX	Sarbanes-Oxley Act of 2002
UCC	Uniform Commercial Code
WARN	Worker Adjustment and Retraining Notification Act of 1988

Glossary of Governance Terms of Art

C-SUITE: The CEO and his or her direct reports.

CHANGE-IN-CONTROL TRANSACTION (AKA CHANGE OF CONTROL): A transaction in which the shareholders of a company lose their status as owners of the common stock of a widely held public company. Paradigm form of a change-in-control transaction is a sale of the company for cash. A transaction in which the shareholders receive stock as all or part of the consideration in the transaction can also be a change in control. Caution: the term can also be used in employment agreements and other HR-oriented provisions and can be defined in terms of a new party acquiring a specified percentage ownership (e.g., 20 percent) or appointing some percentage of the board of directors.

CHARTER: The certificate of incorporation (or in some non-Delaware jurisdictions, the articles of incorporation). Analogous to a corporation's constitution. Requires a vote of both the shareholders and the board of directors to change.

CLASSIFIED BOARD (AKA STAGGERED BOARD): Board of directors in which approximately one-third of members are elected for three-year terms at each annual shareholder meeting.

CLAWBACKS: Policies that require executives to reimburse their employers for compensation and other financial benefits in the event of certain events (principally, restatements of financial statements). Mandated by both SOX and Dodd-Frank.

DIRECTOR PROTECTIONS: Corporate provisions and contracts that insulate directors from monetary liability, including exculpatory charter provisions, indemnification charter and bylaw provisions, and directors' and officers' liability insurance.

FIDUCIARY DUTIES (AKA STANDARDS OF CONDUCT): The obligations of directors, officers, and controlling shareholders to the corporation and its stockholders. Sometimes categorized as "fundamental" (meaning the duties of care and loyalty) and "derived" (the other duties that have been articulated by the courts over time).

FIGHT LETTERS: Communications by each side in a proxy contest that set forth their positions as part of their campaigns seeking votes from shareholders.

FOOTBALL FIELD: The page in a financial advisor's presentation to a board of directors that summarizes the various valuations of the company. So called because each form of valuation is reflected in a dashed line, causing the page to resemble a football field. See Appendix 4.

INDEX FUNDS: A form of mutual fund that follows a passive investment strategy of buying and holding a basket of stocks that are included in an index (e.g., S&P 500). May nevertheless be "active" when it comes to governance issues.

INSTITUTIONAL INVESTORS: Nonindividual owners of a company's securities, including mutual funds (including index funds), exchange-traded funds, hedge funds, insurance companies, pension funds, and endowments.

MAJORITY VOTING: A governance reform adopted on a company-by-company basis that effectively requires candidates in an uncontested election of directors to receive a majority vote as a condition to serving on the board. In contrast to plurality voting.

OVERBOARDING: A term used to describe directors who serve on too many boards. Policies adopted by institutional investors, proxy advisory firms, and companies themselves can deter or prohibit directors from serving on too many boards at once.

POISON PILL (AKA SHAREHOLDER RIGHTS PLAN): A device that can be adopted by a board of directors to deter a hostile takeover and may also have some use in defending against a proxy contest. See note 8 in chapter 4 for a more complete description.

PROXY ACCESS: A governance reform adopted on a company-by-company basis that allows, under certain circumstances, a shareholder to place nominees for director on the company's proxy card. In contrast to a proxy contest.

PROXY ADVISORY FIRMS: Firms that consult with institutional investors about how they should vote their proxies at shareholder meetings, including meetings called to vote on a change-in-control transaction. Some of the firms also issue governance ratings. ISS is the largest and most influential of such firms.

PROXY SOLICITORS: Firms that work for corporations (or activists pursuing a proxy contest) to turn out a favorable vote. In a contest, they often act like a campaign manager.

REGULATION FD: The SEC regulation that essentially mandates that material nonpublic information be made fully public at such time as it is released, preventing selective disclosure.

RETAIL INVESTORS: Individuals who are owners of a company's securities.

REVLON DUTIES: The standard of conduct imposed on directors of a company pursuing a change-in-control transaction. Requires them to take steps reasonably designed to achieve the best transaction (principally based on price) for the shareholders.

RULE 14A-8: The SEC regulation that allows shareholders to require an issuer to include, in its annual meeting proxy statement, subjects to be voted on by shareholders.

SCHEDULES 13D, 13G AND 13F: Filings required under SEC rules by investors. 13D is required for "active" individual investors and groups holding 5 percent or more of a company's outstanding shares, as well as "passive" investors holding 20 percent or more. It includes a statement of "plans and proposals" with respect to the investee company. 13G is required for "passive" investors holding between 5 percent and 20 percent. Active investors that held their positions before the corporation's initial public offering may be allowed to use 13G. 13F is a quarterly filing (due within forty-five days of the end of each calendar quarter) required for any institutional investment manager with at least $100 million of equities under management. The 13F is a list of all the manager's holdings as of the end of the quarter.

SHAREHOLDERS: The owners of the common stock of the corporation. A term used interchangeably with "stockholders" (the term used in the Delaware General Corporation Law).

SHARKWATCH 50: A listing of the most prominent and aggressive activist hedge funds, available at the website sharkrepellent.net.

SHORT SLATE: An activist shareholder's nominees for less than a majority of board seats in a proxy contest.

STAKEHOLDERS (AKA OTHER CONSTITUENCIES): Nonshareholders that have an interest in, or are affected by, the affairs of a corporation. The typical list includes employees, creditors, suppliers, customers, and communities.

STANDARDS OF JUDICIAL REVIEW: The approaches taken by a court adjudicating whether corporate fiduciaries have breached their fiduciary duties (standards of conduct). The most favorable standard is the business judgment rule. When there is a concern about the possibility of director conflicts of interest, courts will apply enhanced scrutiny. When there is a clear conflict, courts will apply entire fairness. When there is an allegation of interference with the shareholder franchise, the courts will require a compelling justification. When the business judgment rule applies, the burden of proof is on a plaintiff. Under the other approaches, the burden is on the directors.

STANDING BOARD COMMITTEES: The audit, compensation, and nominating and/or governance committees of the board (there may be some others). In contrast to special (or ad hoc) committees established for some discrete purpose (e.g., addressing shareholder derivative demands, certain types of transactions, internal investigations).

STANDSTILL AGREEMENT: An agreement entered into between a company and an activist shareholder whereby the activist agrees not to buy shares and/or to seek board seats and other changes for a stipulated period. Such an agreement might also be entered into as part of a confidentiality agreement with the counterparty to a possible M&A deal.

STOCK WATCH: A service provided by firms sometimes hired by a corporation to provide real-time monitoring of stock ownership. More current than reports on Schedule 13F but not always perfectly accurate.

TRANSUNION CASE (AKA *SMITH V. VAN GORKOM*): The Delaware Supreme Court decision in 1985 that started the evolution toward director-centric decision making.

WOLF PACK: The presence of more than one activist hedge fund in a company's list of shareholders, with the expectation that they will work together (but avoid forming a formal "group," as defined in the applicable securities laws).

Note: These are simplified definitions of somewhat more complex concepts that are explained in greater detail in the text and endnotes of the book.

PART I

The Policy, Law, and Market Forces That Have Created the New Era in Corporate Governance

A critical building block to understanding both the practical requirements of corporate governance in the new era as practiced today and the resulting challenges for CEO leadership is an appreciation of the purpose of governance and the interplay of policy, law, and market forces.

1

What Is Corporate Governance and Why Do We Care?

The fundamental issue that public company corporate governance addresses is agency cost derived from the dispersion of ownership. When ownership is widely held and liquid (and thus ever-changing), there is a separation of ownership and control. Such a separation creates the risk that "the agent will not always act in the best interests of the principal."[1] This is not at all a new concept. Adam Smith wrote about the separation of ownership and control in *The Wealth of Nations* in 1776, in the context of joint-stock companies. Berle and Means wrote about it during the Great Depression against a background of the growth of giant companies such as AT&T that, before the growth of institutional shareholders, were extremely widely held.[2]

Even owners with a sizable position in the equity of a corporation may be loath to accept seats on its board. While a seat may allow such an investor to exert some degree of control, it also may come with a price—diminished liquidity resulting from securities laws that prevent buying or selling while in possession of material nonpublic information.[3]

Because agency costs are incurred at the individual firm level, the various definitions of corporate governance take on a decidedly microeconomic orientation. James McRitchie has done a wonderful job collecting definitions of corporate governance—from academics, practitioners, and others.[4] For example, corporate governance is any or all of the following:

- "How investors get the managers to give them back their money."[5]
- "The whole set of legal, cultural, and institutional arrangements that determine what public corporations can do, who controls them, how that control is exercised, and how the risks and returns from the activities they undertake are allocated."[6]
- "The allocation of power within a corporation between its stockholders and its board of directors."[7]
- "[A] field in economics that investigates how to secure/motivate efficient management of corporations by the use of incentive mechanisms, such as contracts, organizational designs and legislation."[8]
- "The relationship among various participants in determining the direction and performance of corporations."[9]

With a special focus on decision making, the following definition provides a framework for much of this book: After determining for whose benefit decisions are to be made, corporate governance is a system for how, and by whom, decisions get made in a corporation and for selecting, compensating, and holding accountable nonowner decision makers.

This book does, in fact, focus heavily on the decision-making aspects of corporate governance. The reason for this is fairly simple. I used to quip that corporate governance is what public company M&A lawyers do in a down market. That is my own background. I have been involved in more than sixty such announced deals, the majority of which were transactions valued at over (sometimes well over) $1 billion. That practice gets me into the boardroom all of the time, where I advise heavily on the decision-making process. When other, nontransactional board decisions (including determining responses to shareholder activism and conducting internal investigations) are required, I am often asked to help in that regard. In the New Era in Corporate Governance, another approach to a governance law practice has developed—more of a regulatory approach outside the context of specific decision making. While it is an overgeneralization, the decision-making-oriented lawyer is largely involved in special situations of the type discussed in chapter 8, and the more purely governance-oriented lawyer deals more with the very important but more routine board activities described in chapter 7. Many do both.

While corporate governance is important on a microeconomic level, it is important on a macroeconomic level as well. Jonathan Macey at Yale Law School states, "We care about corporate governance because it affects the real economy."[10] The Conference Board has declared that "American economic success depends on establishing an effective system of corporate governance."[11] The Financial Crisis Inquiry Commission reported, "We conclude dramatic failures of corporate governance . . . at many systemically important financial institutions were a key cause of [the 2008 global financial] crisis."[12]

One other reason for thinking about the macroeconomic importance of governance is derived from how the ownership of U.S. equities has evolved. According to one estimate, in 2017 more than half of individual citizens held shares either directly as retail investors or indirectly through pension funds, mutual funds, certain types of life insurance products, and ETFs. Stock is owned even by 21 percent of those households that have annual incomes of less than $30,000.[13] In addition, university students and parents of students, recipients of grants from foundations, and those served by other not-for-profits all have an indirect interest in the performance of publicly traded companies because of share ownership by endowments. In 2017, the Federal Reserve reported that U.S. households and nonprofits have a net worth of nearly $100 trillion and that 25 percent of that was represented by directly and indirectly held equities.[14] Because corporate governance affects the performance of the companies in the portfolios of individuals and institutions, governance is a matter of macroeconomic importance.

There is a second macroeconomic effect that may, in part, be attributable to the new era—the decline in the number of U.S. public companies. In 2018, there were 3,671 listed companies, about half the number in 1996—the early years of the New Era in Governance. "Increases in regulations, shareholder lawsuits and activist demands have . . . diminished the appeal of a public listing," and this trend "has benefited private market players at the expense of everyday investors."[15] Another reason for the decline—"Many founders . . . believe that private markets are better at allowing them a long-term perspective."[16] As a result of basic economic laws of supply and demand, this trend may also be a cause of increasing stock market valuations for those companies that are public.[17]

There may well be a third macroeconomic effect. The New Era in Corporate Governance may be driving C-suite-level talent away from public companies. I recently ran into a man who I had observed years earlier as a terrific public company CEO. He left that job to become CEO of a private equity fund's portfolio company. I told him about this book and its main themes. He responded by telling me that he had recently been approached by a headhunter about the job of CEO of one of the most significant public companies in his industry, a company with a market capitalization of more than $50 billion. He told me that he asked the headhunter, "Why would I *ever* want to do that?" This reaction is consistent with one of the comments received in the CEO survey reported on in chapter 12.

2

The Threshold Question of Corporate Governance: For Whose Benefit Are Corporations to Be Governed?

The threshold question for designing a system of corporate governance is this: For whose benefit are corporations to be governed? To use an architectural metaphor, form will follow function. For example, in many countries in Europe, where there is an emphasis on governing for the benefit of employees, the governance structures include two-tier boards—a board of executive directors and a supervisory board. The latter supervises management and has equal numbers of directors elected by shareholders and by employees.

The discussion of the separation of ownership and control and the focus on agency costs foreshadow an answer to this question in the United States that corporations are to be governed for the benefit of the owners—that is, the shareholders. While the primacy of shareholder interests is ultimately the answer that has been arrived at in the U.S., the issue has been the subject of an ongoing policy debate for some time, framed as shareholder versus stakeholder.

In the depths of the Depression, Professors Berle and Dodd conducted a robust debate about "for whose benefit" in the *Harvard Law Review*.[1] Milton Friedman weighed in on the subject in 1970 with his famous *New York Times Magazine* article titled "The Social Responsibility of Business Is to Increase Its Profits."[2] The shareholder-versus-stakeholder debate continues in the current decade. Professor Lynn

Stout of Cornell, writing in 2012, took the position that "the ideology of shareholder value maximization lacks any solid foundation in corporate law, corporate economics or the empirical evidence. . . . U.S. corporate law does not impose any enforceable legal duty on corporate directors or executives of public corporations to maximize profits or share price."[3] A similar position was articulated in 2017 by two Harvard Business School professors in an article in the *Harvard Business Review*. Again, the title says it all—"The Error at the Heart of Corporate Leadership: Most CEOs and Boards Believe Their Main Duty Is to Maximize Shareholder Value. It's Not."[4] And yet, in 2013, Vice Chancellor J. Travis Laster, of the Delaware Court of Chancery, wrote with much greater authority that "the standard of conduct for directors requires that they strive . . . to maximize the value of the corporation for the benefit of its residual claimants"—that is, the owners of the common stock.[5]

The debate has no doubt been energized by political leanings and because it is so easy to conflate the question of "for whose benefit" with another question: "to whom does a corporation owe duties"? So, a more complete answer is that corporations are to be governed (and decisions made) for the ultimate benefit of the shareholders, but at the same time, corporations have many duties to other stakeholders (also called the "other constituencies") by way of specific law and regulation as well as contracts. Another formulation is to say that generalized duties (i.e., fiduciary duties) are owed only to the shareholders.

The specific protections of the nonshareholder constituencies are legion. Employees are protected by OSHA, WARN, ERISA, ADA, ADEA, EEOC, FLSA, NLRA, whistle-blower anti-retaliation laws, collective bargaining agreements, employment agreements and state law limitations on noncompetition agreements. Customers are protected by antitrust laws, the FDA, the CPSA, privacy laws, the UCC, tort laws, and contractual warranties. Utility customers are protected by regulations pertaining to rates. Creditors are protected by corporate statutes defining what a "legal dividend" is, fraudulent conveyance laws, the bankruptcy code, and the contractual requirements of their debt instruments, including an implied covenant of good faith. Even "communities at large" have specific protections, such as zoning and environmental laws, as well as safety requirements applicable to utility companies.

The phrase "primacy of shareholder interests" is a fair summary for explaining the structure of U.S. corporate governance and for describing shareholders as the sole beneficiaries of generalized fiduciary duties. That notion certainly applies without exception when a board is considering a sale of the company in a transaction that qualifies as a "change in control." As the Delaware Supreme Court stated in its historic *Revlon* decision in 1986, "Concern for non-stockholder interests is inappropriate when . . . the object no longer is to protect or maintain the corporate enterprise."[6]

The so-called other-constituencies statutes that were adopted post-*Revlon* suggest legislative dissatisfaction with a conclusion that shareholder interests are to be the primary consideration of managements and boards. Many states (though not Delaware) have statutes that provide that boards may, in considering corporate actions, take into account the interests of employees, customers, suppliers, and even their communities at large.[7] And some companies have included provisions to the same effect in their certificates of incorporation.[8] These interests are in addition to whatever duties law and contract specifically require, as described earlier. In the absence of historical context, these statutes and provisions might be viewed as progressive and even paternalistic pieces of legislation. Not so. They should be viewed as anti-takeover devices because of the timing of their adoption and because they purport to legitimize consideration of nonshareholders as a basis for rejecting an unsolicited bid. It should also be noted that the constituencies statutes are permissive—they use the word "may," not "must" or "shall." Incidentally, when boards have tried to rely on these statutes to accept a lower-priced offer, it typically does not work. Most courts have held that these statutes do not negate an obligation to seek the best deal, principally based on price (the so-called *Revlon* obligation discussed later).[9] Shareholders are not likely to approve the lower-priced deal, anyway.

As a guide to directors and officers in the broader context of decision making outside of a change-in-control transaction, the word "primacy" in the phrase "primacy of shareholder interests" should not imply "exclusivity." A more nuanced understanding is required.

At a minimum, primacy means that shareholder considerations cannot be secondary to the interests of other stakeholders. In 1919, in the celebrated dispute between the Ford and Dodge families, the Michigan Supreme Court addressed the "for whose benefit" question as follows: "It is not within the lawful powers of a board of directors to shape and conduct the affairs of a corporation for the merely incidental benefit of shareholders and for the primary purpose of benefiting others."[10]

"Primacy of shareholder interests" does not mean, however, that the interests of other stakeholders (beyond contractual and other legal rights) cannot be considered at all in general D&O decision making: "A board may have regard for various constituencies in discharging its responsibilities, provided there are rationally related benefits accruing to the stockholders."[11] And those benefits need not be immediate.

In an important 1992 article by then Delaware Chancellor William Allen, he first summarizes the two competing policy conceptions of corporations—social entity and property. Under the first view, because corporations (and the limitation of liability afforded to their owners) exist only because of legislative actions of the state, it would be possible for the state to require that they be governed for the benefit of a group broader than simply their owners. In contrast, under the property conception, corporations are simply property, and the interests of their owners are paramount. He goes on to say that, until the advent of contested takeovers in the 1980s, this debate really did not need to be resolved. The competing views could peacefully coexist. When the debate became more consequential in the context of hostile bids, Allen concludes that, because the courts allow boards to focus on the long-term interest of shareholders, just about any action that benefits the nonshareholder constituencies can be justified so long as it ultimately benefits shareholders![12]

The old-school version of such actions was philanthropy in support of noncontroversial charities and other not-for-profits. In the new millennium, the range of such actions was greatly expanded under the banners of corporate social responsibility (CSR) and environmental, social, and governance (ESG). It is not difficult to justify such actions as ultimately benefiting shareholders, and boards are well advised to consider CSR/ESG as part of corporate strategy. For a consumer products company, CSR/ESG might be viewed as brand building and part of a good marketing strategy. For a public utility, CSR/ESG can be important in the rate-setting context. For a company in just about any industry sector, CSR/ ESG can yield benefits in terms of recruiting and retaining employees. In addition, a "good corporate citizen" is more likely to catch a break from the press, regulators, customers, and even juries at a time of a company-originated crisis. Finally, while not all view CSR/ESG the same way, those activities can be attractive to both current and future investors.

Even investors with a singular focus on financial returns advocate attention to nonshareholder stakeholders through CSR or ESG as a means of serving the long-term interests of shareholders. Michelle Edkins, the global head of corporate governance for BlackRock (which in 2018 had $6 *trillion* in assets under management), had this to say: "We look at [CSR issues] . . . not because we are promoting either a social or environmental agenda. We don't have one. The only thing every single one of our clients has asked us to do is generate a return on their assets. We look at environmental and social factors in a business to get a sense of the quality of leadership and the operational excellence within that firm, because in the long term, when companies don't manage what fits under the banner of environmental and social . . . that is usually when you have a well blow up or you have a product recall or litigation that costs enormous amounts."[13]

In his 2018 annual letter to CEOs of public companies, BlackRock's CEO Larry Fink took these sentiments a step further—"To prosper over time, every company must not only deliver financial performance, but also show how it makes a positive contribution to society." (In his 2019 letter, Fink went even further—"Unnerved by fundamental economic changes and the failure of government to provide lasting solutions, society is increasingly looking to companies, both public and private, to address pressing social and economic issues.")[14] The BlackRock message was spotlighted by *Barron's* in its June 25, 2018, issue (reprinted as a special supplement to the June 26 issue of the *Wall Street Journal*) titled "Investing with Purpose/Larry Fink's Mission." Fink's 2018 letter triggered many reactions, including an op-ed in the *Wall Street Journal* by Andy Kessler—the title of which evoked the ghost of Milton Friedman: "Stocks Weren't Made for Social Climbing." Kessler, a hedge-fund manager, called Fink "only the latest to evangelize this [CSR] fad."[15]

Another recent example of the embrace by Wall Streeters of CSR is the ETF launched in 2018 by Goldman Sachs, described as a "feel-good selection of Russell 1000 companies" that score highly on JUST

Capital's rankings. Those rankings "score[] businesses using a complex formula related to workers, customers, products, environment, jobs, communities and management."[16] JUST Capital was founded in 2013 by hedge-fund manager Tudor Jones. It recently ranked companies by how much of the 2017 tax cuts would flow through to employees.[17]

Other organizations provide ESG ratings, as well. However, different organizations can give very different ratings to the same company; after all, "they are no more than a series of judgments by the scoring companies about what matters."[18] ESG/CSR ratings have become a part of general performance rankings, as well. The *Harvard Business Review*'s 2018 list of "best performing CEOs" was based on four criteria—three traditional financial measures and an ESG index. The Drucker Institute's Management Top 250 rankings use social responsibility as one of its "five dimensions of corporate performance," with a 23 percent weighting—higher than any other criteria.

There are some who express skepticism about CSR as an investment strategy, citing evidence that it is not a vehicle for achieving superior returns: "Investors are increasingly convinced that they can buy companies that behave better than the rest and make just as much money. They are wrong."[19]

There are also examples of corporate advocacy of CSR having a possible negative impact on shareholder interests. CEOs who have been vocal about social issues—such as Black Lives Matter or gun control—have created customer pushback against their companies.[20] It will be interesting to see whether Nike's embrace of Colin Kaepernick and the positions of Dick's Sporting Goods and Levi Strauss on gun violence will ultimately play out positively or negatively with consumers. Other pushbacks have come from the government. In 2018, the Department of Labor (which has jurisdiction over ERISA) released regulatory guidance stating that "fiduciaries must not too readily treat ESG factors as economically relevant to the particular investment choices at issue when making a decision."[21] There was an interesting development along these lines in 2018, when the beneficiaries of CalPERS voted to remove its president and replace her with a union official who criticized the incumbent for her "focus on [ESG] investing."[22] When Delta Airlines canceled its affinity program for the NRA in the wake of school shootings, the Georgia legislature passed a bill to remove a potential $50 million sales tax exemption on the purchase of jet fuel at Delta's Atlanta hub, although those tax breaks were later restored.[23] And when major banks sought to restrict their services to gun retailers and manufacturers, Republicans in Congress threatened legislation and complaints to the Consumer Financial Protection Bureau.[24]

And yet, a failure to address social issues (or being perceived as on the wrong side) can have negative HR consequences. For example, in response to the humanitarian crisis on the southern U.S. border involving the separation of children from their families, one hundred Microsoft employees demanded that the company cancel its contract with U.S. Immigration and Customs Enforcement. Employees of McKinsey, the global management consulting firm, made the same demand, and the firm terminated the relationship.[25]

One way for a company to address a social issue but reduce the risk of pushback is to speak out through an association. It is even better if the position the company takes can be linked to business considerations. A great example was the letter dated August 22, 2018, from the Business Roundtable to the secretary of homeland security on the subject of immigration policy. The letter was signed by dozens of CEOs from the largest companies in the United States.[26]

An example of legislators tangling with the notion of shareholder primacy is exhibited with the advent of "public benefit" corporations. A public benefit corporation is "a for-profit corporation . . . that is intended to produce a public benefit or public benefits and to operate in a responsible and sustainable manner. To that end, a public benefit corporation shall be managed in a manner that balances the stockholders' pecuniary interests, the best interests of those materially affected by the corporation's conduct, and the public benefit or public benefits identified in its certificate of incorporation."[27] Public benefit corporations first appeared on the scene in the United States around 2010, and as of 2017, over thirty states had adopted enabling legislation.[28] B Lab, a not-for-profit, has issued "B Corporation certifications" to nearly 2,700 for-profit enterprises around the world, based on its criteria measuring "a company's entire social and environmental performance." Corporations established under public benefit corporation statutes will qualify for such certification.[29] There are publicly traded B corps (e.g., Laureate) and B corps that are subsidiaries of public companies (e.g., Unilever's

Ben & Jerry's). One publicly traded B corp (Etsy) came under attack from two activists—one sought a change from that status; the other urged a sale of the company.[30]

Further tangling came in 2018, with Senator Elizabeth Warren's introduction of the Accountable Capitalism Act. As she described her bill in a *Wall Street Journal* op-ed, it essentially requires all corporations with more than $1 billion of revenues to "look out for American interests," following the benefit corporation model. The bill would "require[] corporate directors to consider the interests of all major corporate stakeholders," but interestingly would seem to give only shareholders the right to sue for a failure of directors to do so. Additional provisions of the bill include that employees elect 40 percent of the board, that political contributions require the approval of 75 percent of both shareholders and directors, and that equity-based compensation would have to be held for up to five years.[31]

And then there is a school of thought that CSR is simply an effort to "soften capitalism" and doesn't go far enough to address vexing social issues. In his review of the book *Winners Take All*, by Anand Giridharadas, the Nobel laureate in economics Joseph Stiglitz wrote, "Like the dieter who would rather do anything to lose weight than actually eat less, th[e] business elite would save the world though social impact investing, entrepreneurship, sustainable capitalism, philanthrocapitalism, artificial intelligence, [and] market-driven solutions."[32] He didn't say it, but it sounds a bit like "CSR is the opium of the people."

Finally, one author has looked at the subject from a very long-term historical perspective and concluded that, at least in the past, "virtuous business practices can be . . . successfully implemented . . . although . . . have proved difficult to achieve, particularly in publicly traded corporations" and "have had relatively short half-lives."[33]

All of this suggests that Chancellor Allen was *really* onto something when he titled his 1992 article "Our Schizophrenic Conception of the Business Corporation."

• • •

Imagine the decision-making difficulties posed if Senator Warren has her way and directors have a generalized obligation to both shareholders and employees (to pick but one nonshareholder constituency) when considering, say, a capital expenditure on robotics. Such an expenditure that would yield financial benefits for the shareholders (and probably customers through lower prices) but would result in employee layoffs. U.S. corporate governance provides a highly practical decision-making regime by limiting the obligations to the employees (or any other nonshareholder stakeholders) to myriad specific laws and contracts while allowing for *consideration* of the interests of those stakeholders, but only if doing so will ultimately benefit the stockholders.

SHAREHOLDERS, AGENTS, AND STAKEHOLDERS

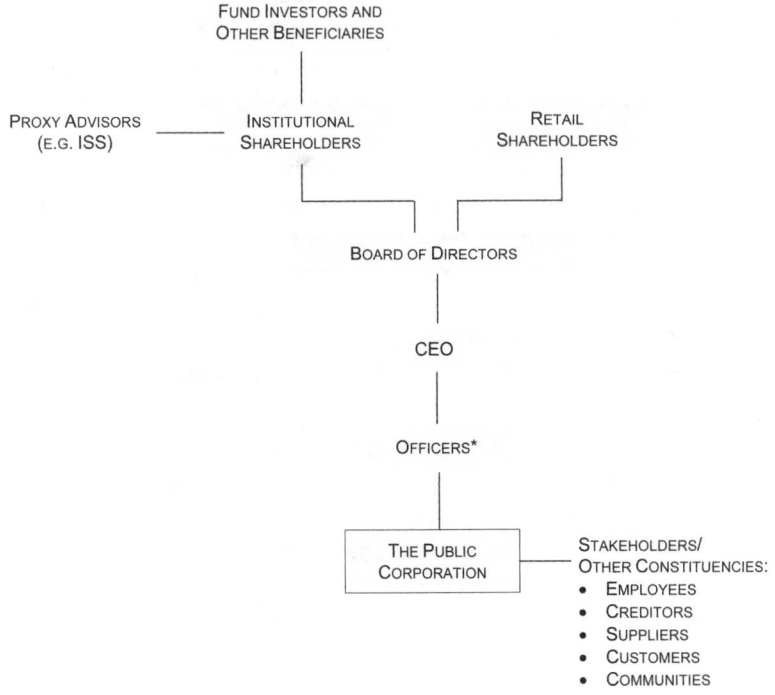

FUND INVESTORS AND
OTHER BENEFICIARIES

PROXY ADVISORS
(E.G. ISS)

INSTITUTIONAL
SHAREHOLDERS

RETAIL
SHAREHOLDERS

BOARD OF DIRECTORS

CEO

OFFICERS*

THE PUBLIC
CORPORATION

STAKEHOLDERS/
OTHER CONSTITUENCIES:
• EMPLOYEES
• CREDITORS
• SUPPLIERS
• CUSTOMERS
• COMMUNITIES

* NOTE: THE GENERAL COUNSEL REPORTS TO THE CEO BUT
HAS ETHICAL RESPONSIBILITIES TO THE BOARD OF DIRECTORS

It is true that European boards seem to manage to deal with obligations to multiple constituencies. In my own experience, however, I have seen U.S. public company boards struggle even with the fact that shareholders are themselves not a monolith.

For example, boards often want to distinguish between long-term and short-term holders. More than one director has said, in the context of a hostile takeover, something like "I don't care about the arbs." "Arbs" are investors who engage in merger arbitrage; a friend once gave me a bumper sticker that read "I don't brake for arbs." A similarly dismissive view of short-term investors was expressed by none other than the CEO of Black-Rock in his 2015 annual letter to CEOs: "Corporate leaders' duty of care and loyalty is not to every investor or trader who owns their companies' shares at any moment in time, but to the company and its long-term owners." These statements are simply incorrect; there is a duty to the shareholders as a whole, without regard to their particular circumstances or holding periods. That said, boards and managements are clearly able to focus on what is good for the long term, as Chancellor Allen stated in his article.

Another example is the struggle that board members will have if they start worrying about high-tax-basis versus low-tax-basis shareholders. In the real world, boards tend not to take into account shareholder tax positions when approving transactions. (In this regard, they can rely on case law asserting that "the duty to act for the ultimate benefit of stockholders does not require that directors fulfill the wishes of a particular subset of the stockholder base."[34]) I recall one time that an octogenarian descendant of a company's founder complained about a cash merger: she had hoped to hold the stock long enough that the tax basis would be adjusted upward upon her death. The solution—drop dead—was not suggested to her.

3

The Forces That Shape Corporate Governance

Corporate governance is shaped by law, markets, and politics.

Law

Delaware's Court of Chancery (trial-level corporate court), Supreme Court, and legislature are a major source of the substantive law of fiduciary duty and, thus, corporate governance. This is because a majority of all public companies, and more than 60 percent of the Fortune 500, are incorporated there. Moreover, it is quite common for courts in other jurisdictions to expressly look to Delaware judicial precedents when their own courts have not previously grappled with a particular issue of corporate law.

These are the big themes in the development of the law of corporate governance over the past fifty years:

- the debate over federal (as opposed to state) substantive corporate law
- a degree of unpredictability about decisions from the Delaware courts
- legal developments lagging of changes in the markets
- cycles of scandals and crises leading to federal reform legislation that effectively sets federal minimum standards for public corporations

The federal-state debate is captured in the phrase "race to the bottom." The notion is that if fifty states are competing to have entities incorporated in their jurisdiction, then they will compete with laws that increasingly favor management. Thus, in the absence of a jurisdiction having a monopoly over incorporations, there will be a race to the bottom, to the detriment of shareholders. During the twentieth century, there were a couple of efforts to establish federal substantive corporate law. One such effort was by Professor Cary of Columbia, who, in the mid-1970s, advocated for federal minimum standards that would at least set the "bottom."[1] Another effort attempted to use the federal securities laws as a source of law on fiduciary duties. That effort failed as well when the U.S. Supreme Court declared in the 1970s that the securities laws were limited to creating a disclosure regime and could not be used to assert fiduciary duties.[2]

Then came the 1980s. Contrary to the race-to-the-bottom thesis, the Delaware Supreme Court, in *Smith v. Van Gorkom* (better known as the TransUnion case), for the first time imposed financial liability on directors for gross negligence in the discharge of the fiduciary duty of care. The TransUnion board had approved (and recommended to shareholders that they vote in favor of) a sale of that company for a substantial premium over the market price. Liability was imposed because the board had, quite frankly, followed an abysmal decision-making process.[3] (This was even before the additional requirements of *Revlon*, discussed later, were imposed.) At about the same time, the Court in *Unocal* placed constraints on what a corporate board could do to fend off a hostile takeover.[4] Maybe the purported leader of the race to the bottom was changing its approach?

Interestingly, Delaware's neighbor to the north made an effort to take the lead in that race to the bottom with the exceedingly management-friendly Pennsylvania Antitakeover Statute of 1990.[5] Going in the other direction was North Dakota, with its adoption in 2007 of its Publicly Traded Corporations Act. The provisions of that act, including a rule of construction mandating that interpretive issues be resolved in favor of shareholders, could be characterized as a governance activist's dream.[6] Corporations have not flocked to either state. There was some hope on the part of Pennsylvanians that corporations might seek to reincorporate in that state. However, for an existing corporation, that would require a shareholder vote, and institutions made clear that they would not support such a move, because it would excessively insulate boards and managements. There was some concern on the part of corporations that shareholders would propose a reincorporation to North Dakota as a way of bundling a set of governance provisions that would otherwise be handled one at a time through shareholder proposals under the proxy rules. That didn't happen, either.

I first heard about the North Dakota statute from the then chief justice of Delaware, Myron Steele, when I was on a panel with him years ago at the San Diego Securities Regulation Institute. He started his remarks with the usual caveat that what he was about to say did not necessarily reflect the position of the Delaware courts. He then added, humorously, something along the lines of "I am not even sure these are my views . . . and they certainly may not be the views of those Young Turks who sit on the Court of Chancery." This comment may be taken to suggest that personnel changes at the courts may contribute to the difficulty in predicting decisions of the Delaware courts.

In 2013, then Chancellor Strine (and now Chief Justice) offered this view about where Delaware sits: "I think . . . judges in Delaware who participate in corporate law in Delaware take legitimate umbrage when folks say that we don't hold managers accountable for breaches of fiduciary duty in Delaware. I find that claim to be astonishingly outdated and simple-minded, when any review of our corporate law will see . . . that [it] is, frankly, much more pro stockholder and more balanced than any of our other states."[7]

The 1985 decision in *Smith v. Van Gorkom* was viewed as a departure from the typical evolutionary, incremental pace of change that is the tradition of common law. The Delaware Supreme Court opinion was a non-unanimous reversal of the trial court. It can fairly be characterized as surprising and revolutionary. Even now, some regard it as wrongly decided. Perhaps the most passionate critic of the decision in the TransUnion case was J. W. Van Gorkom—yes, the company's CEO whose name adorns the caption of the case. He was a leading member of the Chicago corporate establishment, and after the decision came out, he issued what he called a "monograph" to his fellow members of that establishment to "clear up the confusion" about the case created by the media. He referred to Delaware as "a jurisdiction that could act so irrationally" and criticized the "court's distorted reasoning."[8] TransUnion marked the start of a movement from management-centric decision making to board-centric decision making on at least the "big issues."

Boards and those who advise them studied the criticisms leveled at the TransUnion board by the Delaware Supreme Court. In keeping with the business judgment rule (to be discussed later), the criticisms were not about the board's decision per se but rather about the inadequacy of the process that was followed to make its decision. That study of the Court's criticisms led to new approaches to the decision-making process for considering a sale of a company. Those more robust approaches were then applied to other important decisions—takeover defenses, major acquisitions or other commitments of capital, CEO succession, a change in strategy, and even executive compensation.

In the immediate aftermath of TransUnion, boards and those advising them began to wonder whether Delaware was the place to be—that is, to incorporate. Was Delaware "racing to the top"? The Delaware bar and legislature sought to assuage those concerns (and did so successfully) with the enactment of Delaware Section 102(b)(7).[9] That new statute enabled companies to include provisions in their certificates of incorporation eliminating or limiting the exposure of directors to monetary damages for a breach of the duty of care. (Importantly, officers are not covered, breaches of the duty of loyalty are not covered, and injunctions can still be issued if there has been a failure to exercise due care.) Interestingly, there was no resistance on the part of shareholders to vote in favor of amendments to adopt those so-called exculpatory charter provisions. And virtually all the adopted provisions go beyond limiting exposure (say, to the amount of directors' fees). When applicable, they eliminate the exposure to monetary damages. Other states followed Delaware, and these provisions are now ubiquitous.

Other provisions designed to insulate directors against liability (the so-called director protections) are discussed in chapter 6.

In truth, TransUnion may have led to the single most important development in improving corporate governance. As noted earlier, with more being expected of boards, they in turn are more demanding of management. The quality of the process for board decision making was greatly improved, starting with the quality of analysis that now stands behind any management recommendation and including access to experts and the time that boards are given before being asked to make a final decision.

TransUnion may have been the most surprising precedent coming out of the Delaware courts, but there are many other instances of what might fairly be characterized as dramatic changes in position by those courts. For example, as will be discussed in chapter 6, *Graham v. Allis-Chalmers*[10] (which embodied a relatively forgiving approach to board oversight of compliance) was upended by *Caremark*[11] and *Stone v. Ritter.*[12] In what is labeled in later chapters as the "Delaware accordion," a judge-made proliferation of new fiduciary duties (good faith, candor, oversight) was followed by a reconcentration of those duties under the traditional categories of care and loyalty. Standards of judicial review also proliferated. The most forgiving standard, the business judgment rule, was supplemented by standards labeled "enhanced scrutiny" and "entire fairness," which were to be applied under certain circumstances. Recent precedents discussed in chapter 6, however, allow boards to get back under the BJR by following certain procedural steps.

The Delaware courts have also tweaked their own precedents. The holding in *Unocal*[13] (relating to takeover defenses) was "clarified" in the decision in *Mercier.*[14] That latter decision also advocated for narrowing the scope of the application of the "compelling justification" requirement (applied to any interference with the shareholder franchise) of *Blasius.*[15] As a final example, there has been considerable judicial to-and-fro over "shareholder ratification." The plethora of examples lead some to question just how predictable the Delaware courts really are. More on this in chapter 6.

Another element of Delaware law in the area of corporate governance is the interplay between the courts and the legislature. As noted earlier, the exculpatory charter provision was a legislative response to concerns raised by the TransUnion decision. A more recent example relates to exclusive jurisdiction bylaws, which require fiduciary claims to be pursued in Delaware. First, the provisions were validated in the *Chevron* decision.[16] When one Delaware judge went further and validated a provision that stipulated an exclusive jurisdiction over a Delaware corporation, but that exclusive jurisdiction was the corporation's headquarters state of North Carolina,[17] the Delaware legislature stepped in. The new Section 115 validates exclusive jurisdiction provisions but states that "no provision . . . may prohibit bringing such claims in [Delaware]."[18] Another example arose when there was a suggestion that a right to indemnification of directors could be stripped away after the event that gave rise to the need for indemnification.[19] The legislature again stepped in with an amendment to the indemnification statute to generally prohibit such an action.[20] A final example is when the legislature prohibited fee-shifting bylaws after a judge opined on the facial validity of such a provision.[21]

There is another aspect of the role of case law in shaping corporate governance—it often lags developments in the market. One of the most vivid examples is how judges have had to grapple with sophisticated equity derivatives in the context of Schedule 13D, a federal securities regulation that is pertinent to corporate governance (especially shareholder activism). Schedule 13D requires public filings by holders of more than 5 percent of a company's stock. In *CSX v. Children's Investment Fund*, the Second Circuit Court of Appeals addressed a number of issues. Among other things, the Court struggled with the question of "whether and under what circumstances the long party to a cash-settled total return equity swap may be deemed, for purposes of Section 13(d), the beneficial owner of shares purchased by the short party as a hedge." The appeal was argued to the Second Circuit in August 2008, and the Court did not issue its opinion until July 2011. On the question described above, the Court, after ruminating for three years, basically punted and declined to rule on the issue.[22]

Historical cycles of crisis and scandal have led to legal reform at a more revolutionary pace than typically results from case law. Let's start with the stock market crash of 1929 and the Great Depression. Those crises led to, among other things, the enactment of the securities laws in the 1930s. While these laws did not cover fiduciary duties, they did impose on corporate "agents" standards for obligatory disclosures to their "principals." The subsequent evolution of the proxy rules under the Securities Exchange Act of 1934 is more directly related to corporate governance, especially rules related to executive compensation disclosure, shareholder proposals, and the conducting of proxy contests and tender offers.

Corporate misconduct led to the enactment of a number of laws in the 1970s that constrain directors and officers in how they manage a corporation—NEPA, ERISA, FCPA, OSHA. In addition, "some commentators have connected the initiation of a corporate governance project by the ALI [American Law Institute] principally to transient social events of the late 1970s."[23]

The most vivid examples of governance-related reform legislation triggered by crises, though, came in the new millennium. These examples can be thought of as creating the federal minimum standards advocated by Professor Cary.

The spectacular and sudden failure of Enron and others led to the enactment of Sarbanes-Oxley (SOX) in 2002. That statute can be thought of as a reasonably well-deserved scolding of just about every player in the universe of publicly traded companies. No one was spared. There are SOX provisions relating to management and all of the so-called gatekeepers—boards, public accountants, lawyers, rating agencies, and analysts.[24]

More important, because a root cause of Enron and others was believed to be the failure of corporate governance (captured in the then-common refrain "Where were the directors?") and because of the macroeconomic impact of the post-Enron crisis of confidence in public securities markets, Congress moved swiftly to adopt provisions that can be characterized as substantive federal corporate law. Some of this substantive law was imposed directly; an example is the ban on loans to executives. Another is the (very expensive) requirements of SOX Section 404, mandating that management assess the effectiveness of internal controls and that an outside auditor attest to and report on that management assessment. Most were indirect. For example, those effected via requiring the SEC to adopt disclosure rules—such as disclosures about codes of ethics for senior financial officers (Section 406) and audit committee financial experts (Section 407). Other substantive law was effected via requirements imposed by the stock exchanges on their listed companies. Key among these related to audit committees (Section 301).

In an interesting parallel to the states' race to the bottom in corporate law, after SOX was enacted, some thought that the New York Stock Exchange and the NASDAQ would compete to be friendlier to management and boards as they were formulating the rules required of them by SOX. While there are some differences in the rules they adopted, the anticipated "regulatory arbitrage," as it was called at the time, did not materialize in any significant way.

The enactment of SOX was a dramatic event for Corporate America. Shortly after SOX was signed into law, the Economic Club of Chicago held a forum event at seven in the morning in which a panel, including Congressman Oxley and me, discussed the new statute. Despite the early hour (and even accounting for Midwesterners' early rising habits), the ballroom was filled. After the microphones were turned off, I turned to the congressman and asked privately, "Would you go on a corporate board right now?" His candid reply was, "I would probably wait for the dust to settle."

Any number of clients asked for a checklist of the new requirements under SOX. My firm responded by publishing the Sidley Best Practices Calendar for Corporate Boards and Committees.[25] It was designed to cover all the new requirements, but to add them in a logical chronological sequence to the bigger-picture items that all boards should consider, such as strategic planning and succession. This approach was adopted, in part, to address grumblings from some board members that SOX would result in "rules-based" or "checklist-based," not "principles-based," board governance. The Sidley Calendar is periodically updated and can be accessed on the firm's website.

To directors who complained about checklists, I would often note that the airline pilots who brought them to the board meeting used safety checklists to good effect. I am also a big fan of Atul Gawande, the Harvard Medical School surgeon, and his book *The Checklist Manifesto*. Checklists (like processes) can be useful when used as a decision-making "floor" and not accepted as a ceiling.

Only a few years after Enron, there was another and more significant event—the Global Financial Crisis and the Great Recession. While perceived failures of corporate governance (other than at systemically important financial institutions) were not at the heart of this crisis, the resulting federal reform legislation, Dodd-Frank, included governance related provisions. Those largely (but not exclusively) pertain to executive compensation.[26]

Market

At the same time that all these changes were occurring in the legal background pertinent to corporate governance, there were market developments of probably greater importance. Most prominent in this regard was the rise of the institutional investor and the decline of the individual (or "retail") investor. The statistics tell a good bit of the story.

The rise of the institutional investor creates a second-order agency problem—managements and boards (as agents) are dealing with shareholders that are themselves not principals but are agents for others who have the ultimate economic interest. Some have called this "agents watching agents,"[27] or the "separation of ownership from ownership."[28]

In 1973 Burt Malkiel's *Random Walk Down Wall Street* was published.[29] The thesis of that book was that, on an after-fees basis, it makes more sense to passively invest in a basket of stocks that mimic the market as a whole rather than pay an "active manager" its typical fee to try to "beat the market." This led to the development of low-fee index funds. As Jack Bogle of Vanguard, often regarded as "the father of the index fund," put it: "Don't look for the needle in the haystack. Just buy the haystack."[30]

Institutional Ownership of Common Stock, 1900–2006

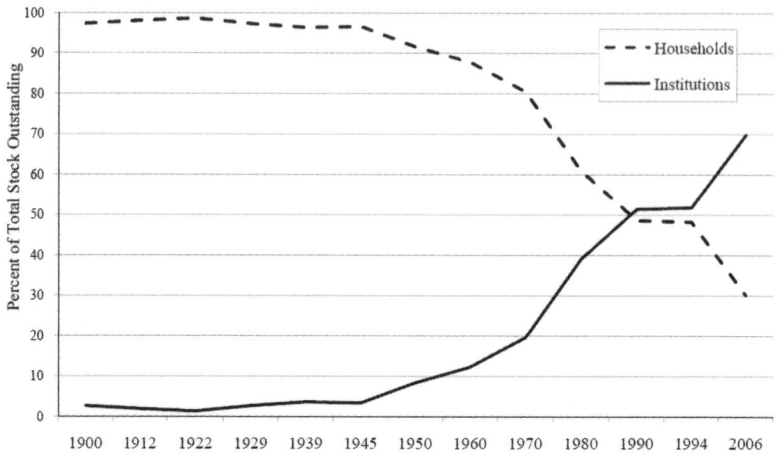

Source: Marshall Blume and Donald Keim, Trends in Institutional Stock Ownership and Some Implications, SPRING 2008 Q-GROUP CONFERENCE, Draft March 12, 2008.

The growth of passive investment management has accelerated. Index funds in 2018 represented a substantial portion of BlackRock's $6 trillion in assets under management, Vanguard's $5 trillion, and State Street's nearly $3 trillion. Those firms are commonly called "the Big Three." A recent study shows that 44 percent of assets in all types of mutual funds and ETFs were held by index funds and ETFs at the end of 2017 (up from about 10 percent in 2000).[31] Bogle has stated that "it seems only a matter of time until index funds cross the 50 percent mark," with the effect that the Big Three "might own 30 percent or more of the U.S. stock market"—a level of concentration that he believes would not "serve the national interest."[32] As a governance matter, if index funds do not like how things are going at an investee company, they cannot simply sell out of that position. As a result, some of the institutions with a passive investment strategy became activist when it came to governance issues.

Beyond the statistics, however, there were a number of related developments. In 1988, the federal government told institutional investors that under ERISA that they must vote their shares.[33] The typical institution was not geared up to read, much less analyze, the proxy statements of hundreds of corporations in their portfolios. To respond to the mandate to vote, the institutions began to rely on proxy advisory firms—most prominent among them being ISS, but including Glass Lewis and Egan Jones. Many commentators publicly, and CEOs privately, have railed against the "outsized influence" of ISS.[34] Others have expressed concern about the conflicts of interest arising when ISS provides consulting services to corporations on executive compensation issues. There is a fairly widely held view that even institutions that have staff to help decide how to vote their proxies will claim they must rely on the ISS recommendation. This is allegedly because they are seeking pension-plan business from the companies, and in voting against management, they want to assert that "the devil made me do it."

In addition to advising on how to vote proxies, ISS (among others) began issuing corporate governance ratings. The general idea is that governance ratings should help with equity investment decisions because of a perceived correlation between good governance and good performance. Post-Enron, the credit-rating agencies also began to look at ratings, under the theory that good governance would stave off sudden meltdowns into bankruptcy.[35] ISS's version has gone through a number of iterations over time—CGQ, Grid Governance Risk Indicators, and also QuickScore 1.0, 2.0, and 3.0. (In addition to governance ratings, ISS launched an Environmental & Social Disclosure Quality Score in 2018.) The various ratings systems were the subject of an academic study that concluded that, at least as of 2008, "the predictive ability of the leading commercial governance ratings . . . is well below the threshold necessary to support the bold claims made for them."[36]

In my own observations, a valid conclusion about the quality of a company's governance is a highly subjective assessment that requires, among other things, direct observation of the interactions between the board and the CEO and also among the members of the board. The commercial ratings systems, perhaps understandably, must rely largely on externally determinable, objective facts.

I have also observed directors who place great emphasis on the ratings, perhaps because, as one said, "I have never received a bad grade in my life." They will seek to tinker with things like structural takeover defenses to get a better grade—this, despite the fact that, in the right hands, those defenses can help achieve more value for shareholders. It is like the excessive concern with US News rankings of professional schools that can lead a dean to accept a 4.0 student from an undistinguished college over a student with a slightly lower GPA from a demanding program at a more selective institution. There are certainly valid reasons for doing so, but getting a better US News ranking is not one of them.

Between the impact of ISS voting recommendations, the attention given to governance ratings and ISS's estimated 61 percent market share of the proxy advisory business,[37] it is impossible to overstate how much influence ISS has over Corporate America. And to fully appreciate the level of detail that ISS focuses on when it comes to corporate governance, one need only skim the table of contents to its annual United States Proxy Voting Guidelines.

The most recent pertinent market development is the growth of financially oriented activist hedge funds. While the traditional institutions (whether following active or passive investment strategies) might not want to take a particularly aggressive position on subjects other than governance, they will on occasion simply rely on (or, it is rumored, encourage through an RFA, or request for activism) hedge funds to do that for them. The activist hedge funds have benefited from the successes of the governance activists. Governance reforms, such as adopting majority voting, giving shareholders the ability to call special meetings, and eliminating a classified board, have made it easier for hedge funds to effectively threaten corporate boards and achieve their goals.

There is another "market" that influences corporate governance— the marketplace of ideas. The principal domestic marketplace is academia. The most prominent example is the Harvard Law School Program on Corporate Governance led by Professor Lucian Bebchuk. He has written extensively, and influentially, on the subject. For example, Professor Bebchuk's writings on classified boards was a catalyst for the movement away from that form of director elections. And the program posts articles on its website, to which other academics also contribute. Topics covered include excessive board compensation,[38] corporate political activity,[39] and short-termism.[40]

Two well-respected professors of corporate law have recently advocated for "outsourcing the board"—that is, creating a new type of firm (called a board service provider, or BSP) to take over the functions of a board of directors. "Our idea," say the professors, "is to do away entirely with having individuals sitting on the board."[41] While recognizing that such an approach would require changes to the corporate statutes, they nevertheless advocate for this approach with a list of reasons, each of which can be challenged:

- "Public corporations simply are too large and complex for the board to have a day-to-day managerial function."[42] That is correct, but it seriously misstates the role of the board.
- "The role of the typical public corporation board [has] shifted from a mainly advisory function . . . to an emphasis . . . on active and independent monitoring of the top management team."[43] In my own experience, boards do both, together with having the final say over the big decisions.
- Directors "do not have the time or the mandate to challenge management's judgments except as to a discrete number of issues."[44] Boards have an unlimited mandate, and in my experience, when it truly matters, boards roll up their sleeves and spend the time needed on important issues. Moreover, because directors today serve on fewer boards, they have more time for those boards on which they serve.
- Boards "have an inherent information disadvantage."[45] Boards have an unlimited right to information. A well-advised board will make demands about both the quality and the format of routine information and will also insist on being provided with the critical information required to make material decisions in special situations (see chapters 7 and 8). A well-advised management team will understand that it is obligated, as a

fiduciary matter, to provide such information to the board even without being asked for it.

- "Directors are generalists . . . with little firm-specific knowledge, skills, or expertise."[46] Most boards are now assembled carefully using a skills matrix. Moreover, because an individual director often has a longer tenure as a director than the CEO's own tenure as CEO, directors can actually have more firm-specific knowledge than the CEO.
- "Directors do not have well-designed incentives."[47] All directors have an incentive to do a good job as a matter of avoiding both financial and, perhaps more importantly, reputational exposure. Some directors have a substantial ownership stake in their company and/or are compensated with stock.

On top of all of these challenges, how does an entity like a BSP participate in shareholder engagement and provide the coaching that virtually all CEOs require from time to time?

Another marketplace for ideas encompasses the pronouncements of organizations that represent institutional investors. Institutional investors have advocated for inclusion and diversity for years. And the Council of Institutional Investors issues policy statements on a variety of governance subjects. In 2017 and 2018, CII was campaigning against dual-class common stock (a subject covered in chapter 5), and in 2019, CII is advocating for more enhanced proxy statement disclosure about the process a board follows during its self-evaluation. In 2016, a group of CEOs, institutional investors, and even one hedge-fund activist got together and published the Commonsense Corporate Governance Principles.[48] An updated version of these principles was released in October 2018. Also in 2018, a report was issued titled "Embankment Project for Inclusive Capitalism" in a collaboration of the Coalition for Inclusive Capitalism, the accounting firm EY, and others.

There is also a global marketplace of ideas. Imports into the United States include separating the chair and CEO positions and the say-on-pay vote, both imported from the United Kingdom. A number of European countries have introduced mandatory quotas for gender diversity on boards. The United States has its own exports, including examples of hedge-fund activism in Europe and Asia.[49]

Politics

Professor Roe of Harvard makes a compelling case that populist distrust of financial institutions led to legislation in the 1930s that prevents banks from controlling industrial enterprises: "Main Street did not want to be controlled by Wall Street."[50] (This is in stark contrast to the keiretsu of Japan.) But there are now huge accumulations of stock in institutional hands, as well as a "shadow banking" system. These developments place significant control of industry in the hands of financiers.

The politics of populism is reflected in a number of federal law provisions relating to executive compensation—Internal Revenue Code sections covering "golden parachutes" and annual compensation greater than $1 million,[51] as well as "clawback" provisions of both SOX and Dodd-Frank.[52] The populist attention to income inequality is clearly behind the Dodd-Frank pay-ratio disclosure provision, which is awfully hard to justify as a matter of investor protection. Perhaps the best evidence of what Congress was really driving at in requiring pay-ratio disclosure is the fact that it intentionally used "median" rather than "mean" employee compensation as the denominator. Mean (i.e., what most would call "average") would have been much easier (and cheaper) for companies to calculate. Because the mean is typically higher than the median, however, using the mean would also have resulted in reporting a lower (and less embarrassing) ratio. The ratios are all over the map, vary by industry, and tend to be higher for companies with larger numbers of employees.[53] Perhaps as a "preview of coming attractions," and another example of the global marketplace for ideas about corporate governance, it should be mentioned that 2018 UK legislation is requiring the disclosure of a comparison of median hourly pay for men to median hourly pay for women.[54]

Politics clearly entered into the SEC's disclosure requirements for conflict minerals.[55] Those requirements were adopted pursuant to a Dodd-Frank mandate based on concerns that the profits from mining those minerals are used to fund violence in the regions where they are found and thus contribute to humanitarian crises. Presidential politics was clearly behind Senator Warren's introduction of her 2018 bill entitled the Accountable Capitalism Act. Her avowed purpose of the bill is to address the fact that "corporate profits are booming, but average wages haven't budged over the past year." Evoking President Roosevelt, she stated, "We should insist on a new deal."[56] Similarly, "at least five declared or likely Democratic presidential candidates [for 2020] want to restrict how much stock U.S. companies can buy back from shareholders," despite the fact that "some studies show that research, development and other capital expenditures are unaffected at companies that offer buybacks."[57]

PART II

The Board-Centric Corporation

Once upon a time, decision making in U.S. public companies was totally management-centric. There was no requirement that a majority of board members be independent. Board members were selected largely by CEOs, not a committee of independent directors. In the 1970s Armand Hammer of Occidental Petroleum kept undated director resignations in his desk! In 1986, the *New York Times* ran an article entitled "America's Imperial Chief Executive." The "Last [Corporate] Emperor" may have been Jack Welch at General Electric. It has been reported that, when Welch was CEO, a new GE director was surprised by the lack of discussion at board meetings. When he asked a long-tenured director, "What is our role?" the reply was, "Applause."

The net effect of much of what was described in Part I was an evolution to the board-centric corporation, which is what has always been the intention of corporate statutes. As a result, it is critical that both board members and CEOs fully and accurately understand what is required of a board, how boards are held accountable, and how to make a board effective (in both routine matters and special situations). It is equally important to understand where to draw the line between the roles of the board and management. Providing those understandings is the goal of Part II.

4

The Role of the Board

Understanding the role of the board begins with appreciating the statutory mandate. Virtually all corporate statutes contain a charge along the lines of Section 141(a) of the Delaware General Corporation Law: "The business and affairs of every corporation . . . shall be managed by or under the direction of a board of directors, except as may be otherwise provided in this [statute] or in its certificate of incorporation." This provision has been summarized in the case law as "the bedrock statutory principle of director primacy."[1]

The principal focus should be on the words "under the direction of"—this is the statutory authorization for delegation to management. Before the New Era in Corporate Governance, there seemed to be an assumption that, unless required by statute or expressly retained by the board, all decision-making authority resided with management. For a variety of reasons (including how directors were selected), there was little such "express retention." In those bygone days, there were even references in the financial press to the "Imperial CEO."[2]

In the new era, though, the default setting has changed to be much closer to what is contemplated by the statute. (There will still be references to an imperial CEO, but that typically refers to the CEO's interaction with employees, not the board.) The act of delegation from board to management should involve a conscious exercise of the board's business judgment. A best practice is to engage in a periodic review of "standing resolutions" that spell out the matters that must be presented to the board for action—matters such as acquisitions and borrowings greater than a certain size, reductions in force above a specified threshold, or settlements of litigation above a specified dollar amount. Of course, certain actions cannot be delegated: those for which the statute requires board (or in some cases board committee) action, such as issuances of stock, declaration of dividends, and approval of mergers. There are other subjects for which board action (indeed, action by independent directors) is required by rules of the stock exchanges, such as executive compensation and selecting candidates for membership on the board. In the new era, the role of the board also includes setting its own agendas and having a hand in determining the flow of information to the board. Standing resolutions should also address which information should immediately be brought to the attention of the board, such as allegations of misconduct on the part of a CEO, material inquiries from regulators, and a potential acquirer's approach.

A business judgment about delegation requires answering the question, Where do we draw the line between the role of the board and the role of management? This involves both allocating decision-making authority and determining the appropriate level of intensity of board oversight. While there have been some very helpful generalizations offered,[3] the correct answer for any particular company is highly contextual. It is dependent on, among other things, how well the company is performing, whether the company is engaging in "business as usual" or launching a new strategy, and how much confidence the board has in the CEO and the management team. Of course, if there is a low degree of confidence in management, the solution might be a change in CEO rather than closer monitoring. Conversely, if there is a high degree of confidence, there might be a concern that a board that hovers too closely might demoralize or, worse, drive away the CEO.

Making sure that directors stay on the right side of the line between the roles of the board and management is a recurring challenge. Failure to observe boundaries often involves the actions of a single director or two rather than the entire board.

In my survey of CEOs (discussed in more detail in Part IV), one of the questions was "Have you ever . . . had to admonish a board member about 'stepping over the line into management matters'?" Another question was "Have you experienced board members seeking information from members of the management team in a manner that is inconsistent with agreed upon protocols?" Both questions were frequently answered in the affirmative.

On more than one occasion, I have been asked to speak to an individual director about "stepping over the line." One instance involved a company in a highly regulated industry where the chair of the board's compliance committee believed that it was the prerogative of the chair to hire and fire the chief compliance officer. I typically suggest that, rather than singling out one individual, I give an "education session" to the entire board on the subject. The comment I make that seems to carry the most impact is noting the theoretical possibility that an overactive director could be deemed to be playing an officerlike role and lose the benefit of the exculpatory charter provision.

I have often advised that good governance on the part of a director is like spelling "banana." The hardest part may be knowing when to stop.

Wherever the line is drawn, the board will have decision-making responsibility (not just an oversight role) over the "big subjects": succession, strategy, executive compensation, material transactions (including especially a change in control). Depending on the circumstances, a board may also have the final say on internal investigation.

Of these "big subjects," the biggest of all is CEO succession. One of the reviewers mentioned in the acknowledgements is my colleague for over forty years, Newton Minow. The same Newt Minow who, as President Kennedy's Federal Communications Commission chairman, coined the phrase "vast wasteland" in reference to television. In the governance context, he is the father of Nell Minow, the cofounder of ISS, and has also served on numerous significant public company and not-for-profit boards. (He loves to tell the story about how ISS recommended a vote against him at a corporate annual meeting because of his attendance record—refusing to take into account that he had health issues that year!) His advice to me on reviewing a draft of this book was as follows—"I have witnessed succession failures at least 40 percent of the time. Of all the responsibilities of a board, this is the most important. Give it more emphasis." I have always benefited from Newt's advice and hope that I have given the subject the emphasis it deserves. I seriously considered having a separate chapter on CEO succession. While I devote a good bit of text to the subject, as a matter of organization, I have opted to distribute the discussion of that subject in several places: planning for succession (and what to do about the predecessor) is in chapter 7, executing on succession in chapter 8, and helping a successor actually succeed as a leader takes up a good bit of chapter 13 and, in some way, is the overarching theme of this book.

There is an ever-increasing focus on the importance of corporate culture, which leads to an interesting question about the proper role of the board with respect to this intangible. Indeed, the NACD devoted one of its recent Blue Ribbon Commission Reports to this subject. Corporate culture can be considered a board level subject in a variety of ways:

- Culture can be manifested in the company's position on CSR/ESG, which the board should address as a matter of strategy.
- A culture of compliance can have a favorable impact on the risk profile of the company and, thus, should be a part of the board's routine risk management exercise (see the discussion in chapter 7).
- A culture of collaboration can yield positive results in terms of recruitment, retention, productivity, and innovation. Thus, the success of the CEO in fostering collaboration might be part of the board's evaluation of the CEO's performance as a leader.

- If there is evidence that the culture is toxic (or even deeply suboptimal), the board should encourage the CEO to address a transformation. The success of the CEO in effecting the transformation should also be part of his or her evaluation.

That said, the role of the board with respect to culture is essentially one of oversight. The culture of a company is driven by its history, tradition, and the messaging and personal behaviors of individuals (especially the CEO) in day-to-day leadership positions.

A discussion about the role of the board doesn't end with understanding board versus management. It also includes an understanding of board versus shareholders. While that will be covered in more detail in the chapters on shareholder activism in Part III, some general concepts are useful here. First, the statute grants shareholders a limited number of subjects on which they must vote, such as the approval of mergers, the approval of a sale of "all or substantially all" of the company's assets, and amendments to the certificate of incorporation (but in each case, only upon the prior recommendation of the board), as well as the election of directors. (Additional subjects for shareholder approval are required by stock exchange rules[4] and recommended by ISS[5]). Shareholders cannot, as a matter of law, invade the province of the board to manage (or direct the management of) the company. Indeed, the duty of a board to manage (or direct the management of) the company "may not be delegated to the stockholders."[6] If the shareholders are dissatisfied with how the board is doing its job, then their recourse is to make changes to the board. To preserve this authority on the part of the shareholders, under the *Blasius* case, the courts aggressively protect the shareholder franchise.[7]

When it comes to a decision to sell the company, it might be intuitive to think that such a decision belongs in the hands of owners of the company—that is, the shareholders. However, even in this context, the law places tremendous authority in the hands of the board. As noted earlier, a sale effected by a merger requires both board and shareholder approval. Even in the case of an offer made directly to shareholders (i.e., a tender offer) that the owners of a majority of outstanding shares wish to accept, the board has authority to prevent that from succeeding because of the judicial validation of the so-called poison-pill defense (discussed at some length in the endnotes), which can be implemented and removed only by the board.[8] Indeed, case law states that in the event of a coercive tender offer at an inadequate price, the board is *obligated* to prevent shareholders from taking the offer.[9] Again, the shareholders are not without recourse; they can change the board to put in directors who will redeem the poison pill. It is for this reason that hostile tender offers are typically accompanied by a proxy contest and why a classified board is an important structural anti-takeover device.

This description of board-centricity should not be taken to suggest that boards are all-powerful or immunized against shareholder pressure. That is the subject of Part III.

5

Assembling an Effective Board

There are number of factors to consider in assembling an effective board.

Board Size

The process of assembling an effective board starts with deciding how big the board should be. The formal requirement for the size of the board is often set in the certificate of incorporation or bylaws (and most typically expressed as a range or an "up to" number). Setting the specific size involves a practical judgment. The board should not be so large as to run the risk of what social psychologists call "social loafing," or the tendency to slack off because "the other folks will do it."[1] It should also not be so large as to impede meaningful discussions of matters that the board as a whole should take up. In contrast, the board should be large enough to populate the various required standing committees (audit, compensation, and nominating and governance) and any other committees that the board determines should be empaneled (e.g., technology) or that may be required under terms of a litigation settlement or consent decree (e.g., compliance). This is an important practical consideration if it is desired that those committees meet concurrently. A board also needs to be large enough to accommodate all the skills and experiences required to be represented on the board, which will of course vary by company.

Skills Matrix and Diversity

Determining which skills should be represented on the board involves creating a "skills matrix" delineating the expertise and experience needed to pursue the company's strategy and address its challenges. All boards need to have directors with the skills mandated for an audit committee—one "audit committee financial expert" and a number of others who meet the requirements for financial literacy.[2] A retail company should have real estate experts and (to address the challenges of online marketing) technology experts. Companies with global footprints should have directors with international business experience and, possibly, those who live outside the United States. Companies in highly regulated industries should have directors with relevant experience in dealing with the government. Consumer products companies need marketing experts. And so on.

In addition to pertinent skills, a board should consider gender, racial/ethnic, and even age diversity. The substantive reason for this is to bring together the varying perspectives for problem solving that mitigate against "groupthink" (another term favored by social psychologists).[3] There is some body of evidence supporting the notion that companies with diverse boards perform better.[4] Certainly, for a company with a diverse employee base and/or global operations, there can be human resources considerations for diversity "at the top of the house"—the boardroom and also the C-suite. And shouldn't a company with a predominantly female customer base have a board that somewhat reflects that fact? Consideration should be given to anticipated demographic changes in the company's markets.

The other reason for boardroom diversity is because "the market" is demanding it. Other than a 2018 California statute and similar legislation in other states, the United States does not have the mandated diversity that has appeared in other countries.[5] Nevertheless, institutional investors and others have articulated goals for gender diversity percentages in the boardroom,[6] and/or a policy to oppose the election of all directors at companies that fail to have any female directors.[7] In its policy update for the 2019 proxy season, ISS announced that beginning in 2020, it will generally recommend against nominating committee chairs at companies with no female directors. Glass Lewis announced the same policy, but effective a year earlier, in 2019. Having more than one female director protects against marginalization and claims of tokenism. The percentage of U.S. public company directors who are female is increasing but still lagging the aspirational goals. The percentage of female directors in board leadership positions (chair or lead independent) is even lower. Unfortunately, racial/ethnic diversity does not seem to receive the attention it deserves.

One approach to achieving diversity and its benefits is to adopt a "Rooney rule." The NFL adopted the policy (named for the former owner of the Pittsburgh Steelers) in 2003 to require that teams interview at least one minority candidate whenever there is an opening for head coaching positions. The corporate version (which has been the subject of shareholder proposals under SEC Rule 14a-8) would require that, for any opening on a board that lacks diversity, there must be at least one diverse candidate considered.

Some boards include a "celebrity" director. Over the years, I have observed directors who were former governors and congressional representatives, former generals, business school deans, one former chairman of the Federal Reserve Board, and even former professional athletes. There is also a category of celebrity CEOs. There can be no generalization about "value add" from such board members, other than to urge nominating committees to apply strict merit-based standards in selecting any nominees. Some celebrities (especially governors and deans) can be terrific directors. Others, not so much. I recall attending a number of board meetings including a director who was an iconic sports figure but literally never spoke. I am proud that I resisted asking for his autograph.

One could argue that a board that is overpopulated with celebrity directors should raise red flags for investors. Exhibit A for this proposition is the board of Theranos, the health-care tech company that failed in spectacular fashion and whose founder was indicted in 2018. Its independent directors included two former secretaries of state (Kissinger and Schultz), one former and one future secretary of defense (Perry and Mattis, respectively), two former senators (Nunn and Frist), and two high-profile CEOs (Kovacevich and Bechtel).

At one point in time, many boards included a senior partner from the company's principal outside law firm as a director. That person was often effectively the company's general counsel. Beginning in the mid-1980s, this became much less commonplace and today is actually quite rare for several reasons. First, there was the "inside counsel revolution," beginning with the hiring by Jack Welch of Ben Heineman Jr. as GE's general counsel.[8] As a related matter, it became much more difficult to decide which was the principal outside law firm. Then, there are the chilling effects of proxy statement disclosure requirements about fees paid to the law firm and independence requirements that may prevent the lawyer from serving on any of the standing committees. From the perspective of a law firm's risk management, it became less desirable to have a partner sit on a board as law firms became more of a target of litigation and as conflict-of-interest rules were tightened. As I have told many CEOs, it is easier to simply "rent" advice from a lawyer by the hour.

Independence

Another critical criterion for selecting board members is independence. This is because a majority of board members (and all members of the standing committees) must meet the definition of independence imposed by rules of the stock exchange where the company is listed.[9] In addition to a general requirement, there is a higher standard of independence for membership on the audit committee.[10] This is part of the package of SOX reforms, predicated on the notion that greater independence would prevent the Enron-type debacle.

The stock-exchange rules are not the only source of requirements for and definitions of independence. ISS has its own categories: inside, affiliated outside, and independent outside.[11] In populating a compensation committee, it is necessary to consider the independence requirements of the 1934 Act Section 16(b),[12] and prior to the Tax Cuts and Jobs Act of 2017, it was necessary to consider independence requirements of Internal Revenue Code Section 162(m).[13] In populating a special litigation committee (or any other special committee set up to address management or other conflicts of interest), consider whether social, philanthropic, or other relationships can be successfully argued to impede the ability of a director to reach a decision purely in the best interests of the corporation.[14] There is even case law holding that some directors have been so intimidated by the CEO that they cannot be counted as independent.[15]

Finally, some suggest that after a long period of board service an individual director loses a degree of independence. (ISS says nine years; note, however, that the average tenure of directors in the S&P 1500 during the period 1998 to 2010 was 8.2 years.[16]) Such people are uncharitably labeled "zombie directors."[17] Even worse, a shareholder of Boeing, in a Rule 14a-8 proposal that the SEC would not allow to be excluded from that company's proxy statement, labeled its longest serving director a "lapdog."[18] Apart from such pejoratives, there is another reason to be cautious about having excessively long-tenured directors—they are the most vulnerable to being targeted and voted off in a proxy contest. Having said all of that, it is unusual for a company to set term limits (although age limits are somewhat more common).

Two stories about independence.

Ben Heineman Sr., the industrialist who ran the conglomerate Northwest Industries in the 1970s and 1980s (and the father of the long-standing general counsel of GE), was the only inside director of that company. When asked why he took that position (which at the time was fairly unusual), he stated, "How can someone be my peer on the day of board meetings and be my subordinate the rest of the time?" He was reflecting on the reality that some inside directors simply give the CEO an additional vote on the board. Under the Delaware statute it is actually possible (though unheard of for a public company) to provide in the certificate of incorporation for one director to have more than one vote.[19] As a somewhat related matter, it is common to hear a director say near the end of a conference call that is running over, "I have to get off, but I will give my proxy to the chairman." Obviously shareholders can vote by proxy, but this is not allowed for directors.

One time I told a CEO, who was making a bid to buy his company, that there would need to be a special committee comprising independent directors to respond to his bid. He listened carefully and then said: "Great! So Dad [a director, but not an employee] can be on the committee?" You can guess my answer.

Nominating Candidates

After establishing the size of the board and criteria to be considered for membership, a nominating committee will review the candidates.

The starting point will be the incumbents. While there is a default expectation of reslating, every incumbent should be considered in terms of how long he or she has served and, more importantly, how each has *recently* contributed to board discussions and decision making. Consider also whether there have been changes in the skills matrix that would cause any of them not to be considered if they were new candidates. For example, has there been a divesture of a business unit such that the director's expertise is less relevant to the remaining enterprise? Finally, there can be changes in an incumbent's life that are relevant to a reslating decision. Have any incumbents lost the job that they had at the time they joined the board, and what were the circumstances? (Many companies have policies requiring that board members tender a resignation in such a case.) Have they taken on a new job that will detract from the ability to perform or that will create a conflict of interest? As a general matter, does the board need to be "refreshed"?

When a decision is made not to reslate an incumbent, there will be thoughts about providing a "soft landing." The easiest thing to do is give the incumbent director the opportunity to inform the company that he or she does not wish to stand for reelection. A decision by an incumbent director not to stand for reelection triggers an SEC disclosure (which can be tricky if the decision is based on a known disagreement on "operations, policies or practices").[20]

On rare occasions, the title "director emeritus" can be given to a long-standing director whose personal reputation will continue to add luster to the reputation of the company. (For the sake of that person, public disclosures, such as websites and annual reports, should not suggest that he or she is a "real" director.) More controversial would be to offer the departing director a consulting agreement. Caution should be exercised about compensation under such an agreement; anything in excess of the level of board fees, and certainly any equity-based compensation, will attract unwanted attention. A retiring director should be aware that, unless otherwise provided for contractually, a consultant is held to a simple negligence standard (not the gross negligence standard applicable to directors) and does not have the benefit of the suite of director protections. Gifts to the departing director's favorite charity can also be controversial.

In considering new candidates, a nominating committee will first consider the skills matrix. This should include whether the candidate could serve as a successor to an incumbent who is filling a particular role but who is about to cycle off (e.g., the audit committee financial expert, for example, if there is no current incumbent who could so serve or is willing to be so identified). Independence, general reputation, and diversity are obviously high on the list of considerations. Does the candidate have any conflicts of interest that are problematic from a business perspective, or is the candidate on the board of a competitor such that there is a legal problem under the antitrust law's prohibition on director interlocks?[21] Other considerations are whether the candidate be "overboarded" in the view of ISS or under the company's own governance guidelines,[22] whether the candidate will have scheduling conflicts around board meeting dates, whether the candidate will likely be available to serve for some appropriate number of years, and what references say about the candidate's boardroom demeanor.

Vetting is, of course, a two-way street. During the process of recruitment, the candidate should be undertaking his or her own due diligence by reading documents, understanding the company's recent history and prospects, and asking a series of questions. Among the questions a candidate should ask are the following:

- Do I have the time to serve, and given the schedule of at least regular meetings, am I available when I need to be? (This is important, because proxy rules require disclosure of the name of any director who has a less than 75 percent attendance record, and ISS will recommend a withhold vote for any such director.[23])
- Do I have the expertise and experience that will allow me to contribute in a meaningful fashion, and am I sufficiently interested in the company, its business, and its challenges to make that contribution?
- What is the quality of the group of executives who deal with "public company issues"—CFO, GC, head of internal audit, head of investor relations? Does the GC recognize his or her ethical responsibility to the board?
- How do I feel about the risk profile of the company, and do the board members have appropriate levels of formal protection from personal liability (see discussion in chapter 6)? As a related matter, what is the quality of the board's involvement in risk management and of the company's chief compliance officer and chief information officer (see chapter 7)?
- What is the dynamic in the boardroom, and does the CEO actually look to the board for advice?

In addition to action by a nominating committee, shareholders can put forward a candidate. The two mechanisms for that are a proxy contest and what is known as proxy access. In a proxy contest, an insurgent publishes its own proxy statement and collects votes on its own proxy card (all discussed in detail in Part III). Proxy access, in contrast, is a process, adopted on a company-by-company basis, to allow shareholders to add to the slate of director nominees listed in the company's proxy statement and on its proxy card. This company-by-company approach (also called "private ordering") was established after an SEC rule mandating proxy access at all public companies but later struck down on procedural grounds.[24] The SEC's failed rule would have given the right to use proxy access to a holder of more than 3 percent who had held at that level for three years and wished to nominate three directors. Most shareholder proposals for proxy access, or company-volunteered provisions, have been along the same lines. As of 2018, approximately 65 percent of the S&P 500 provided for proxy access.[25] It has turned out that, so far, financial activists who are intent on changing a board are not using proxy access to do so. They will engage in a threatened (and sometimes actual) proxy contest.

Electing Candidates

Once nominated, the candidate needs to be elected. Most companies elect all directors annually. The exception to this is the "staggered" or "classified" board, in which approximately a third of the directors are elected each year for a three-year term. As a result of successful efforts by governance-oriented activists, the incidence of staggered boards went from a majority of S&P 500 companies at the beginning of the twenty-first century to only 10 percent as of 2016.[26] Elimination of the staggered board became a goal of governance activists after it was observed that the combination of a staggered board and a poison pill was an extremely effective set of structural defenses against hostile takeovers.[27] This is because it would take two annual meetings (approximately thirteen months) to attain a majority on a staggered board, which would be needed to redeem the pill.

Years ago, McDonald's Corporation was presented with a shareholder proposal to eliminate its staggered board. The then-nonexecutive chairman of the board convened a "panel of experts" to debate the wisdom of staggered boards in front of the proponent. The panel included individuals on "both sides of the aisle," including me. I argued then, and continue to believe, that one benefit of three-year terms is that they enhance the ability of a director to be independent—that is, to speak his or her mind at least in a nonelection year. Think of the difference between the U.S. House and the Senate. (I also think the staggered board should be the last structural takeover defense to give up.) The argument that carried the day with the proponent (and led to withdrawal of the proposal) came from the CEO. He noted that McDonald's had many suppliers for whom the company was their sole customer. Those suppliers needed some assurance that the management they knew and trusted would be in place when they were asked to make capital expenditures to expand capacity. McDonald's has since declassified its board.

When a hostile bidder engages in a proxy fight and puts up candidates to replace one-third of a staggered board, it will typically nominate individuals who are independent of the bidder itself in order to improve its chances of success in the election. Even when the bidder succeeds in getting those individuals elected, its candidates can turn against it. This can be achieved by a combination of a lecture on the law ("you have a duty to *all* shareholders") and a dose of facts and analysis that convince the new directors that the incumbent board's position on inadequacy of price or opportunistic timing is correct. We succeeded in doing this on a number of occasions.

If a new candidate is found between annual meetings of shareholders, most companies have the ability to elect the candidate by board action—to fill a vacancy created by a death, resignation, or retirement or a vacancy created by a board action to expand the size of the board. While in this instance directors can be elected by the board, at least in Delaware, there are no situations in which the board can remove a director, even for cause. That is, only shareholders have the power to remove a director and can do so generally with or without cause. (In the case of a staggered board, it is possible to provide for "for cause" removal only. In the absence of a staggered board, a provision of the certificate of incorporation purporting to require cause to remove an annually elected director is unenforceable.[28]) The inability of directors to remove a fellow director is one of the reasons that a well-drafted CEO employment agreement will provide that, upon any termination of employment, the CEO is deemed to have resigned from all boards in the corporate family.

Both new and incumbent candidates are elected at shareholder meetings by vote of the shareholders. Separate and apart from the detailed disclosure requirements for proxy statements, the complexity of the system for simply voting proxies boggles the mind. It is graphically illustrated in an SEC release from 2010 that was devoted to possible reform of the entire proxy system.[29] That chart is reproduced in appendix 1.

While most companies elect on the basis of one share, one vote, it doesn't have to be that way. The most common departure is a dual-class common stock capitalization (sometimes called an A/B structure) in which one class has a high number of votes (e.g., ten votes per share) and the other class has one or even no votes per share. This structure is sometimes put in place at the time of an initial public offering to give the founders or their families the ability to attain liquidity and the other benefits of public ownership, and yet remain assured of being able to control the enterprise. The structure can have the effect of giving founders controlling votes (say, 80 percent) at a time when their percentage economic interest is quite low (say, 20 percent). While some dual-class capitalized companies provide for a "sunset" of the high votes, either based on time or on when the economic ownership dips below a certain level, that is not always the case. Dual-class structures (especially without a sunset or that do not provide for equal treatment of the two classes in a merger) have been subject to criticism.[30] There is some movement toward making them ineligible for inclusion in various stock indices.[31] Nevertheless, it is probably the case that, without the assurance of ongoing control that the structure provides to founders, many companies (e.g., Ford Motor, Hyatt Hotels, News Corp, Tootsie Roll, Facebook, and Google's owner Alphabet) may not have gone public.

While dual-class capitalizations have been criticized (in many cases quite fairly) as an entrenchment mechanism, they can work for the benefit of all shareholders. For example, Helene Curtis had such a capitalization. It allowed the founding family to take steps necessary to "fix" the company even though those steps penalized short-term results. Even more important, when the family supported the board in its decision to explore a sale, it gave total credibility to the price demand—"hit our asking price or the company will stay independent." An even rarer utilization of the dual class came with the sale of Renaissance Learning, during which the founders holding the high-vote stock agreed to take less than the public shareholders to facilitate a sale.

When a founder has voting control as a result of a dual-class capitalization (or otherwise), while it may seem intrusive, the board of the company has a legitimate interest in knowing whether the founder and his or her spouse have entered into a prenuptial agreement covering what happens to the controlling interest in the event of a divorce. This can be an even more complicated subject when the spouses are the cofounders.

Another departure from one share, one vote is tenure-based voting. In this approach, shares that are in the hands of long-term holders are entitled to additional votes. The rationale given for such an approach is that it rewards long-term holders and may facilitate managing with a longer-term perspective. The real motivation is, again, control. Tenure-based voting has been approved as a concept by the Delaware courts,[32] but there are issues with it in securities law and stock exchange listing.[33]

Then there is the question of what vote is required to be elected. For the longest time, the answer was a plurality. In plurality voting, if there are ten board seats and ten candidates for those seats, the required vote to win election is literally one share. In the early 2000s, this became a target of governance-oriented activists, who decried that system as a "Soviet-style election." As a result of successful activism, by 2018, 90 percent of the S&P 500 corporations had adopted one or another form of "majority voting" to apply in any uncontested election.[34] In simple terms, if a director does not receive a majority of votes cast, he or she is elected but must tender a resignation. The board then has the discretion to accept or reject that resignation. The discretion is limited, however. In the absence of a good reason for refusing to accept the resignation, ISS may (under its "responsiveness" standards[35]) recommend a "withhold vote" against some other directors the following year, thus leading to the specter of another failure to obtain a majority of votes.

Cumulative voting, under which (to oversimplify the formula) a holder of, say, 10 percent of the stock would be assured of being able to elect 10 percent of the board, has gone the way of the dinosaurs.

On a truly exceptional basis, holders of preferred stock are entitled to elect directors. Most "series resolutions" that authorize the issuance of the security provide that, if dividends are not paid out, then the holders of the preferred are entitled to elect some number of directors. This is obviously designed to create an incentive for the incumbent directors to declare the stipulated dividends (which, unlike interest payments on debt, must always be left to the discretion of the board from time to time). Another instance for holders of preferred (or sometimes a special class of common) to elect directors is when shares are issued to labor unions in settlement of claims in bankruptcy. For example, two of the unions representing United Continental employees are entitled to one director each. Those directors recuse themselves from matters relating to labor relations.

When a new director joins a board, there should be an onboarding process to bring the director up to speed so as to be able to contribute immediately. Sometimes this will involve conveying information that was perhaps too sensitive to provide in the director's preelection diligence and was explicitly deferred. For example, to preserve attorney-client privilege, counsel will not want to go much beyond what is publicly disclosed about material litigation until after the election. A really well-organized board will provide a new director (especially one who is joining a public board for the first time) with a "mentor."[36]

One topic for a mentor to cover with a new board member is "boardroom etiquette." Boardroom etiquette is about more than just "making nice." A board is a team. A team functions better if there is a "virtuous cycle of respect, trust and candor."[37]

Indeed, some incumbent board members can use coaching on this subject. A colleague described to me an extreme example of this. He told me about a board's conference-call discussion of a possible transaction that became so heated that one director said to another, "If we were in the room together right now, I would invite you outside to settle this like men." That kind of outburst may not be "coachable."

A less charged example relates to discussions about politics. I did interviews for a board self-evaluation around the time of the 2016 presidential election. A director complained to me about the banter that took place in the boardroom concerning the two candidates. For him, it exceeded a level that could be fairly characterized as "good natured," felt like "baiting," and (while he didn't use the term) bruised that "virtuous circle."

Mentoring about etiquette can include proper demeanor toward members of management who are making presentations and understanding which discussions and opinions should be deferred to executive sessions of the nonmanagement directors (discussed in chapter 7).

Finally, I have witnessed more than one example of directors who would have benefited from being told not to monopolize the conversation. Often the director with the greatest power of persuasion and impact on deliberations is the one who sits back, picks the best time to offer a view, and delivers it concisely.

6

Duties, Accountability, and Protections of Directors

In light of the vast level of authority bestowed upon directors, as described in chapter 4, it is logical that there would be related duties and that, when directors do not properly discharge those duties, there should be legal accountability. Without protections that limit the personal financial exposure of directors, however, boards would become too risk averse and corporate innovation would suffer. Moreover, it would be very difficult to assemble an effective board. Boardrooms would be populated largely by judgment-proof directors, for whom the fees would be so important that their independence could be compromised. While it may seem anomalous, shareholders benefit when directors have an appropriate level of protections against legal accountability. Those protections, of course, do not immunize directors against potential reputational damage.

Duties of Directors under Corporate Law

Directors' duties come from many sources, starting with the corporate law, which imposes fiduciary duties that are owed to the corporation and its stockholders.[1] The fundamental duties are care and loyalty. Delaware courts, which preside over litigation involving a majority of U.S. public companies, went through a period of articulating additional types of duties, sometimes described as being "derived" from the fundamental duties. More recently, those courts seem to be reverting to a focus on the basics. This proliferation, followed by reconcentration, might be called the

Delaware accordion. (There has been a similar approach to standards of judicial review, discussed later.) In an example of perhaps protesting too much, one judge wrote, "How we understand duties may evolve and become refined, but the duties themselves have not changed."[2]

There is a good argument that the Delaware pronouncements are relevant even to companies incorporated in other states. Many of those other states have statutes that follow the American Bar Association's Model Act. Under statutes based on the Model Act, directors are expected to behave in a manner in which a similarly situated prudent person would behave.[3] And, of course, the greatest number of examples of such persons sit on the boards of Delaware companies. It is also common for courts presiding over non-Delaware corporations to expressly look to Delaware courts' opinions in the absence of their own precedents.

The courts usually articulate the duty of care as a requirement that directors take into account "all material information reasonably available" to them before making a decision and to consider that information with a "critical eye" and act in a "deliberate manner."[4] This requirement should be viewed through a lens of proportionality. That is, the more consequential the decision, the more information should be considered and the more time and process devoted to the decision. For example, a very consequential decision is a decision to sell the company. A similarly consequential decision is the selection of a CEO. Approaches to discharging the duty of care in relation to those decisions are detailed in chapter 8. Less quantitatively "material" to most companies but nevertheless highly consequential are decisions about executive compensation.

Discharging the duty of care can be as much about process as about information. "Optics" can also be important because of what they suggest about quality of process and seriousness of purpose. Any student of the TransUnion decision can recite that the Court noted in its opinion that the merger agreement was signed by Mr. Van Gorkom when he was in white tie at the opening night of the Lyric Opera of Chicago. Because of disclosure considerations and concerns about leaks, it is common for a board meeting to approve a merger to be held on a Sunday.

For one of my deals, the Sunday was the day of the Super Bowl. A director asked if we could arrange for a TV set to be in the boardroom during the meeting. It was actually a matter of legal advice to say no. Appearances matter!

Both substance and appearance will enter into a decision about whether to hold an in-person meeting or a meeting by telephone or video conference. The more consequential or complex the subject of the meeting, the more appropriate it is for it to be in person. If one or two directors cannot attend in person, they should participate by phone or video conference. In one meeting to approve the sale of a company (scheduled for a weekday but after the close of the U.S. markets), only one director of our client could not attend in person. He was in Europe. Due to the time-zone differences, he had already had dinner (and perhaps a libation or two). I like to think that it wasn't caused by our refresher on fiduciary duties or discussion of the terms of the merger agreement, but as evidenced by his loud snoring, the director on the phone had clearly fallen asleep. Efforts to rouse him (shouting into the speaker phone and even having the hotel concierge knock on his door) were unsuccessful. This created a bit of a challenge about how to record his vote.

The duty of care can be weaponized as a delaying tactic by a director who opposes an action that the board seems to be on the verge of approving. A comment by one director made in front of the other directors to the effect that "I don't think we yet have enough information to make this decision right now" can rattle the resolve of the others in moving forward. I once said to a board that, in my legal judgment, the board members had sufficient information and had spent sufficient time on a decision involving the sale of a subsidiary that they had an excellent record of discharging their duty of care. As a result, I advised that, if they so desired, they could vote on the pending matter. The director who, up to that point had done an excellent job of delaying the decision, said, "Cole, are you trying to railroad this through?" My reply—"I don't think that is a fair comment, given that this is the fourth hour of the seventh meeting devoted exclusively to the subject." The directors proceeded with the vote, and it passed with only one dissent.

The duty of loyalty is a requirement that directors make decisions that are unencumbered by either self-interest or divided loyalties. The Delaware statute expressly provides a mechanism for dealing with director (and officer) conflicts of interest, and even for allowing directors to vote on transactions in which they have financial interest.[5] Compliance with this provision prevents the approved transaction only from being "void or voidable"; it is not a safe harbor against a breach-of-loyalty claim.

Accordingly, in such cases the best practice is either recusal of the conflicted director or appointment of a special committee of disinterested directors. A special committee has the advantage that the interested director can be thoroughly insulated from the proceedings and deliberations of the other directors (e.g., no need to receive notices of meetings). If recusal is the path selected, the recused director should be asked to waive notice of meetings and also waive rights to accessing information pertaining to the issue that led to the recusal.

One articulation of the duty of loyalty states that it "embodies not only an affirmative duty to protect the interests of the corporation, but also an obligation to refrain from conduct that would injure the corporation and its stockholders or deprive them of profit or advantage."[6] This notion about not depriving the corporation of profit underlies the corporate opportunity doctrine. Under that doctrine, if a fiduciary (director or officer) is provided a business opportunity that the corporation might take advantage of and the fiduciary doesn't present it to the corporation but takes that opportunity for himself or herself (or another entity that he or she is associated with), that constitutes a breach of the duty of loyalty. Interestingly, this is one fiduciary duty that the Delaware statute allows a corporation to waive by including a provision expressly to that effect in the certificate of incorporation.[7] Such a provision is perhaps most common in the case of a corporation that has venture capital representatives on its board of directors or that is majority owned by another corporation and has representatives on the board.

The duty of loyalty also underlies the fiduciary obligation (that supplements the securities law prohibition described later in this chapter) not to trade on the basis of inside information.[8] In addition, if a board

member has concerns that management is stealing from the corporation, he or she may have a duty not to quit, again derived from the duty
of loyalty.[9]

In the mid-1990s, the Delaware Supreme Court added another
duty—the duty of good faith—which was initially described as part of
a "triad," together with care and loyalty.[10] There was some confusion,
though, about what good faith really meant. A decade later, that court
in *Disney* provided "some conceptual guidance to the corporate community." It stated that a breach of good faith would involve more than
gross negligence; it would require showing an "intentional dereliction
of duty, a conscious disregard for one's responsibilities."[11] The court
later provided further clarification in a different case. In *Stone v. Ritter*,
the Court wrote "the obligation to act in good faith does not establish
an independent fiduciary duty that stands on the same footing as the
duties of care and loyalty." Rather, it is a breach of the "duty of loyalty
[to fail] to discharge [a] fiduciary obligation in good faith."[12] This leads
to the following question—If a board is advised about what it must
do to discharge its duty of care but consciously decides to decline to
take the required steps, would that elevate a breach of the duty of care
to a failure to act in good faith, and therefore, a breach of the duty of
loyalty?

Stone v. Ritter also addressed another newly articulated duty—the
duty of oversight. In another case from the mid-1990s, *Caremark*, Chancellor Allen had "reassessed" the holding in a 1963 decision (*Graham v.
Allis-Chalmers*). The earlier case pertained to the obligation of a board
to affirmatively engage in oversight about a company's compliance
with law. *Graham* held that "absent cause for suspicion there is no duty
upon the directors to install and operate a corporate system of espio-
nage to ferret out wrongdoing which they have no reason to suspect
exists."[13] In *Caremark*, Chancellor Allen in essence said that times had
changed. While "dicta" (i.e., language not needed for the decision and
thus without the precedential impact of a "holding"), the Chancellor wrote that "it is important that the board exercise a good faith
judgment that the corporation's information and reporting system is
in concept and design adequate to assure the board that appropriate
information will come to its attention in a timely manner." He went

on to say, however, that "only a sustained or systematic failure of the board to exercise oversight . . . will establish the lack of good faith that is a necessary condition to liability."[14] A decade later, the Delaware Supreme Court approved the *Caremark* standard in *Stone v. Ritter*, with something of an extension. Liability can be established not only by a failure to implement a good reporting system. There can also be liability "having implemented such a system . . . [by] consciously fail[ing] to monitor or oversee its operations."[15]

Caremark established a duty of oversight pertaining to legal compliance risk. After the housing bubble led to the Great Recession and the Global Financial Crisis in 2008, shareholders attempted to expand the duty of oversight to apply to business risk. Plaintiff shareholders of Citigroup alleged that the directors failed "to properly monitor Citigroup's business risk, specifically its exposure to the subprime mortgage market." In rejecting the application of *Caremark*, the Court of Chancery stated that the plaintiff shareholders were "attempting to hold the director defendants personally liable for making (or allowing to be made) business decisions that, in hindsight, turned out poorly for the Company."[16]

The *Citigroup* case (and a later case against the directors of JP Morgan relating to the "London Whale" trading debacle) can be read to stand for the proposition that directors are to be held more accountable as a legal matter for compliance risk than for business risk. There may be some irony in that outcome. In any event, reputational accountability can be meted out at the ballot box and by the financial press for a failure of oversight of business risk.

Another duty that the Delaware courts have established is the duty of candor or of disclosure. This arises in two different contexts. When directors are seeking shareholder action, the duty requires that directors "disclose fully and fairly all material information within the board's control." Unlike securities law disclosure claims, a fiduciary disclosure claim in this context "does not include the elements of reliance, causation and actual quantifiable monetary damages." When directors are not seeking action on the part of shareholders, liability requires proof that the directors are "deliberately misinforming shareholders about the business of the corporation."[17] Similar to what the Court did in clarifying the duty of good faith, the Delaware court had to decide whether a breach of the duty of candor implicated care or loyalty. In *Arnold v. Society for Savings Bancorp*, the Delaware Supreme Court found, on the facts of that case, that a fiduciary disclosure violation was shielded by the exculpatory charter provision—that is, was a duty-of-care issue.[18] In *Chen v. Howard-Anderson*, the Delaware Chancery Court said, in effect, "It depends"—if the disclosure violation were intentional, it would breach the duty of loyalty; if inadvertent, it would be a breach of the duty of care.[19]

The flip side of the duty of disclosure is the duty of confidentiality. That duty covers not only information about the company but also information about board deliberations. While the obligation to preserve confidentiality of company information is clear as a matter of law, confidentiality of board deliberations has received less attention in the case law. Nevertheless, company policies typically cover both types of information.[20]

There is an interesting question about whether directors may share confidential information with others for purposes of seeking assistance in discharging fiduciary duties. The "others" may be personal counsel or, in the case of a director who is representing a major shareholder (e.g., a fund, a family), the shareholder who is being represented. On this point, a Delaware judge wrote in a law review article that "directors generally must have the right to consult with their own counsel and other advisors to assist in their evaluation of the materials presented to them by management or their fellow directors."[21] As a practical matter, and to address potential Regulation FD issues, the sharing of information by a "representative director" is usually covered by a confidentiality agreement between the company and the others with whom the director plans to share the information. Even with a confidentiality agreement in place, privileged information should not be shared with persons outside the umbrella of privilege.

Beyond these generalized fiduciary duties created by case law, there is a very specific duty created by statute—not to pay dividends or repurchase shares other than out of funds that may be properly used for such purposes, or the so-called legally available funds.[22] A failure to comply with this requirement can expose directors, jointly and severally, to personal liability for the full amounts unlawfully paid out.

Other duties articulated by the Delaware courts include a raft of duties in the M&A context (discussed in chapter 8).

To Whom Are Fiduciary Duties Owed?

In keeping with the notions discussed in Part I, it is clear that the generalized fiduciary duties are owed to the residual owners—that is, as a general matter, the shareholders. That statement does not fully answer the question, however. Subsidiary questions follow.

Do boards of controlled corporations owe duties to the controlling shareholders (who can, after all, take care of themselves), or are the duties somehow limited to being owed only to minority holders? The answer is that duties are owed to *all* of the shareholders by *all* of the directors. This point is illustrated in another case from the mid-1990s—*Mendel v. Carroll.* In that case, the controlling family (owning about 50 percent of the outstanding stock) proposed a merger in which the family would acquire all shares owned by the public for $25.75 per share in cash. This proposal triggered an offer by a third party to acquire all shares of the company for a higher price—$27.30 per share in cash. The outside bidder asked the board of the company to issue it an option to buy 20 percent of the company's stock, so as to dilute the family interest and clear the way for the public shareholders (as well as the family) to take the higher offer. In its opinion approving the directors' decision not to grant the option, the Court held as follows: "The board's duty was to respect the rights of the . . . Family," and "the board's fiduciary obligation . . . requires it to be a protective guardian of the rightful interest of the public shareholders . . . but . . . it does not authorize the board to deploy corporate power against the majority stockholders, in the absence of a threatened serious breach of fiduciary duty by the controlling stock."[23] In this instance, the courts refused to force the issuance of an option eliminating a control position to facilitate a better price for the entire company. In a different case, however, it allowed such an issuance with the effect of diluting corporate control "for a proper corporate purpose" (to fund renovations of a company's restaurants).[24]

While boards of companies that have controlling shareholders owe duties to all shareholders, not all controllers see it that way. To the extent that they are too explicit in their expectations of fealty (especially to directors who greatly value the fees they receive), questions could be raised about independence. A candidate for a seat on the board of a controlled corporation might add one more question to the list set forth earlier, addressed to the controlling shareholder: "Do you accept the notion that I will have fiduciary duties to all of the shareholders, and not just you?" A candidate for a seat on a controlled company board should be fully apprised of all the ways such a company is different, under special rules of the stock exchanges and otherwise.[25]

The presence of a controlling shareholder can create potential issues for corporate lawyers as well as directors. When representing any corporation (controlled or not), under ethical and SEC rules, a lawyer has a responsibility to the corporation and is required to respond to the highest authority in the organization—namely, the board of directors. On many, if not most, matters, the lawyer will take direction from the CEO and other members of management. However, there will be times when he or she is duty-bound to elevate issues to the board of directors—a requirement that can certainly put the lawyer in an awkward spot.[26] This awkwardness is exacerbated when the CEO is also the controlling shareholder.

I was once asked to represent a household-name public company that had a controlling shareholder due to a dual-class common stock capital structure. During my conversation with the GC, he quite candidly said, "There should be no ambiguity here; the client is [name of controlling shareholder]." That was one of the reasons that we declined to take on the representation.

Do directors owe fiduciary duties to holders of preferred stock, which (after all) is a form of equity? The answer is no. Those holders are entitled to have their contract rights (embodied in the preferred stock series resolution or otherwise in the charter), but no more.[27]

Do directors owe fiduciary duties to holders of convertible debt, options, and warrants, and does it matter if those instruments are "in the money"? Again, the answers are no and no.[28]

Do directors of a company that is about to spin off a subsidiary have a fiduciary duty to those who become shareholders of the company to be spun off? No again.[29]

Do directors of an insolvent corporation owe fiduciary duties to its creditors, who (at the end of the day) will become the residual owners following a bankruptcy proceeding? The answer to this question provides another example of how the Delaware courts have meandered. In 1944, the Delaware Supreme Court held that, upon insolvency, the duties of directors shifted to the creditors.[30] In 1991, Chancellor Allen in *Credit Lyonnais* stated that directors owe duties to creditors, as well as to the shareholders, when the company enters the "vicinity of insolvency."[31] Then, in 2007, the Delaware courts held that "as a practical matter . . . directors never owe fiduciary duties directly to creditors," but that creditors have shareholder-like standing to pursue derivative claims against directors on behalf of the corporation whenever the company is insolvent or in the "zone."[32]

Finally, one of the more interesting questions is whether individual directors have fiduciary duties to each other. Suppose, for example, one director is aware of information that is material to an important issue being brought before the board for decision. Does that director have an obligation to his or her colleagues on the board to share that information? In the 1988 case of *Mills v. Macmillan*, three directors were aware that one of the parties interested in acquiring their company had been given a "tip" about the process. They did not share that fact with the rest of the board. The court applied the duty of candor to this situation with the following language: "At a minimum, [the duty of candor] dictates that fiduciaries . . . may not use superior information or knowledge to mislead others in the performance of their own fiduciary obligations. . . . [T]here can be no dispute but that such silence [i.e., failing to disclose the tips] was misleading and deceptive. In short, it was a fraud upon the board."[33] If there is a breach of duties among board members, it might be characterized as a breach of the duty of loyalty if it is intentional.

Directors like those in *Macmillan* who leak confidential material information create problems under the securities laws for both their companies and themselves. A leak emanating from the company can force a premature disclosure of material information by eliminating the basis (under *Basic v. Levinson*) for nondisclosure.[34] Such a leak may also expose the company as a violation of Regulation FD (discussed at some length in the endnotes).[35] The problem for the individual director is illustrated by the infamous case of Rajat Gupta, the Goldman Sachs director who served a two-year prison term, was fined $5 million, and ruined his personal reputation as a result of his leak to a hedge-fund manager within minutes after a board meeting.[36]

There are times when concerns are raised about a "leaky" director. Most people will think (mistakenly) that there is a difference between deception by failing to volunteer information and deception by declining to give information when asked. As a result, when there is suspicion that a director is improperly speaking to a bidder about a confidential possible deal, I will suggest that each update meeting of the board begin with a statement from the chair something like "Any one of us might be hearing from bidders trying to get information about our process, and so on. So, as part of our update, let's go around the table (advisors and board members alike) and ask if anyone has had any contact with any bidder." In response to this statement, on one occasion, one director came up with a fairly preposterous story (not earlier volunteered by him) about how he had been walking down the street and the CEO of a possible bidder just happened to pull up in his car, and they had a chat. I am fairly sure we did not get the full story, but I do believe the exercise chilled his subsequent actions. The same approach can be used when there is a report in the press citing an unnamed source. The exercise of "going around the table" can be supplemented with some research into prior relationships between the reporter who got the scoop and anyone privy to the confidential information.

Duties of Directors under the Federal Securities Laws

Directors' duties under the securities laws generally relate to reporting requirements. There is the requirement that a majority of the directors sign the Form 10-K, and there are requirements for disclosures under the proxy rules. There is no requirement to disclose material nonpublic information simply because it exists. Well-advised companies give a "no comment" response to inquiries about rumors and unusual market activity.[37] Such information can remain confidential so long as there is no trading in the company's securities by either the company of directors and officers and so long as there are no rumors that originate from the company.

There are also requirements relating to insider trading. One, the requirement not to trade on the basis of material nonpublic information, parallels the fiduciary duty of the same proscription. Directors (and others and even the company) can create a safe harbor for trading by adopting a plan under Rule 10b5-1 that contemplates purchases or sales at some time in the future. Three caveats: First, such a plan can be adopted only when there is no undisclosed material information.[38] Second, the SEC Enforcement Division will be on the alert for the possibility that executives could be manipulating earnings to be announced ahead of scheduled transactions contemplated by such plans.[39] Finally, there is a question of whether the 10b5-1 safe harbor is also protection against a claim of fiduciary duty. It should be, because it breaks the causality chain—that is, a trade under such a plan would not be based on material nonpublic information.

There is also the prophylactic rule under Section 16 that requires disclosure of transactions in company stock by directors, officers, and 10 percent shareholders, and also presumes that any purchase and sale by any such person within six months of each other may have been based on inside information. Without any need to prove that there actually was such information, any profits from such "short swing" transactions will be required to be "disgorged" to the company. When a director is affiliated with a shareholder who owns less than 10 percent, under some circumstances the deputization theory is applied, by which the shareholder is deemed to be a director and trades by that share-holder are also subject to Section 16(b).[40]

Finally, there are filing requirements under Rule 144 for sales of company stock by affiliates.[41]

Other Sources of Directorial Duties

Corporate and securities laws are not the only source of duties of directors. They can be imposed on directors by the board itself—governance guidelines, codes of ethics, committee charters.

An announced policy that is used to solicit shareholder votes can take on contract-like enforceability. For example, in 2005, News Corp. was sued under the theory that it had induced a favorable shareholder vote by adopting a policy requiring shareholder approval of any extension of its poison pill. While policies can typically be modified at the board's discretion, the Court gave sufficient credence to the plaintiff's reliance theory to lead News Corp. to enter into a settlement agreement.[42]

Obligations with respect to corporate governance (and especially compliance oversight) can also be imposed in civil litigation settlement agreements with shareholder plaintiffs or with the government, as well as in deferred and nonprosecution agreements with the Department of Justice.[43]

Sources of Expectations, If Not Duties

In addition to the expanding legal obligations imposed on directors, as described earlier and to be covered in following chapters, there are expanding expectations. While they do not have the force of law, at least not yet, they have a significant influence on boards and contribute to the theme of board-centricity. As these expectations lead to standard board behavior, they might also be used by a plaintiff seeking to establish in a lawsuit what a prudent person would do.

In some cases, these increased expectations are created (or, at least, articulated) by the NACD, the leading organization for directors, via its occasional Blue Ribbon Commission reports.[44] Examples include the following:

- 2018—"Adaptive Governance: Board Oversight of Disruptive Risks"
- 2017—"Culture as a Corporate Asset"
- 2014—"Board-Shareholder Communications"
- 2013—"Talent Development"
- 2006—"The Role of the Board in Corporate Strategy"

Another source of increased expectations is governance-oriented activists. For example, following *Citizens United*, in which SCOTUS removed barriers to corporate political contributions, activists began demanding increased board oversight of political spending, along with increased disclosure of political contributions and lobbying efforts.[45]

Institutions have established expectations that directors will be directly involved in "shareholder engagement." In 2015, Vanguard sent out letters to five hundred CEOs asking that portfolio companies provide for direct communications between investors and directors, including the possible creation of a board-level "shareholder liaison committee."[46] Vanguard was essentially touting an approach advocated by the 2014 Shareholder-Director Exchange Protocol.[47] In the letter, Vanguard sought to anticipate and dispense with arguments against such an approach, saying it would "disintermediate management" and "we'll get tripped up on Reg. FD issues." To the great frustration of some companies that attempted to abide by the suggestion, institutional investors rebuffed some offers to meet with claims of "not enough time" or "not during proxy season." Boards sometime express frustration if the meetings are held only with governance professionals and do not include portfolio managers. Some institutions offered cautionary advice to the effect that the meetings could have a negative impact—for example, if the investor wanted to discuss executive compensation and the chair of the compensation committee seemed poorly prepared or uninformed. One mitigator of this risk is to ask the institution for an advance agenda of what they wish to discuss.

In other instances, increased expectations on boards are caused by changes in the business environment. Perhaps the most important current examples of this are cyber-risk (a concept, indeed a term, that was unheard of twenty years ago) and the focus on sexual misconduct brought about by the #MeToo movement (regrettably, a plague that has been around probably forever and, happily, is just now getting an appropriate level of attention).

Legal Accountability under the Corporate Laws

TYPES OF LITIGATION: DERIVATIVE OR DIRECT. When there has been a breach or alleged breach of fiduciary duty by directors, the principal procedural path to hold them accountable is a shareholder derivative suit. (Another possible path is direct litigation, discussed later.) A derivative suit is litigation brought in the name of the corporation and initiated by shareholders. If pursued and successful, any damages are recovered by the corporation; that recovery benefits the shareholders proportionately, because the value of the corporation itself is increased.

A derivative suit typically begins with a demand being made on the board to commence the litigation. The theory for this approach is that litigation is like any other management decision and should be made by the board. When the demand is made, in most instances a special litigation committee is appointed to consider whether a claim should be brought. The committee must be populated by directors who are both independent (see chapter 5 and cases cited at note 14 in chapter 5) and also disinterested in the outcome—that is, not potential targets of the suit. The committee will then retain independent counsel to guide them through the process and investigate the allegations. The committee might conclude that the allegations have no merit and determine not to pursue the suit. Even if the allegations are found to have merit, the committee may conclude not to pursue the litigation on the basis of the kinds of factors that would lead a board not to pursue litigation against any third party—for example, the cost of litigation will exceed the potential recoveries on a risk-adjusted basis. Such a determination will be respected by a court so long as it is satisfied that the committee was truly independent and disinterested and did a thorough job.[48]

There are situations in which the demand on the board is "excused" because of "futility"—that is, there could not be a legitimate special litigation committee because all the directors participated in the acts that allegedly constituted a breach of fiduciary duty.[49] During the course of the litigation (which can take years), the makeup of the board can change—some of the defendant directors may leave and be replaced by new directors who are not defendants. In this situation, a special litigation committee comprising these new, independent, and disinterested directors can be appointed to decide whether the corporation should continue the litigation. The new committee can dismiss the pending case—even if properly commenced by shareholders—so long as

- the decision to dismiss does not involve a breach of fiduciary duties; and
- the committee has concluded "after an objective and thorough investigation" that the continuation of the suit would be "detrimental to the company" and that conclusion is not "wrongful."

However, because of the legitimacy of the commencement of the suit and because "directors are passing judgment on fellow directors," the courts impose a strict standard of review before agreeing to such a dismissal. "The corporation should have the burden of proving independence, good faith and a reasonable investigation," and then the "Court should determine, applying its own independent business judgment, whether the motion should be granted."[50]

Whether a special committee is appointed for considering a derivative claim or for some other reason, the appointment is usually followed by the committee's selection of independent counsel. Invariably, when I am that counsel, one of the first things I do is reconfirm that all members of the committee are truly independent and disinterested. I do that to increase the likelihood that the decisions of the committee will be given deference by a court and otherwise be viewed as legitimate. In this context, a rather conservative reading of what is required seems appropriate. It is a rare director who objects to being removed from a committee.

When a special litigation committee determines that a suit should be brought, it often results in settlement discussions that will involve the shareholders who initiated the demand.

It is interesting to note that a pending derivative action will be extinguished when a company is sold and the plaintiff shareholders no longer have an ownership interest in the company. The only exception to this outcome is if the merger was for the purpose of extinguishing the claim.[51]

There are some circumstances in which shareholders can bring fiduciary claims directly. If the alleged breach benefits some of the shareholders, to the detriment of the others, then a recovery by the corporation would make little sense because the improperly benefited shareholders would share in it proportionately—as when a board has agreed to overpay one of the shareholders for an asset.[52]

When a company is being sold and the shareholders wish to make a claim of breach of fiduciary duty, that claim is brought directly and, typically, as a class action. This makes sense. The remedy being sought before the transaction is completed is an injunction. Any recovery for monetary damages would come after a closing, and the shareholders would not be able to benefit if the damages were to be paid to the corporation that they no longer own.

At one time, there was virtual certainty that the announcement of a deal would trigger a lawsuit (or multiple suits) from plaintiffs' law firms that had found a shareholder to be their client. While the incidence of these suits has declined somewhat (because of a new attitude of the Delaware courts about "disclosure-only" settlements announced in 2016[53]), boards must still plan for them. Ironically, these "strike suits" can be a source of comfort to directors. This is because these suits are brought as class actions; the percentage of "opt-outs" is small; typically the only financial exposure is to modest payments of plaintiff attorney's fees, which come from the company or the D&O carrier; and the directors receive a release from liability to the company's shareholders for any claims arising out of the transaction.

An alternative path for redress on the part of a shareholder who believes the company was sold for too little consideration is not to sue the directors but to pursue dissenters' rights to receive "fair value" under an appraisal statute.[54] The exposure from this kind of suit belongs, where it should, on the shoulders of the buyer.[55] (Shareholders bringing such a suit also have some exposure—a court can conclude that the merger price *exceeded* fair value.)

Appraisal cases are yet another example of unpredictability on the part of the Delaware courts. Recent commentators have said, "It's easy to throw up your hands at the current state of the law on appraisal rights in Delaware."[56] While the Court of Chancery is given broad latitude in how to weigh various valuation methodologies (see the primer in appendix 4), the Delaware Supreme Court has frequently criticized its determinations along those lines, remanding cases for further proceedings. The methodologies most pertinent to fair value "exclusive of any element of value arising from the accomplishment or expectation of the merger"—according to Section 262(h) of the statute—are the discounted cash flow, or DCF, calculation, the comparable companies analysis, and the negotiated merger price. The DCF calculation can vary significantly depending on the projections utilized and the discount rate applied. For example, in the *Dell* appraisal case, the expert retained by the stockholders came up with $28.61 per share, the buyer's expert came up with $12.68 per share, and the Court of Chancery declared the DCF to be $17.62 per share. While there has seemed to be a bit of a trend toward heavy reliance on the deal price (especially when there has been a robust sales process), when the buyer is another company in the same industry sector, there can be a good argument that the value of synergies should be deducted from the deal price to arrive at the fair value of the company on a stand-alone basis.[57] In one recent case, the Court found the target company's unaffected thirty-day average trading price to be reliable evidence of value, despite the fact that trading prices include no element of control premium.[58]

STANDARDS OF JUDICIAL REVIEW. Distinct from the standards of conduct established by fiduciary duties are the judicial standards of review for determining director liability.[59] When there is litigation against directors, a pivotal (and sometimes outcome-determinative) issue is a procedural determination about the applicable standard that a court would apply in assessing director liability, coupled with the assignment of the burden of proof. This is another example of the Delaware accordion, a term used above to describe the proliferation, then reconcentration, of fiduciary duties. The Chancery Court itself observed that "particularly during the 1980s, standards of review seemed to proliferate."[60]

Until recently, it was fairly easy to describe the standards of review as a static continuum.

The most forgiving standard, applied in most instances, was the business judgment rule (BJR). The rule "operates as both a procedural guide for litigants and a substantive rule of law."[61] When the BJR was applicable, a board's decision would not be second-guessed unless a plaintiff could carry the burden of proof that the decision was reached through a breach of the duty of care or loyalty. The court would give deference to the decision—right or wrong—if there was any "rational" basis for making it. The court's inquiry was largely focused on the decision-making process. Finally, the BJR "has no role where directors have either abdicated their functions, or absent a conscious decision, failed to act," although "a conscious decision to refrain from acting may . . . be a valid exercise of business judgment."[62]

Because a board is made up of individuals, the question arises whether a breach of fiduciary duty by some, but not all, of the directors would render the BJR inapplicable. Because all directors are typically made privy to the same information (and thus all have the same factual basis for satisfying the duty of care), this issue most likely arises in the event of a breach of the duty of loyalty. As a starting point, if "at least half of the directors who approved a business decision are not independent or disinterested . . . the court reviews the directors' decision [not under the BJR but] under the entire fairness standard."[63] That exacting standard is discussed later in this chapter. If less than a majority of the directors functioning on a business decision are tainted, it is possible that even one director who is so tainted could upend the application of the BJR. The Delaware courts have held that, to rebut the application of the BJR due to a breach of the duty of loyalty by one director, a plaintiff is "required to prove that the disloyal director either dominated the board or in some way tainted the presumed independence of the remaining board members" and that the one director's self-interest was "so 'material' as to persuade the trier of fact that the independence of the board 'as a whole' had been compromised."[64]

If a plaintiff cannot rebut the BJR in a lawsuit attacking a transaction, is the case over? Technically no, but practically yes: "[A] plaintiff who fails to rebut the business judgement rule presumptions is not entitled to any remedy unless the transaction constitutes waste" and "[a] claim of waste will arise only in the rare, 'unconscionable case where directors irrationally squander or give away corporate assets.' "[65]

Next in the continuum was an intermediate standard to be applied to a category of board decisions that warranted "enhanced [judicial] scrutiny," for example, decisions relating to a change-in-control transaction,[66] decisions relating to resisting hostile takeovers,[67] or decisions to dismiss a shareholder derivative claim.[68] Under enhanced scrutiny, the burden is on the directors to prove the "reasonableness" of their actions.

The principal justification for enhanced scrutiny is the potential for subtle director conflict. In the case of resisting takeovers, the concern expressed in the *Unocal* case was with "the omnipresent specter that a board may be acting primarily in its own interests" and resisting the takeover to retain the directors' board seats. In the case of dismissing a derivative claim, the Court in *Zapata* stated, "We must be concerned that directors are passing judgment on fellow directors," and as a result, there is a risk of "abuse, perhaps subconscious abuse." In the case of a change-in-control transaction, an additional rationale was applied. In such a situation, enhanced scrutiny is justified not only because of "the omnipresent specter" but also because of the significance of the transaction—"there is no tomorrow for the corporation's stockholders, meaning that they will be forever shut out from future profits generated from the resulting entity as well as the possibility of obtaining a control premium in a subsequent transaction."[69]

Should enhanced scrutiny be applied to CEO succession decisions? After all, those are arguably as consequential as a decision to sell the company, and unlike a sale of the company, there is not a shareholder vote required to implement CEO succession. The answer is clearly no for all kinds of reasons—including the fact that, as many CEOs have experienced, CEO succession (unlike a sale of the company) is a highly reversible decision.

Even more stringent standards were applied in two instances: cases involving director interference with the shareholder franchise and cases involving approvals of transactions with a controlling shareholder. If there was an allegation of a manipulation of voting rights, then the burden under the *Blasius* case was on the board to prove a "compelling justification" for doing so. This extremely rigorous standard was applied because of "the central importance of the franchise to the scheme of corporate governance" and the fact that "the shareholder franchise is the ideological underpinning upon which the legitimacy of directorial power rests."[70] If there was a transaction with a controlling shareholder, then the burden of proof was on the directors to show "entire fairness"—defined as both fair price and fair dealing. If such a transaction was either approved by a fully empowered special committee or required approval by a majority of the minority of the shareholders, then the standard of entire fairness still applied, but the burden of proof shifted to the plaintiff to prove the absence of entire fairness.[71]

In recent years, the Delaware courts have altered this continuum in meaningful ways, making it *dynamic*—that is, providing some opportunity for relief from the standards that were less forgiving than the BJR. There appears to be a deliberate shift back to the BJR.

In the 2015 decision in *Corwin*, enhanced scrutiny of a change-in-control transaction was held to apply only up to the time of a "qualifying" shareholder vote—that is, a vote that was fully informed and uncoerced. This had the effect of applying enhanced scrutiny to only an injunction proceeding. Thereafter, if the qualifying shareholder vote was favorable, the standard of review reverted to the BJR, effectively applying the most lenient standard to claims for damages. Even better, the required showing for liability was waste (virtually impossible to prove) rather than gross negligence.[72] The next year, that approach was applied in the context of a tender offer implemented under DGCL Section 251(h). That is, if a majority of shares were tendered, that had the same effect as a favorable vote and the BJR would be applied.[73]

In 2007, the original requirements to meet enhanced scrutiny of takeover defenses were rearticulated. The original 1985 *Unocal* formulation, as modified in the 1995 *Unitrin* case, was that takeover defenses would be upheld if "the board of directors had reasonable grounds for believing that a danger to corporate policy and effectiveness existed" (as there would be in the event of an inadequately priced tender offer) and "the defensive response was reasonable in relation to the threat posed" (e.g., a buyback program or adopting a poison pill but not a "scorched earth" action).[74] In 2007 in *Mercier*, the Delaware Chancery Court noted that "there was probably too much emphasis on the word 'threat' in the test." The court went to say that the test would be for the "directors to: (1) identify the proper corporate objectives served by their actions; and (2) justify their actions as reasonable in relationship to those objectives."[75]

Also in *Mercier*, then Vice Chancellor Strine advocated that the compelling justification standard, to be applied in circumstances of alleged manipulation of the shareholder franchise, should be limited to circumstances in which the vote involves an election of directors. Thus, directors worry less about moving the date of a shareholder vote on a sale of the company when they see that the votes are not coming in favorably.[76]

In 2013, the entire-fairness standard applied to a related party transaction received a major change. As indicated above, earlier case law did nothing more than shift the burden of proof if a special committee was used and/or if there was a majority of the minority shareholder vote required. In the *MFW* case, the Delaware Supreme Court held that if, from the outset of the transaction there was both a special committee and a majority of the minority vote required, then the standard reverted to the BJR.[77] It is interesting that the Court went directly to the "bottom" of the continuum rather than applying the approach applicable to a third-party change in control—enhanced scrutiny followed by the BJR as articulated in *Corwin*.

In theory, if defendants survive enhanced scrutiny or the application of entire fairness, then their actions will be reviewed under the BJR. But to have prevailed under either standard of review means that the issue of discharging the duties of care and loyalty would have been favorably decided, the defendants would prevail under a BJR review and, thus, the case is over.

JUDICIAL STANDARDS OF REVIEW (AS OF 2018):
A SIMPLIFIED SCHEMATIC

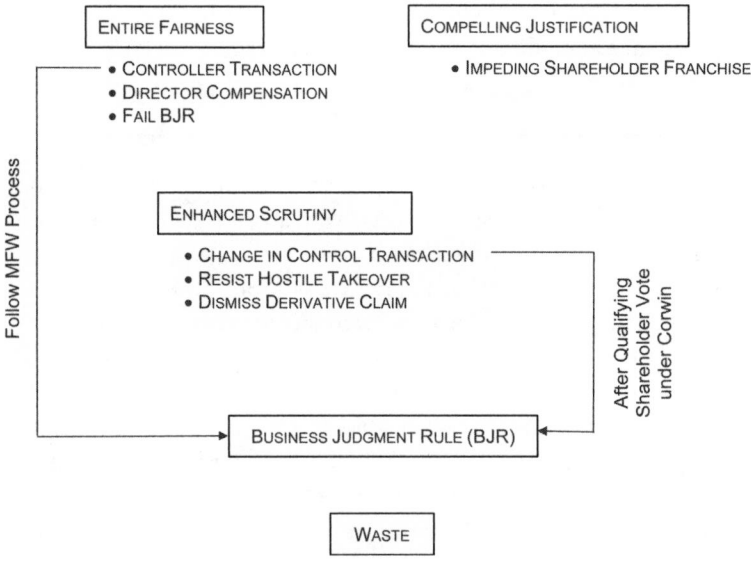

If a transaction is subject to the BJR from the outset (e.g., not a sale of the company but a material acquisition), the question becomes, What if the plaintiffs are successful in defeating the presumption that the BJR should apply—then what is the standard?" In a transactional setting, in at least one case the Delaware Chancery Court stated that if the BJR "is rebutted, the burden shifts to the defendant directors, the proponents of the challenged transaction, to prove to the trier of fact the 'entire fairness' of the transaction to the shareholder plaintiff."[78]

Director Protections

Regardless of the type of litigation or the judicial standards of review, a significant issue in the minds of defendant directors is "Who is going to bear the cost of litigating and bear the financial liability for a breach of fiduciary duties?" That is, "How am I protected from financial exposure?" Director protections fall into two categories: those that cut off financial exposure to liability and those that shift onto others cost of litigation as well as, if it comes to it, financial exposure to liability. In each instance, there are exceptions to availability, but the net effect of the entire suite of director protections is that the number of times directors have actually had to write a check is tiny.

In the early 1980s, I was advising the special committee of a board that was established to deal with an offer to buy the company by the management team (with the support of a private equity firm). One of the directors was a burly, former college football player who ran a manufacturing company. He looked as though he would be equally comfortable on a loading dock as in the boardroom. After I gave the briefing about their duties and the risk of litigation, he asked, "Would it be entirely chicken shit of me to quit right now?" My response was a definitive "kinda." (He stayed.) Ever since then, I have coupled my talk about duties with a discussion of the robust suite of protections available to directors.

The provisions that cut off exposure start with the exculpatory charter provision. As noted in chapter 3, after the decision in the Trans Union case, the Delaware legislature enacted provisions that allow Delaware corporations to "eliminate" exposure of directors to monetary damages for breaches of fiduciary duty through provisions in their certificates of incorporation. The limitations are important. Among other things, they do not cover breaches of the duty of loyalty; they do not prevent injunctive relief; they do not cover officers; they do not cover illegal dividends.[79] Especially because of the first limitation, plaintiffs seek out any conflicts of interest that can implicate a loyalty breach as a means of improving their leverage in settlement negotiations.

Another provision that protects directors is reliance in good faith on reports of officers and opinions of experts.[80] Again, the limitations are important. For something to rise to the level of a report, it requires a degree of formality. One of the lessons of the TransUnion case is that an oral comment from an officer at a board meeting may not qualify.[81] One issue that can arise when relying on the advice of a general counsel is whether his or her comments are delivered as an expert legal opinion or as (perhaps less expert) business advice. (This issue also has implications for the availability of the attorney-client privilege to statements from a GC.)

To establish good-faith reliance on an expert's opinion, the expert should be selected with care and be free of undisclosed or unmanaged conflicts. Also, the expert should present the analysis that supports the opinion and be quizzed about the opinion with a critical eye. There is a particularly troubling decision of the Delaware Chancery Court on this subject. In *Emerging Communications*, all the board members but one were entitled to rely on a banker's fairness opinion. The one director who was not so entitled was a former investment banker who the Court held that, despite the fairness opinion, "knew, or at the very least had strong reason to believe, that the . . . price was unfair" because he "possessed a specialized financial expertise." This is a troubling concept for, say, any audit committee financial expert or any professional serving as a director. There is some comfort in the fact, however, that (despite the quoted language) the real basis for the finding of liability was a conflict of interest on the part of the director.[82]

There are two different protections available for directors against claims that dividend payments or stock repurchases were made unlawfully. First, the statute provides that directors shall be "fully protected in relying in good faith upon the records of the corporation and upon such information [etc.] . . . presented by any of its officers [etc.]"[83] relating to a dividend or repurchase. So, a best practice is to have a detailed CFO's certificate presented to the board establishing legally available funds. (That certificate might also cover debt-covenant compliance and, possibly, solvency.) Second, the statute relating to dividends and stock repurchases states that directors "who may have dissented . . . may be exonerated . . . by causing his or her dissent to be entered . . . [in] the minutes."[84] This latter protection is infrequently used.

Provisions that shift (rather than cut off) litigation costs and liability exposure to others are indemnification (and related provisions providing for advancement of expenses) and D&O insurance.

By statute, indemnification in Delaware has an important limitation—it does not cover liability in a derivative suit. Indemnification is typically provided for in a provision in the certificate of incorporation or bylaws, calling for indemnification "to the full extent provided by law." Because of a case that held that mandatory indemnification did not compel advancement of expenses,[85] those provisions are now typically written to mandate expense advancement as well. Another limitation can arise from public policy against indemnification for violations of securities laws.

Some companies also provide directors with indemnification agreements.[86] While those agreements do not really change the underlying obligation, they can supplement a bylaw or certificate of incorporation obligation in a variety of ways, including these:

- Where there is a required finding to qualify for indemnification, the burden of proof can be placed on the company.
- The agreement can provide for reimbursement of expenses if the director has to sue for payment.
- There can be an affirmative duty to carry D&O insurance.
- There can be a requirement to fund a trust to support the indemnification obligations in the event of a threatened hostile takeover.

There is also the practical limitation that a right to indemnification is only as good as the creditworthiness of the indemnitor.

The gaps in indemnification are filled with D&O insurance, although that can be limited by policy exclusions and, ultimately, the amount of coverage available under the policy. D&O policies are "claims-made" policies and can provide three basic types of coverage—Side A directly protects the insured directors and officers; Side B compensates the corporation for payments it must make to directors and officers under indemnification obligations; entity coverage protects the corporation against claims made directly against it.[87]

A limit to both indemnification and insurance can result, in extreme cases, from the terms of a settlement agreement. In Enron and other cases, the indemnitor companies were bankrupt, and the exposures of the directors were many multiples of the amount of available insurance coverage. On these facts, the plaintiffs succeeded in negotiating provisions that prohibited the director defendants from availing themselves of the benefits of either insurance or indemnification. Happily, this has been an extremely rare occurrence.

Shortly after Enron imploded, I was the moderator of a panel comprising three Delaware judges. An audience member asked, "In light of the exculpatory charter provision, isn't it likely that the chair of the audit committee of Enron will pay nothing?" As an illustration of the receptiveness of judges (or at least one judge) to arguments against exculpation, one judge (chillingly) answered as follows (paraphrasing all but the first two sentences, which were memorable and are verbatim)—"Oh, no. I could *get him*. The chair of the audit committee was a retired academic. As chair, he received over $300,000 in compensation from Enron last year. That is a multiple of what I make in my full-time job. The compensation was so significant to the chair that he had every incentive not to make waves . . . to put his head in the sand. And that is a breach of the duty of loyalty."

Shareholder ratification as a source of director protection is a noteworthy subject. The history of Delaware jurisprudence on this subject is a great example of the unpredictability of the Delaware courts. In 2009, an opinion of the Supreme Court in *Gantler* noted that "the scope and effect of the common law doctrine of shareholder ratification is unclear, making it difficult to apply that doctrine in a coherent manner." The opinion went on state: "To restore coherence and clarity to this area of our law, we hold that the scope of the shareholder ratification doctrine must be limited to its so-called 'classic' form; that is, to circumstances where a fully informed shareholder vote approves director action that does not legally require shareholder approval in order to become legally effective. Moreover, the only director action or conduct that can be ratified is that which the shareholders are specifically asked to approve. With one exception [described in a footnote as a claim that directors lacked authority to take an action], the 'cleansing effect' of such a ratifying shareholder vote is to subject the challenged director action to business judgment review, as opposed to 'extinguishing' the claim altogether."[88]

The language of *Gantler* was a rather strong dose of cold water on the efficacy of ratification as a defense in the case of a merger, which does legally require a shareholder vote. Nevertheless, in 2013, the Chancery Court in *Rural Metro* seemed to ignore the "coherence and clarity" of the Supreme Court's guidance and considered, in a merger case, whether the shareholder vote would lower the standard of review to the BJR. (It declined to do so, on the basis of misleading disclosure and omissions in the proxy statement.)[89] In a later case (*Corwin*), the same Chancery Court judge again ignored *Gantler*. His decision to do so was supported by the Supreme Court in an en banc opinion written by the Chief Justice—"No doubt *Gantler* can be read in more than one way."[90] It would have been more direct to simply state that *Gantler* was being overruled.

Last category of protection: Directors can protect themselves in practical ways, by being careful about note taking and, especially, emails and texts. A note can be something as simple as circling a number in a banker's presentation or an exclamation point in a margin of a memo. Some companies have taken the prophylactic step of blocking the note-taking feature on digital board books. Notes cannot be destroyed after there has been a threat of litigation; to do so can amount to "spoliation" of evidence or obstruction of justice. As practical matter, emails and texts can never be destroyed. In a major M&A deal, there was an email exchange that came out in discovery and received considerable attention. During the board meeting to approve the transaction, one director sent another the following message—"it's screw the shareholders."[91]

I often caution directors about note taking. Because I never want to say, or be quoted for saying, "Don't take notes," I usually just observe that "the prize for the director with the most notes is the longest deposition." Once, after delivering that message, I observed a director typing away on his laptop. I asked him if there was something about my advice that he didn't understand, and he replied, "I'm not taking notes; I am answering emails." At that point I mentioned as diplomatically as I could that the duty of care also required paying attention. That exchange came before the era of smartphones!

Legal Accountability under the Securities Laws

Directors can be held accountable to shareholders for disclosure violations under the securities laws. Because of the incidence of frivolous lawsuits, Congress enacted the Private Securities Litigation Reform Act in 1995, requiring a higher standard of proof to initiate litigation. If litigation goes forward, there is effectively a negligence standard for director liability under the Securities Act of 1933 (the act that applies in securities offerings, such as an IPO) for material misstatements or omissions in the registration statement. There is a requirement of "scienter" in the case of a claim under the Securities Exchange Act of 1934, which, among other things, covers periodic reports such as the 10-K and 10-Q. (Scienter under the securities laws is established by intent, knowledge, or deliberate recklessness.)

Directors can also be subject to enforcement actions brought by the SEC. Included in the possible remedies are a lifetime ban on service as a director of a public company for "conduct [that] demonstrates unfitness to serve."[92]

Other Sources of Accountability

In many ways, directors are most concerned about extralegal accountability, principally damage to reputation. Public company directors tend to be highly accomplished individuals with good reputations. They are appropriately concerned that a misstep by a company on whose board they serve will damage that reputation and perhaps limit their opportunities for future board service. Such damage can come through bad publicity—think of the box appearing in *Wall Street Journal* articles identifying the board members of a company under stress. An even more direct source of damage can come through the ballot box. If a director is singled out by ISS and subjected to a withhold or vote-against campaign, he or she may have to contend with a failure to receive a majority favorable vote.

So, what should a director make of all of this—duties and expectations that seem to ratchet upward; dynamic judicial standards of review with distinctions that perhaps only a lawyer would love; a pretty robust set of protections against financial (but not reputational) exposure; courts in Delaware that may be more than a little unpredictable? As goes a famous quote attributed to Satchel Paige, "Work like you don't need the money . . . love like you've never been hurt . . . dance like nobody's watching." If he were an advisor to a board of directors, Paige might have said, "Work hard, rely in good faith on experienced and unconflicted advisors, discharge all of your duties (especially the duty of loyalty), and make decisions like it's all your own money, and assume you *may* have to prove they were reasonable . . . reasonably expect that director protections will keep you from getting hurt financially . . . behave as though everyone (a judge, the shareholders, ISS, and the financial press) is watching."

In 1990, there was a *Harvard Business Review* article entitled "Why Sane People Shouldn't Serve on Public [Company] Boards." As I stated in my cranky letter to the editor, I think that is nonsense. So, apparently, do the hundreds of people who are just dying to be invited to serve on their first public company board. Board service is demanding but a great way to be around intelligent and interesting people, to address, important issues, and to contribute to commerce.

In particular, it is the decision-making aspects of corporate governance that make serving as a public company director (or CEO) so stimulating and challenging. Reaching a thoughtful decision to take any important action (or to decline to take such an action) requires a board to consider a broad range of factors and implications, including business strategy, operations, and risk; finances and tax; legal (including disclosure); reputational (with all important constituencies); and the reactions of shareholders, proxy advisors, securities analysts, and the stock market. When an action involves a counterparty, negotiating strategy and tactics also enter into the equation.

7

Routine Board Operations

What constitutes "routine" board operations has evolved throughout the New Era in Corporate Governance. This evolution (growth, really) of the routine tracks the growth in the duties and expectations of directors discussed in the prior chapter. Long gone are the "good old days" when a board could plan to meet four times a year for a single day, from breakfast through lunch or maybe midafternoon, with exactly sixty minutes allocated to concurrent committee meetings.

The increase in the number of hours to be devoted to even routine board matters (much less the special situations discussed in the next chapter) is one of the reasons that directors now serve on fewer boards than in the past and why standards about "overboarding" make sense.[1] This fact, though, has actually created opportunities for improving board diversity, which was discussed as a goal in chapter 5, because nominating committees are forced to look beyond sitting and retired CEOs to be candidates. The logical next candidate pool is CFOs and others in the C-suite, and there is currently more diversity in those positions than there is in the top job.

What must be covered as a matter of routine is set forth in a calendarized, summary fashion in the Sidley Best Practices Calendar.[2] The big categories of subjects to be covered by a board (either as an entirety or through committees) every year are as follows: the board's own organization; financial reporting; strategy, budget, and projections; executive compensation; succession planning; CEO performance evaluation;

talent management; risk management; shareholder relations; and planning for shareholder activism and unsolicited takeover attempts. A board should also be thoughtful about executive sessions, minutes of meetings, and opportunities for ongoing education about governance.

The Board's Own Organization

Separate and apart from assembling the right people on the board (discussed in chapter 5), the board needs to organize its own efforts. A global view of that effort is typically set forth in a document entitled something like Governance Principles. The first such document was introduced to great fanfare in 1994 by General Motors. Subsequent versions have become more elaborate.

A first step is to decide on which committees to establish and, then, what their roles should be. Stock-exchange rules essentially require three standing committees—audit, compensation, nominating.[3] Some companies have other committees. A company in a regulated industry or that is operating under a consent decree may have a compliance committee. Some companies, especially public utilities and consumer products companies, have an ESG or CSR committee. Risk committees can be common at financial institutions. There can also be technology committees, and so on. Because it is so easy to convene the full board by telephone or video conference, it is certainly less necessary and is becoming less common to have an executive committee. Moreover, having an executive committee has an undesirable connotation of there being a varsity and a junior varsity. When there is an executive committee, it usually comprises the board chair, the CEO, any lead independent director, and chairs of the other committees.

Committee charters are required by stock-exchange rules.[4] While those rules dictate to a considerable degree the substantive content of the charters, boards nevertheless have some latitude in both substance and language. A caution on substance: especially with regard to the audit committee charter, there can be some risk of "charter creep." That is, when a new expectation about oversight gains currency, the default reaction seems to be "let the audit committee do it." A caution on drafting: too many boards write that the role of a committee is to "ensure" one thing or another. Because these charters are published, there is some risk that a plaintiff's lawyer will use such language as a "promise" that was unfulfilled. A better formulation would be that the committee "is to take steps reasonably designed to ensure." This caution might also be applied in the drafting of governance principles and of codes of conduct.[5]

An even more important organizational matter for a board is deciding whether to separate the roles of chairman and CEO. This separation is an example of the global market for governance ideas and was imported into the United States from the United Kingdom. A chairman who is not the CEO can be "executive" or "nonexecutive." A nonexecutive chairman should not be listed in bylaws or elsewhere as an officer; this is to avoid an assertion that some of his or her actions are not covered by exculpation.

The principal distinctions between executive and nonexecutive are what the chairman gets paid and whether the chairman has an outward-facing role (e.g., communicating with Wall Street).[6] If the chairman is "executive" or if the CEO is also the chairman, the board will need to select an LID. Once a CEO is also the chairman, it is difficult to reverse course and take that title away. It has happened, though, in the case of pressure from shareholders (e.g., Bank of America in 2009). Once a CEO has lost the title of chairman as a result of shareholder pressure, it can be difficult to give it back. Again, in the case of Bank of America, that happened, in 2014. The best time for a separation of titles and roles is when there is a change in CEOs. One reason for doing this is to help a first-time public company CEO transition into his or her new role. Thus, it may be an interim step toward combining the roles. Sometimes the chairman is the outgoing CEO. In this case, the board needs to be attuned to preventing "leadership ambiguity" and to making sure that the chairman is truly of a mind to step down as CEO.

There can be real issues associated with having an outgoing CEO serve as chairman. One practical issue needs to be grappled with even before the effective date of the change—executive compensation. First, should the outgoing CEO still have a golden-parachute severance package that provides for a significant cash payment in the event of a change in control? Arguably, providing such a package is inconsistent with the rationales for providing parachutes (meeting "market" and making an executive indifferent about losing the job in a change in control). This is separate from the golden-parachute effect of accelerated vesting of equity-based compensation, which likely will remain in place. Second, what salary should the outgoing CEO receive during the period of chairmanship, and should he or she be granted equity-based compensation, which (after all) is designed to have a longer-term orientation? Many individuals in that position (especially those who are advised by one of the aggressive "talent-side" lawyers) think that the compensation arrangements during the CEO period should simply carry over. Compensation committees should carefully consider both issues.

Another issue that can arise during any period in which an outgoing CEO serves as chairman can be captured by the phrase "old habits die hard." I remember sitting in a boardroom when a director asked the new CEO a question and his predecessor, the chairman, answered. Similarly, like children appealing to their grandparents, members of management will sometimes go to the former CEO to discuss issues that are really within the proper purview of the new boss. This latter issue can be partially addressed by having the outgoing CEO move to an office "off campus."

Some of the reluctance of a CEO to fully let go relates to the loss of stature. As one former CEO told me, "When you retire, you go from 'who's who' to 'who's he?'"

Organizing the board to be most effective in its routine operations should involve a periodic assessment of both delegated authority (discussed in chapter 4) and information flow. Delegation should be revisited periodically because "things change." Regarding information flow, it is incumbent upon the board to speak out about the quality, quantity, and timeliness of the information it receives—both in anticipation of board and committee meetings and between meetings. Directors value receiving executive summaries as a guide to detailed facts and analysis.

Addressing information flow is one of the most important aspects of the role of the chairman or LID.

The authority of each director to receive essentially anything he or she asks for is embodied in the Delaware statute.[7] And the courts have taken the position that managements should be proactive, not merely reactive—"Officers also have a duty to provide the board of directors with the information that the directors need to perform their statutory and fiduciary roles."[8]

A caution about the formatting of information flow to the board: The centerpiece of public company reporting under the securities laws is the "Management's Discussion and Analysis," which requires describing the company's performance "through the eyes of management." As such, the information supplied to the board can be used to impeach the quality of the company's public disclosure. This is not a theoretical concern; there has been SEC enforcement activity along these lines.[9] The format of information given to the board can also have implications for "segment reporting" under the accounting rules.[10]

Another aspect of board organization is deciding on independent director compensation. When directors set their own compensation, as they invariably do, this is the ultimate conflict of interest. Until recently, however, it has not attracted much attention—perhaps in part because it seems to have been relatively modest in amount as compared to the fees of senior outside consultants or counsel. For example, if a typical director is paid $200,000 to $300,000 annually and puts in two hundred hours at meetings and in preparations for meetings, that works out to $1,000 to $1,500 per hour, or about the level of the billing rate of a senior partner in a law firm.

When director compensation based on equity has had at least the potential for being much more significant, it has attracted litigation. In 2015, in a case relating to the compensation of directors of Citrix Systems, shareholders challenged the award of restricted stock units to directors. Under a plan that was approved by shareholders, there was a limit of one million restricted stock units (RSUs) for a grant to any individual. The plan did not have sublimits based on the role of the individual. Thus, even a director could receive a one-million-share RSU grant. The problem arose because, at the time the action was filed, one million

RSUs were worth $55 million, not a "modest amount" by any measure. The court rejected the "shareholder ratification" defense raised by the defendant directors. Instead, it applied the entire-fairness judicial standard of review and offered the view that, as a preliminary matter, "it is reasonably conceivable that the total compensation received by the non-employee directors was not entirely fair to the Company." Citrix is not the only case challenging independent director compensation.[11]

There are some special situations in which being a director can amount to a short-term, nearly full-time job. For example, the chair of a special committee empaneled to consider a bid by a controlling shareholder to acquire the company will preside over numerous meetings of the committee and will put in many hours between those meetings in consultation with the committee's outside advisors and sometimes in negotiations. It is quite common to be asked, "What should that person be paid?" Clearly, there should not be a "success fee," although I have been asked about that more than once. I usually suggest that the chair keep a log of hours spent and that compensation on an hourly basis at the rate a senior law partner might be paid would be appropriate. It may also be appropriate to solicit the views of a compensation consultant.

The last major category of board organization is the board self-evaluation—an annual assessment by the board about its satisfaction with its own organization. This is required by stock-exchange rules.[12] There are a few options along these lines. First, the board can evaluate the operations of the board and committees as a whole, or it can extend the self-evaluation to cover individual directors. Where the self-evaluation process does not cover the performance of individuals (and most boards do not do this), individual board members are, nevertheless, evaluated by the nominating committee as part of the reslating process. Second, the self-evaluation can be a written exercise (i.e., filling out a survey form) or oral (an interview based on questions supplied in advance). If it is an oral exercise, the general counsel, outside counsel, or some other third party can conduct the interviews (see appendix 2 for a template to be used in an oral exercise).

I am not a fan of written board self-evaluations. The biggest concern is creating a record that, if directors are candid about concerns, can be used in litigation against the board. That, in turn, can cause directors to be less candid. So, in my judgment, an interview process is preferable. Moreover, for the sake of candor, an outside party should do the interviews and follow the Chatham House Rule—that is, report on what people said but not who said what. Finally, if the outside party is counsel, there is some chance of having the notes of the interviews, and the report out, covered by privilege.

Some companies ask managements to evaluate the board. The bottom-line questions in that exercise are whether directors are well prepared, ask good questions, and provide useful advice.

Financial Reporting

One of the most important roles of the board of a public company relates to financial reporting. This important "gatekeeper" function falls most heavily on the members of the audit committee, who under stock-exchange rules must meet special qualifications and independence requirements.[13] Under those same rules, audit committees must review earnings releases and "earnings guidance provided to analysts and rating agencies," although this "may be done generally," and the committee "need not discuss [each] in advance."[14] Among the questions that the audit committee should ask when reviewing a draft earnings release are the following:

- Will the themes and key messages in the release be consistent with what is going to be disclosed in the earnings call script and in the MD&A to be included in the next SEC periodic report on 10-Q or 10-K?
- Is this release compliant with the requirements of SEC Regulation G (pertaining to non-GAAP financial measures)?
- In respect of earnings guidance, are we taking full advantage of the safe harbor for forward-looking information, and as articulated, are we creating a duty to update?

In addition, the audit committee must report annually on its processes in a company's proxy statement.[15]

Audit committee members do not have sole responsibility for financial reporting as among the board members, however. All board members are asked to sign the company's SEC annual report on Form 10-K, and a very significant part of that document is devoted to financial reporting.

Aside from the formal requirements, a key role of the audit committee (and especially its chairman) is relationships with the CFO, the chief accounting officer, the head of internal audit, and the outside auditing firm. A good relationship is key to providing the kind of transparency that allows the audit committee to fulfill its responsibilities. That relationship will facilitate getting candid answers to questions such as "Are we aggressive in our accounting?" and "What is the quality of our accounting staff?" Transparency is aided by the requirement of executive sessions with the outside auditor and others.

One element of due diligence that an audit committee might consider undertaking is to ask to see the minutes of a management disclosure committee (if there is one), as well as copies of the subcertifications that are delivered to the CEO and CFO to support their certifications required under SOX Section 302 about accuracy and fair presentation of financials. Any identified exceptions from a "no issues" subcertification could be significant "red flags." Whistle-blower reports and SEC comment letters relating to accounting and financial reporting must also be brought promptly to the attention of the audit committee.

While all board members should be conversant with the concept of materiality, that concept plays a major role in the workings of an audit committee. Too often, and frequently at the encouragement of accountants, the directors and officers fall back on mechanical rules of thumb—5 percent or 10 percent of this or that metric. Under the securities laws, the definition of materiality is much more fact-intensive and based on both quantitative and qualitative factors. In the context of the requirements of the proxy rules, the U.S. Supreme Court in *TSC v. Northway* held that "an omitted fact is material if there is a substantial likelihood that a reasonable shareholder would consider it important in deciding how to vote . . . [that] the omitted fact would have assumed actual significance in the deliberations of the reasonable shareholder . . . would have been viewed by the reasonable shareholder as having significantly altered the 'total mix' of information made available." Importantly, the fact need not be outcome-determinative.[16]

This standard of materiality has been applied by the Delaware courts to information to be supplied for a merger vote in duty of candor cases.[17] It is also applicable under the securities laws to much more than proxy voting. The SEC staff issued an accounting bulletin in 1999 echoing the language of *TSC v. Northway*—"The omission or misstatement of an item in a financial report is material if . . . it is probable that the judgment of a reasonable person . . . would have been changed or influenced by the inclusion or correction of the item." The staff further stated that "exclusive reliance on . . . any percentage or numerical threshold has no basis in the accounting literature or the law." It gave a number of examples in which a quantitatively small item could be material, including if it were the difference between reporting a loss or a profit, meeting or missing analyst expectations, complying with or failing to comply with a loan covenant, or having the effect of increasing management bonuses.[18]

Audit committees (and others) should also be aware of the SEC's position on "improper influence on the conduct of audits."[19] The relevant provisions prohibit actions to "coerce, manipulate, mislead, or fraudulently influence" an auditor if "such action, if successful, could result in rendering the financial statements materially misleading." Among the examples given by the SEC are "threatening to cancel or canceling existing non-audit or audit engagements" and "seeking to have a partner removed from the audit engagement," in each case if the auditor or partner "objects to the issuer's accounting."

Audit committees will need to be conversant in the differences among, and implications of, a "clean" auditor's opinion and one that is "qualified" or contains an "emphasis on a matter." Similarly, audit committees will need to focus on any report about internal controls that calls out either a "material weakness" or a "significant deficiency."

The SEC also has views about the obligation of oversight by an audit committee and may seek to impose responsibility more readily than a Delaware court would under *Caremark*. In a 2003 SEC enforcement action involving Chancellor Corporation,[20] the SEC alleged that a member of the audit committee violated the anti-fraud provisions of the securities laws by "ignoring clear warning signs that financial improprieties were going on at the company and by failing to ensure that the company's public filings were accurate." It sought an order "permanently barring [the director and others] from acting as officers or directors of any public company." This may be an extreme case designed to send a strong message in the post-Enron era, but it is a cautionary tale in any event.

Strategy, Budget, and Projections

On a routine basis, boards should be involved in strategy—the development of a plan that will allow for the corporation to have a sustainable competitive advantage.[21] While this should be a routine activity, the strategic planning exercise need not be an annual event, and by its nature as a long-term-oriented exercise, it should not be. A strategic plan should be developed by management on a preliminary basis, vetted with the board, then (as needed) revised, and vetted again.[22] A board that has been thoughtfully populated with reference to a skills matrix will have a great deal to contribute. Many will advocate for a strategy that pursues ambitious goals (sometimes referred to as BHAGs, or big, hairy, audacious goals), but strategies must be realistic in terms of available capital—financial, human, and intellectual. One of the subjects to be considered as a matter of strategy is the long-term benefit to shareholders of CSR/ESG (discussed in chapter 2). Many companies choose to do strategic planning in an off-site meeting that is not encumbered with the business of a regular board meeting. Occasionally, outside experts with industry knowledge (and a reputation for being able to keep confidences) will be invited to present or even participate in discussions. While there should not be a new strategic plan every year, boards will often have an annual check-in to monitor execution against milestones and, as appropriate, make revisions to the strategy and its milestones.

I recall a conversation with an old-school CEO about board involvement in strategic planning. He commented: "I would never discuss strategy with the board. They are so risk averse that we would never take any bold steps." At about the same time, board involvement in strategy got a boost in a rather unpredictable way. In the 1989 decision in *Paramount v. Time*, the Delaware court noted that in defending against a hostile takeover, the board could conclude that it should not abandon its strategy.[23] As a result, takeover defense lawyers issued client alerts urging that boards be involved in strategy.

I have used two approaches to starting a conversation about strategy. For my own law firm, we employed the well-known SWOT exercise—strengths, weaknesses, opportunities, and threats. It is critical to place a heavy focus on opportunities. It is hard to strategically advance an enterprise if there is an overemphasis on simply addressing problems. The other approach is something I have used in teaching my leadership seminar. It involves facilitating a conversation oriented toward answering three questions: What are we competing for? A typical answer for a public company might be all of customers, talent, and investor dollars. Who are we competing against? The answer might be other producers of goods and services, other employers, and alternative investments. How do we differentiate ourselves from the competition to attain the sustainable competitive advantage we are seeking? The answer relating to customers might be quality, innovation, reliability, and responsiveness of our goods and services (all of which contribute to brand equity). The answer with respect to talent might be compensation, training, opportunity for advancement, culture, and reputation. The answer with respect to investors might be predictability and reliability of financial reporting, as well as total shareholder return, or TSR.

Annually, a board will review a budget (sometimes labeled the business plan) for the following year. Again, the budget is initially developed by the management. In a typical company, this is a bottom-up exercise. Business units offer their plans. Those plans are then consolidated or "rolled up," given a "corporate adjustment," and presented to the board. A board should understand the process by which the plan was developed; the key assumptions; and management's track record of, and confidence level in, achievement. The board may make suggestions for revision, but ultimately a final plan will be "owned" by management. For purposes of preserving the director protection of reliance, it may be preferable that the board "accept" rather than "approve" or "adopt" the plan.

A budget is more than just a tool for managing the business. It serves many purposes. It is an input into executive compensation. It provides the support for any publicly disclosed "outlook" for earnings and other targets. It is provided to debt-financing sources and can be used to set covenant requirements. It is provided to debt rating agencies. And, finally, it is the first step toward the preparation of multiyear projections.

Even though multiyear financial projections would seem to be a logical part of strategic planning and a focus on the long term, not all companies develop projections beyond the next year's budget on a regular basis. Projections are often required, however, in the context of many of the special situations discussed in the next chapter—such as to support M&A negotiations and any related valuation or solvency analysis. Projections (or at least those going out three to five years) should, like a budget, be a bottom-up exercise and go through a vetting process with the board before they are ultimately "accepted." To support an M&A fairness opinion, the three- to five-year projections are often extended to, say, ten years. That extension is often a top-down exercise, and the board should review critical assumptions (e.g., about growth and margins).

Projections are typically updated each year. Ideally, the board will be provided a bridge from the previous to the current projections. Finally, projections are often presented in three cases—a base or achievable case, a downside case, and an upside or optimistic case. Alternatively, a base case may be subject to a more mechanical "sensitivity analysis."

In reviewing a budget and projections, a board should consider the following, among other things:

- Because the starting point is the most recent set of historical financials, there must be confidence in that history. In the unusual circumstance that the accounting of those historical financials is under review (by the SEC or otherwise), the potential impact of the review should be understood.
- The budget and projects should reflect anticipated, future changes in accounting rules, taxes (including tariffs), and the business. Business changes can be the result of, among other things, a new strategy, a major capital expenditure, an anticipated recession or industry cycle, loss of patent protection, and new competition (from disruptive new technology, change in business practices, or otherwise).
- The process for the development of the budget should also be understood.

Executive Compensation

Executive compensation is one of the most important of elements of routine board operations. Decision making is lodged in the compensation committee, which operates under special rules of the stock exchanges.[24] (Those same rules require shareholder approval of equity plans, material revisions, and repricing decisions.[25]) Compensation committees preside over a complex range of subjects: salary, short-term incentives, long-term incentives (usually based on equity grants), deferred compensation, golden parachutes (including accelerated vesting of equity-based compensation), and clawbacks.[26] Setting compensation has accounting,[27] tax,[28] securities law,[29] and public relations implications. Compensation committees have their own consultants, who must be independent of the consultants used by the corporation for general HR matters.

Short-term incentive compensation frequently focuses on financial targets and the achievement of transactional goals, but it can also be used to promote ESG/CSR goals. Royal Dutch Shell announced "plans to set short-term carbon-emissions targets and link them to executive pay."[30] Safety metrics are used in compensation plans of many companies in the utility, energy, and manufacturing sectors.[31]

Executive compensation has been called "the top area of [governance] focus across the globe."[32] This may be a result of the fact that it is one of the most visible aspects of governance. Consider the level of detail and the number of pages required to be devoted to the subject in any proxy statement and the attention given to the subject by the financial press. Consider further that the compensation committee is given a report card for its work, through the "say-on-pay" vote,[33] and that the ISS grading scale requires a 70 percent favorable vote to pass.[34] An ISS recommendation on this vote will consider its list of "problematic pay practices."[35] A compensation committee that receives a failing grade and does not address the cause may be the subject of a withhold recommendation from ISS and a withhold vote, leading to a requirement for a resignation offer under majority voting.

Executive compensation is a subject that captures popular attention and is also a subject frequently raised in discussions of income inequality. The most frequently identified cause of increasing CEO compensation is the capillary (or Lake Wobegon) effect of benchmarking.[36] Another cause is the increased use of equity-based compensation, coupled with a rising stock market that can "float all boats." The increased use of equity-based compensation, designed to align management and shareholder interest and pay with performance, really took off in the 1990s and coincided with a historically long and steep bull market.[37] One antidote—indexed strike prices for stock options—has not gained much traction.[38] Evidence of popular attention to this subject is the fact that Professor Steven Kaplan published his vigorous defense of high CEO compensation in, of all places, *Foreign Affairs*.[39]

The special standard of quantitative materiality applied to executive compensation is well illustrated by the *Disney* case involving the severance payment to Michael Ovitz. The short version of the facts is that Ovitz received a payment of $130 million for doing a bad job for fourteen months. That resulted in shareholder litigation in Delaware that had thirty-seven days of live testimony, resulted in a nearly hundred-page opinion from the Chancery Court (with a table of contents, no less),[40] and a ninety-page opinion from the Delaware Supreme Court,[41] affirming the decision of Chancery. The directors escaped liability in that case, but not for a lack of materiality. While $130 million is a large sum, its quantitative materiality might have been disputed in light of the fact that, in 1996, the year of the payment to Ovitz, the Disney company had cash flow from operations of nearly $5 billion and shareholders' equity at year end of $16 billion.

Of course, executive compensation is qualitatively material. Compensation design can incentivize excessive risk taking.[42] Boards focused on diversity and inclusion should consider relative compensation of male and female executives. Finally, excessive compensation for a CEO can be evidence of "board capture," although what is "excessive" is highly debatable, and high compensation may be evidence of something else—for example, that the CEO is highly valued and the board has concerns about retention.

Two stories (and a digression) about CEO compensation.

Many years ago, I was on a panel at the Tulane Corporate Law Institute with Nell Minow, a founder of ISS who is not exactly an apologist for Corporate America. To the question "Aren't you shocked by the amount of compensation Michael Eisner was paid last year by Disney?" she surprised everyone by telling the following story. "Babe Ruth was asked whether it was right that he was paid more than the president of the United States and Ruth answered, 'I had a better year.'" This was an early endorsement of pay for performance.

Minow's reference to Babe Ruth triggers a digression. The notion that high CEO compensation is *the* prime example of income inequality and a failure of governance is interesting in contrast to silence about professional athletes' and entertainers' compensation, which can rival that of CEOs. There is, perhaps, one way that corporate governance has contributed to income inequality, however, but it has virtually nothing to do with what CEOs get paid. Pressure on management teams for short-term financial performance leads to an unrelenting effort to control costs. That, in turn, leads to a number of different HR strategies. Outsourcing can be argued to eliminate the "corporate ladder"; there will be fewer stories about the middle manager who started in the mailroom when a separate entity operates the mailroom. A similar point can be made about the use

of temporary employees. Offshoring of manufacturing also reduces HR costs. Much of the benefit of the adoption of technology (robotics and other) is through reducing headcount. While
strategies for holding down HR costs may contribute to income
inequality, they can also lead to reduced prices for goods and
services (benefiting consumers) and to improved financial performance, which translates into positive stock prices (benefiting
the significant part of the population that directly or indirectly
benefits from equity market performance). There is, no doubt,
an inevitability to income inequality. Rather than focusing on
CEO compensation through pay-ratio "shaming," those who are
sincerely concerned about income inequality should attend to
the unacceptable causes (e.g., unequal opportunities for quality education and mass incarceration) and unacceptable consequences (e.g., unequal access to health-care and legal services,
homelessness, and the scourge of inner-city violence). Boards
that conclude that CSR is an appropriate part of their corporate
strategy may wish to focus those efforts on such matters. Investors who are interested in relative compensation as a matter of
governance would do well to focus not on the mandated disclosure about pay ratio but on the spread between CEO compensation and either the compensation of the next-highest-paid
member of the C-suite or the average of the compensation of
the named executive officers (the NEOs). End of digression.

The SEC disclosure regime can, unfortunately, sometimes inform not just the shareholders. I was hired by a compensation
committee that for the first time had realized the degree of their
largesse in previously approving a golden-parachute arrangement when they saw a draft proxy statement prepared under
new rules that required a vivid disclosure of the amount the CEO
would receive in a hypothetical change in control. As I recall,
the number was astronomical, in part because it included a tax
gross-up. The full board was delighted with the performance
of the CEO but concerned about the embarrassment or worse
that would follow the disclosure. The solution was to ask the
CEO to give up a contract right, but that was unlikely to happen without some quid pro quo. Fortunately, the company had
had a dynamite year and shareholders would not have objected
to a large bonus. With the help of an economic consultant, the
board calculated the net present value of the entitlement to the

change in control payment: a calculation of the amount it would pay out if the CIC occurred some years hence, multiplied by the probability of that event taking place, discounted by an appropriate rate. Using a similar formula, the board then calculated the net present value of a substitute, less embarrassing change-in-control provision. The first number minus the second number became the basis for the discretionary bonus.

Succession Planning

On a routine basis, boards should engage in succession planning. (Executing on CEO succession is covered in chapter 8.) Many boards think of succession planning as covering who will be the next CEO when the time comes for the incumbent to retire. As a result, they take up the subject most earnestly in the year or two before an expected retirement age. This approach is often favored by incumbent CEOs, although a supremely self-confident CEO will encourage succession planning early in his or her tenure.[43] An effective board will do more than just "normal" planning for the CEO position.

First, the scope of succession planning should cover not just the CEO but also other critical positions. This should be done with due deference to the CEO, as those other positions constitute his or her team.

Second, but perhaps more important, the board should plan for emergency CEO succession in the event of a sudden, unexpected departure of the incumbent and, in addition, plan for what to do in the event of an incapacitated CEO. Sudden departures can result from death or serious medical conditions, having the CEO hired away or (in the age of #MeToo) revelations or credible allegations about sexual misconduct at the company or the CEO's prior employer that warrant immediate termination. A sudden departure of an heir apparent to the incumbent CEO can also raise concerns. Being able to communicate stability and continuity to shareholders, employees, and other constituencies is critical. The single best example of this being done right was McDonald's Corporation. In 2004–2005, that company experienced the death of not one, but two, CEOs within nine months of each other.

Incapacitation can result from heart attack, stroke, or some other serious medical condition that will not necessarily prevent the incumbent's return. In many ways, incapacitation raises more issues for a board than a sudden departure and should be given at least a much planning attention as succession. To be able to assess whether the health issue is indeed temporary and to make decisions about disclosure requirements and content, the board will need to have access to the CEO's medical team and be authorized to make public statements. Privacy requirements of the Health Insurance Portability and Accountability Act (or HIPAA) aside, this can be a sensitive issue for the CEO's family. Requisite consents should ideally be obtained in advance, in part to remove the consent request from the emotion of the event and because of the possibility that the incapacitation is so significant that the CEO is unconscious or otherwise not able to grant consent.

I may be so focused on advance planning for CEO incapacity because, over the course of four decades, I have advised companies on a number of CEO heart attacks, cancer surgeries, and at least one debilitating stroke and coma. My favorite story, including for its happy ending, follows.

In the days before cell phones, I was paged at an airport. The pager was the CFO of a client who told me that the CEO had a serious heart attack and asked, "Do we need to put out a press release?" A number of factors went into my analysis—the heart attack was "serious," and the CEO would be out of commission for a while (among other things, he would have to cancel many meetings, with cancelations likely leading to market rumors); the CEO was the company's largest shareholder; he was the "face" of the company (e.g., he appeared in its television commercials); and while he had a terrific number two, it was unclear whether that person would be a successor. On the basis of all these considerations, I responded, "Yes, put out a press release." A few days later, the CEO called me from his hospital room, with one question—"Why did the stock go up?" I replied, "Because the Street thinks the company will be sold." He harrumphed: "The Street is wrong." It wasn't. The CEO recovered, but we sold the company within twelve months.

That story played out in the late 1980s. Since then, despite a few examples to the contrary (e.g., Steve Jobs's illness at Apple), the default seems to be to make a disclosure. The debate then turns to "how quickly and in what detail." In one instance that I advised on, a disclosure within twenty-four hours of a heart attack was criticized in the press as "too slow." In another instance, there was a disclosure was that the CEO was on an indefinite medical leave and an interim CEO had been named, but it did not describe the medical condition. This was designed to convey the severity of the medical issue while protecting the privacy of the CEO and family. Criticism included the statement from a governance activist to the effect that CEOs relinquish all rights to privacy. Come on!

In 2018, Sergio Marchionne, CEO of Fiat Chrysler, died suddenly following shoulder surgery. The company's stock cratered on the news. It later came out that he had been battling a serious illness for over a year. The company stated that it had "no knowledge of the facts relating to Mr. Marchionne's health."[44] Given the fact that knowledge on the part of a CEO is knowledge of the company, this is a rather untenable position.

It may sound ghoulish, but the announcement of a sudden death or incapacity of a CEO can trigger an unsolicited approach to buy the company that may or may not go all the way to a public, hostile bid. For this reason, routine preparation for hostile takeovers (discussed in a later section) is a companion piece to succession planning.

CEO Performance Evaluation

Implicit in executive compensation and succession planning is, of course, evaluating the performance of the CEO. As a matter of good practice, this should be made an explicit part of the board's annual routine. A starting point is an assessment of the CEO's execution of the company's strategy and of the company's financial performance relative to budget and in the context of macroeconomic forces. A more

complete evaluation includes an assessment of the CEO as commu-
nicator to the Street. Most important is an assessment of the CEO a
leader, applying the criteria under "CEO Succession" in chapter 8 and
the considerations set forth in chapter 12. Finally, it is fair for a board
to include in the performance evaluation an assessment of how well
the CEO addresses the needs of the board in fulfilling its proper role.

Talent Management

Whether part of executive compensation or succession planning, many
boards feel that talent development beyond the C-suite is a proper part
of their routine responsibilities. This notion was espoused by the NACD
in one of its Blue Ribbon Commission reports.[45] The importance of
employee engagement and development to the success of a company
has been demonstrated by the Drucker Institute's "gauge of corporate
effectiveness."[46]

When diversity and inclusion are a strategic goal of the company's talent management, having diversity in the boardroom
will certainly increase the chances of achieving that goal. While
it need not be the case, I have observed that directors who are
women and/or minorities will, more reliably than white men, re-
mind management of the importance of employee diversity and
pay equity. Indeed, one director who I have observed on numerous boards will speak up (appropriately and diplomatically, yet
firmly) whenever presentations by middle management or even
outside advisors are made exclusively by white men. In fact, *all*
directors should speak up in such a situation.

Taken too far, board involvement on this subject can step across the
line into a management function, but certainly it is a fair subject for
oversight. A related subject is whether the board should go beyond
oversight and have actual approval authority over hiring and firing for
certain positions. The most obvious positions that would be covered

by such authority would be the CFO and the GC. There can be an argument that other positions that serve as "staff" to standing committees of the board might also fall into this category—head of internal audit (for the audit committee) and CHRO (for compensation committee). The best practice seems to be for the board to be consulted and to give guidance on personnel decisions relating to key management positions but to give a CEO full discretion about populating his or her team.

Risk Management

Risk management has received a great deal of attention in the New Era of Corporate Governance. The SEC has required disclosure of important aspects of risk management in annual reports since 2005, both how compensation design might create incentives for excessive risk taking and "the extent of the Board's role in . . . risk oversight."[47]

The relationship between risk management and crisis management (discussed in the next chapter) can be analogized to a concept in high school physics. Risk management is like potential energy (the rock when perched at the top of the cliff). Crisis management is kinetic energy (which the rock has when it falls off the cliff). If you live at the bottom of the cliff, it's a good idea to think about preventing the rock's fall or, while the rock is still up there, what to do if it does fall. Thus, risk management has two components: prevention and mitigation of loss.

Any enterprise has all kinds of risk, and the starting point of risk management is to list the pertinent categories. The inventory for most public companies includes the following: operational, financial, compliance, and cyber.

Operational risk can depend on the type of business. For example, the production of products that are meant to be ingested (food or pharmaceuticals) carries the risk of causing harm as a result of contamination. Risk management for this kind of business may involve quality control and quality assurance (for prevention) and tabletop recall exercises (for mitigation). In other types of business, compensation design can be a big factor. For example, bonus structures for traders in a financial institution can have the flavor of "heads I win, tails the bank loses." Proper design coupled with authorization limits (which are strictly adhered to and not waived even for big producers) can prevent or at least mitigate that risk. For other businesses, a change in operations can create risk if the potential impact of the change is not fully considered. A toy company that leans on its overseas suppliers around pricing may need to increase its quality controls to make sure that it hasn't led those suppliers to cut corners (e.g., use cheaper, but dangerous, materials). A manufacturing company that is considering adding a sales office in a territory that is known for governmental corruption should first consider whether it has sufficient infrastructure in that territory to monitor bribery and kickbacks. A sales-oriented company that increases quotas should increase monitoring of its sales practices. For many companies, risk comes from potential "disruption"—for example, the impact on grocery-store chains when Walmart decided to sell groceries.

Financial risk can come from many directions. Most obvious is leverage. Debt can create an "efficient" balance sheet, and debt taken on to buy back stock can improve earnings per share. Nevertheless, in a high-leverage situation, risk can be created by changes in interest rates (for either floating-rate debt or fixed-rate debt that must be refinanced) or if budgets and projections, and thus covenants, are not met. Management of financial risk for financial institutions often involves "stress testing," and this exercise can be useful to other kinds of businesses as well. Stress testing typically games out the impact of changes in interest rates. For companies with convertible securities or that have been financed with PIPES (private investment in public equity), changes in their own stock price can be relevant. For manufacturing companies, changes in commodity prices and tariff proposals might be an appropriate subject. For transportation companies, understanding the implications of swings in fuel prices will be important. Hedging transactions to mitigate financial risk may be appropriate.

Compliance risk management starts with "tone at the top" and a healthy corporate culture. This is useful both for prevention and mitigation. When leaders set the right tone in word and deed, the followers may actually follow. A collaborative culture reduces the risk of the lone wolf, rogue employee who can drag the company down. A culture of respect for individuals can reduce the risk of a toxic work environment that can lead to claims of discrimination, bullying, and sexual harassment. A zero-tolerance policy covering all levels of employees must be more than just words. When noncompliant employees (especially high performers) are appropriately and consistently dealt with, the deterrent effect can prevent the next episode. The mitigating effect arises from the fact that, under Department of Justice guidelines, a good tone at the top that involves the board can enter into a prosecutor's decision not to charge a company for an employee's misdeeds,[48] and is relevant to the penalty assessed by a judge if the company is charged and convicted.[49]

Compliance risk management also involves education. This often starts with a comprehensive code of business conduct applicable to all employees. Those employees who interact with investors need to be attuned to Regulation FD (through baseline education and occasional boosters) as well as to a company's "no-comment policy" when it comes to responding to rumors. As the #MeToo era has made even more evident, training about sexual harassment (including bystander training to encourage peer intervention) is critical.

Cyber is the risk du jour, but one that is likely to be with us for decades. It is now cliché, but true, that there are two kinds of companies—those that know they have been hacked and those that don't know they've been hacked. Hacking comes from thieves, competitors, disgruntled current or former employees, "hactivists," and state actors. Sensitive and proprietary information may reside in the company's own servers or in the servers of vendors (including management consultants and financial and legal advisors). Prevention comes from staff, technology, and education. Mitigation requires knowing in detail who must be notified in the event of a hack (or in some cases even an attempted hack). Notification requirements can be extensive (states and federal agencies under laws and regulations and customers under contractual provisions) and may need to be done in a very short time frame.

In the old days, a corporation's "risk manager" was the man or woman who purchased insurance coverage. While the breadth of risk management has greatly increased, insurance remains a useful mitigator that should not be forgotten. Coverage includes property-casualty, business interruption, employee matters, cyber, and, of course, D&O.

Reputation management can mitigate risk. A company that has a reputation as a good corporate citizen might be more likely to "catch a break" from prosecutors, regulators, and important constituencies when a crisis arises.[50]

Paying attention to corporate organizational structure can also mitigate risk. Separation of various activities into subsidiaries can prevent a failure in one area from having a domino impact on the rest of the enterprise. For this approach to work in insulating one business unit from another, a company must take steps to reduce the risk of "veil piercing," which occurs when a judge is convinced that the separate identity of a subsidiary should be ignored because, for example, the subsidiary has not followed corporate formalities. Intercompany financing arrangements can also cause veil-piercing-like outcomes. This is a fair subject for inquiry by a board of directors, especially if there is a substantial difference in the inherent riskiness between or among various business units.

A key governance issue is where, within the board, does responsibility for risk management oversight reside. Some companies have formal "risk committees." These committees are mostly found in financial institutions and mostly cover financial risk. Other companies seem to default to placing risk management in the audit committee charter. The best approach is to recognize that different committees should address different risks, and some risks are sufficiently important that the full board should address them. Whether risk management is lodged in a committee or in the full board, if a competitor is in crisis the directors should be asking, "Are we at risk for the same issue, and what have we done to prevent or mitigate it from happening to us?"

When risk management was first getting a great deal of attention at the board level, one director said to me, "I confess, I really don't understand what risks this company faces." I suggested that the director start by reading the risk factors section of the Form 10-K he had just signed.

Following the Global Financial Crisis, I was asked, in the context of risk management, "Should we be contemplating so-called black-swan events"? That was a reference to a rather quirky best seller by Nassim Nicholas Taleb entitled *The Black Swan: The Impact of the Highly Improbable*. That book was first published in 2007, but it became much more of a topic of discussion after the crisis. A black swan is, to use a phrase in Taleb's book, "the extreme, the unknown, and the very improbable." Focusing on the probable (and continuing to update one's understanding of what that means) seems sensible from a cost-benefit analysis. Moreover, trying to anticipate and plan for a black-swan event could lead to decision-making paralysis.

Shareholder Relations and Engagement

On a routine basis, the board should be apprised of investor relations—who owns the stock, especially any activists; what is the quality of the investor relations personnel and program; what are the investors (and analysts and ISS) saying about the company; and what are the positions of the major investors on CSR/ESG? The board should also consider how, if at all, it wishes to respond to the call for "engagement" (described in chapter 6).

Preparation for Activism and Hostile Takeovers

Activism and the potential for unsolicited offers for the company, which may or may not turn into a hostile public bid, are a fact of life for any public company. As a routine matter, boards should be reminded about how such matters arise and proceed, as well as how well the company is prepared to anticipate and address them.

Advance planning for an activist campaign includes the following steps:

- Identifying who will be on the team in the event of an activist attack. A fully staffed team includes members of management, experienced financial and legal advisors, special situations PR advisors, proxy solicitors, and (possibly) a stock-watch service.

- Understanding the likely arguments that an activist will mount. This involves having financial and legal advisors prepare a "mock attack." Management and advisors then prepare draft rebuttals to each element of the attack, so as to reduce the amount of time needed to respond to arguments put forth in a real attack. At times, it may make sense to moot such arguments through preemptive action.

- Having in place, or at the ready, structural defenses. These include enhanced advance notice bylaws. Advance notice bylaws provide an "early warning" that a shareholder intends to nominate directors or propose business to be considered at a shareholder meeting. They create a "window" during which nominations or proposals must be put forward—often between 90 and 120 days before the one-year anniversary of the date on which the prior annual meeting took place. Such bylaws are "enhanced" by information requirements, such as the shareholder's ownership of derivatives on the stock and agreements with any candidates, and by requiring candidates to complete a detailed D&O questionnaire. Some companies have a bylaw that disqualifies any candidate who has a "golden leash" agreement with a shareholder, providing for compensation to the candidate, if elected, from the shareholder under certain specified circumstances. A poison pill should also be on the shelf for possible use either in the activist attack or in a hostile bid, if the activist attack triggers one. The board should also be apprised of how change-in-control provisions in HR-related contracts and debt instruments are implicated by a wholesale change in the board but should be cautious about dead-hand provisions.[51]

- Monitoring the shareholder list. Particular attention should be given to the presence on the list of well-known financial activists (e.g., those on the SharkWatch 50) and whether a "wolf pack" of activists seems to be forming. A wolf pack develops when "like-minded" activists all show up on a company's shareholder list but avoid any formal arrangement that could cause them to be required to file as a "group" on Schedule 13D. Some companies hire a stock-watch service to monitor ownership in real time and to provide an early warning of the accumulation of shares. Others simply rely on 13F filings.

- Having an effective "clear day" investor relations program.

- Drafting some first-day communications for employees and shareholders for use when and if an activist goes public. For employees, these should essentially be along the lines of: "The board and senior management are handling this. You can best serve the company and our shareholders by doing your jobs well and without distraction." For shareholders, the message is: "We welcome the views of all of our shareholders and will respond as appropriate in due course."

- Making sure that both management and the board are briefed on how to respond to a first call from an activist. This is critically important, because every single interaction between an activist and the company has the potential to be used publicly in a proxy contest. (Similarly, colorful emails from a CEO to others about the activist can come out in discovery and play into an activist's hands.) The posture of management should be to listen, not preempt the board, and remember that the activist is a shareholder. How the activist is treated can have an influence on institutional shareholders whose votes may be needed in the near future. Board members should understand that they are to deflect any call to the management team.

A mock attack is an extremely useful tool. A real attack from an activist often comprises a detailed "white paper" that the activist posts on its website. It is often months in the making and can be more than one hundred PowerPoint slides. (For examples, visit the website of any of the more formidable activists—Pershing Square, Trian, Elliott.) The defensive reason to anticipate the arguments is to keep the time between the attack and the thorough rebuttal to a minimum, so as to keep the activist's arguments from attaining legitimacy solely by the absence of a counter. Management teams will have different reactions to the notion of a mock attack. I saw a CEO reluctantly agree to the preparation of a mock attack, but he insisted on a preview before it was presented to the board. At the end of the preview, his only comment was "My board will never see this." More enlightened and self-confident CEOs will sometimes use the mock attack as part of strategic planning. To the extent that the arguments in a real or mock attack are other than for purposes of short-term profits in the stock, they can present some ideas that merit consideration.

"Clear day" engagement with shareholders is critical. In a proxy contest that I was helping to defend against, the nonexecutive chairman, the CEO, and the head of investor relations (IR) visited a major shareholder to ask for its vote. At the start of the meeting, the shareholder's representative asked the head of IR, "Why haven't we met before?" The head of IR lost that vote and his job in one fell swoop.

Advance planning for an unsolicited takeover bid is similar to planning for activism. It includes the all-important first-day communication—a "stop, look, and listen" message to be issued in the event of a public offer or "bear hug." This advance planning places a somewhat greater emphasis on structural defenses and, in particular, the poison pill, also known as a shareholder rights plan. The operation of a pill can be explained in two ways, much as one would explain a nuclear weapon. First, there is the technical description of how it operates if triggered. Second, there is the deterrent effect. The "magic" of a pill is the fact that it can be adopted by a board and can be dismantled as a defense only by the board. For a more complete discussion, see note 8 to chapter 4.

When pills were first validated in the 1980s, many companies adopted them and had them in place for a ten-year period. Now, most companies simply have them on the shelf—that is, the board is briefed on how they operate and what the key variables (e.g., the "triggering percentage," duration, and exercise price) are that the board will need to decide on when the time comes. The pills are not adopted until needed, because they tend to engender negative reactions from institutions and ISS. If the board has been briefed in advance, there is always time for adoption when the need arises.

It is really important to make sure that outside directors, as well as CEOs, are prepared for how to act in the event of a call from a potential hostile bidder for the company. On one occasion, an outside director of a client received such a call. When the caller inquired about the possibility of acquiring the company, rather than saying, "Talk to the CEO," the director said, "What an interesting idea . . . send us a letter." That was exactly the wrong thing to say and encouraged the bidder to go public with an offer. As André Meyer of Lazard supposedly said, "M&A is 10 percent financial analysis and 90 percent psychoanalysis."

Executive Sessions

In many ways, the "sleeper" reform of the post-Enron era is the mandate for executive sessions of the board. Interestingly, the sessions are to be of "nonmanagement" directors, a broader category than independent directors.[52] Before this mandate, it was thought to be something of an act of sedition for directors to gather or speak outside the presence of the CEO. Indeed, Jack Welch (the legendary former CEO of GE, whose legend is now undergoing something of a rewrite) once said that he would have quit if his directors wanted to meet without him.

Before executive sessions were mandated, but when the idea was first gaining some traction, I was acting as counsel to the independent directors of a company that was struggling against foreign competition and dealing with a failure to invest for the long term in its manufacturing processes. The CEO was very smart and charismatic but not an effective manager. As a leader, he was a bit insecure, as evidenced by the fact that he never had strong personnel in the C-suite. (He thought they might be too handy as successors.) Despite this insecurity, during a board meeting he made a comment to the effect that, if the board ever wanted to meet in executive session, he would be fine with that. One of the board members reflexively said something like "We would never do that." At the end of the meeting, I was standing outside headquarters with several of the board members as they were waiting for cars to the airport. I suggested that they consider taking the CEO up on his generous offer. They reconsidered, started to meet in executive session, and it was the beginning of an appropriate end to the CEO's tenure.

Some boards hold executive sessions with the CEO at the beginning of the board meeting to hear from the CEO about his or her expectations for the meeting before the rest of the management team arrives in the room. Even when there has been a session at the start of the meeting, executive sessions are held at the end of the meeting. They start with the CEO in the room and continue after he or she leaves. Unfortunately, if the meeting has not been run in a disciplined fashion, this can result in a rather abbreviated session, as directors pack up for their flights.

Aside from the discussion at the session itself, the most important aspect of an executive session is the subsequent feedback to the CEO. Most boards are happy for messages to be carried by the nonexecutive chair or LID, either after the meeting or a few days later. Other boards would like to be present when feedback is given—in some cases to make sure that any constructive criticism is not excessively diluted. In either case, the independent directors should agree on the key messages to be delivered, and it is always good to ask the CEO not to respond immediately. Some delay in a response will reduce the risk of defensiveness and allow for more thoughtful reflection. Depending on the issues raised in the feedback, the CEO's response might wait until the next board meeting.

Board Minutes

An important element of routine board matters is to make sure that record of the board's and its committees' good work is properly memorialized. The principal vehicle for this is corporate minutes. In the past several years, this subject has received greater judicial attention than ever before. Delaware Supreme Court's Chief Justice Strine wrote an article about documentation of M&A transactions that is devoted significantly to minutes.[53] Lawyers typically prefer "short-form" minutes, capturing the subject that were covered but not so much about what was said about each one. There may be instances that warrant a "longer-form" treatment.

One thing to keep in mind in preparing minutes—they are read by directors, of course, but also auditors, underwriters, counsel, and (in discovery) plaintiffs' lawyers, among others. As a result, legal advice should be noted as having been received, but if the substance of that advice is summarized in the minutes read by outsiders, it can lose its privileged status. Moreover, discussions of acquisition targets or potential acquirers should use code names.

A good set of minutes also reduces the risk that an individual director will feel a compulsion to take notes or, even worse, prepare a memo to file.

Board Education

As a matter of routine, a board should be engaging in continuing education. There are a number of approaches to this. Many companies send their directors to conferences and directors' colleges. Specialized programs for audit committees are also available.[54] These events are useful for supplying substantive information, as well as providing networking opportunities for directors. The downside is cost—both in dollars and in time. Because of that downside, many boards prefer to invite in outside speakers to cover new developments. Law firms, investment banks, and others will often provide those updates for free as a matter of business development.

I was once invited to give a presentation on "expanding expectations about board oversight" to the directors of a very large consumer products company. Following my usual practice, I sent the draft of my slides to the GC, who shared the draft with the CEO. The only comment from the CEO was "delete the slides about oversight of political spending." I declined to do so, explaining that there would be some board members who were aware of that "expanded expectation," and by not covering it, my entire presentation might be suspect. Fortunately, that argument carried the day.

Another source of director education could be "client alerts" on governance matters prepared by the major corporate law firms. General counsel are inundated by these documents but might be asked to forward particularly useful ones to directors. Finally, subscriptions to periodicals from the NACD and others might be supplied to directors.

8

Special Situations

In any given year, the typical public company board and its committees address their routine matters over the course of four to six regular two-day meetings. It is a rare board that does not have some number of additional special meetings—special meetings for the special situations that inevitably arise. Special situations can involve, among other things, crisis management, CEO succession, internal investigations, financial distress, M&A, or some other material transaction and shareholder activism. Virtually all benefit from advance planning undertaken as a routine matter. Many will create material information that may not be ready to be fully publicly disclosed and, therefore, will require the closing of the securities trading window for at least some persons for some period of time.

While a board will be active in each of the special situations described in this chapter, in the absence of a conflict, the CEO should generally take the lead in addressing them.

Crisis Management

As noted elsewhere in this book, crisis management deals with risks that come to fruition. There is an element of crisis management in all of the other special situations described here. The degree of involvement of the board will be dependent on its level of confidence in the management to address the crisis: Is management sufficiently disinterested?

Does management convey the appropriate sense of urgency without appearing to panic? Does it have sufficient bandwidth and experience to assess the situation, handle the crisis, and run the company at the same time? Even when management takes the lead, the board should provide close and frequent oversight.

Board oversight includes pursuing the following kinds of questions (which management will do well to preemptively ask and answer and then update as needed):

- Do we have the right team and leadership in place to address the crisis? Does the team include all the right disciplines to address the inevitably multidimensional aspects of the crisis? Have the internal experts agreed to be appropriately supplemented with outside experts, or are they being turf conscious? Have outside experts been retained through counsel to increase the chance that their work will be privileged? The optimal response to the crisis may differ according to discipline. For example, the lawyers often advise that, beyond disclosure required under the securities laws, less is more when it comes to communications. In contrast, the operating, HR, and PR people will want to be expansive in communications—perhaps even before all the facts are in. In light of this, is the leader of the team capable of appropriately arbitrating between and among those conflicting perspectives and using sound judgment to get to the right result?
- When it comes to communications, is the company thinking of all the constituencies, and is there consistency of communications across them? Paul Verbinnen, one of the leading crisis communications experts, recommends thinking in concentric circles. Verbinnen advises that the most important (and, thus, inner) circle comprises employees and others who will be most affected by the crisis and its implications. Particular attention should be given to mission-critical team members—those whom competitors might seek to pick off. The communications focus should then move outwardly toward customers, funding sources, investors, and (lastly) the media. Verbinnen also urges caution in selecting the messenger. In the case of a financially or reputationally material crisis, the logical messenger is almost always the CEO. Indeed, the CEO who ducks this task may be accused of cowardice. The messenger should be watched for

symptoms of fatigue (which could lead to unscripted missteps, such as the BP CEO's "I want to get my life back") and cautioned about the dangers of attempts at humor (the Goldman CEO's "We are doing God's work"). Because the company should speak with one voice, in most cases board members should not take on any communications role. Because crises evolve and communications (including mandatory SEC disclosure) cannot typically await ascertaining all facts and analysis, communications should always have the caveat "This is what we know now, and things can and will likely change."[1]

- What are the financial and accounting implications of the crisis? Relatedly, are we keeping our auditors apprised? Keep in mind that what is told to the board (especially in writing) and communications among board members can have disclosure implications, so words need to be chosen with care. Too often people write about "what we know," when it would be more accurate to say, "This is what we believe."

- What are we doing to anticipate the potential litigation—whether from those affected by (or government agencies interested in) the underlying events, or triggered by our disclosure posture and a "stock drop," or a fiduciary duty claim? If litigation has been threatened, has a "document-hold notice" been issued? Are we preserving privilege? Have we notified insurers?

- If the crisis has caused the reputation of the company to take a hit, are there "acts of redemption" that should be considered? For example, if the company caused an environmental crisis, will a contribution to a community organization in the affected area be useful and should it be publicized? Or would such an action be attacked as "too little, too late"?

- Because a company in crisis often means that there are individuals in crisis as well—perhaps the individual who had some direct responsibility for the crisis-creating event—what are we doing to support that person (the rest of the employees will be watching)? Is that person so distraught that he or she may not be able to function properly or might do something stupid (like destroy documents or try to delete computer files)? Should he or she be given paid leave?

- Finally, when the dust settles, are there things that we should be doing to improve our risk management program, and are there any appropriate employment actions?

A corporate crisis can have a profound impact on individuals who are at the center of the underlying facts or are tasked to deal with the crisis. This is illustrated by reactions I got when I asked executives at two different companies in crisis, "How are you handling all of this?" One said: "I survived the Tet Offensive . . . I guess I will make it through this." The other said, "Much better, thanks . . . I am now sitting up and taking solid food."

CEO Succession

While succession planning should be a routine matter, actually executing on succession is anything but.

Planning often leads to a preliminary conclusion that the successor will come from within the organization and will often focus on a single candidate. That is thought to be evidence of a healthy organization. Moreover, veteran executive-search professionals state a rule of thumb—"unless the external candidate is twice as good as the internal candidate, take the insider." One of the reasons that this is a wise rule of thumb was articulated in the book *Chasing Stars*.[2] Simply put, it is unclear that an outsider who is a "star" at his or her current employer can always transfer that star power to a new job. Taking a star away from the team that provided support, or putting the star into a different corporate culture, could lead to a very different leadership profile.

Even when it appears almost certain that the internal candidate will be the successor, a certain amount of due diligence is appropriate before a final decision is made.

With consent, there should be a background check done on the internal candidate even if he or she has been at the company for years.[3] There have been instances of résumé exaggeration or fraud that have come to light after a promotion announcement. There have been situations in which the new CEO had been involved in personal litigation of an embarrassing nature that had not been brought to the attention of the board but would have surfaced in a simple, noninvasive, computer-based search of court records. When it does come to light after the person was promoted to CEO, it can be a source of embarrassment for the board. Similarly, social media (and even yearbook) postings by a candidate could be a source of embarrassment and are worth checking. Finally, because the new CEO is to be the leader of a team made up of his or her current peers, if possible, it would be good to know how they feel about him or her.

Again, even when the internal candidate is likely to be chosen, it is recommended that some degree of diligence is done on possible external candidates. This can be limited to having an executive recruiter do a "desktop" exercise—research that does not require contacting candidates or interviewing them. The internal candidate should be apprised of the exercise and its largely confirmatory purpose. It would be awkward for the heir apparent to learn about it indirectly.

Finally, because the internal candidate will be vacating an important position, the board needs to give thought to that additional succession decision.

When there are multiple internal candidates, there can be an issue about how to handle the disappointed "also-rans." Jack Welch implemented an extreme solution. He reportedly told three people that they were in contention, and that on a date certain, one would be selected and the other two would be fired. The reason given was a concern that the individuals who were not selected would undermine the successful candidate.

The other approach would be to work to achieve Abraham Lincoln's "team of rivals."[4] Depending on the circumstances, this may not be easy and takes work on the part of both the successor CEO and board leadership. It is a great example of the cliché that "hope is not a plan." A typical plan includes clear communication with the "also-rans" and providing them with opportunities for further career enhancement within the organization under the new CEO. Under some circumstances, a board seat might even be warranted. Increased compensation or some form of "golden handcuff" without anything else is typically not a long-term solution. Whatever approach is to be taken, it should be ready for execution right at the time of selecting the successor CEO and even before there has been a public announcement. Executive recruiters will be calling the "also-rans" immediately post-announcement.

Dick Thomas was the CEO of First Chicago (which later became BankOne and was then acquired by JPMorgan Chase). Dick became CEO after being passed over for the position more than once. On the occasion of his retirement, he explained the reasons that he didn't leave when he was passed over. He said: "There were three reasons: I liked the job I had. I never defined my self-worth in terms of my job title. And, until I became CEO, I didn't fully realize what I was missing!"

When there is no internal candidate or if it is unclear whether he or she will be selected, external candidates will need to be considered in more depth. With the help of a recruiter, a list of potential candidates can be developed and sorted into tiers. The top tiers can be contacted and, with their consent, background checked. This due diligence should include understanding whether the candidate is subject to any noncompetition agreement with a current employer or whether that employer might potentially raise trade secret concerns that would impede the ability of the executive to operate.

The leading candidate or candidates should be interviewed. This raises the question, Interviewed by whom? Because most external candidates will be employed and sensitive to having their current employer apprised of their interest in moving on, they will sometimes ask that only a small number of directors be involved, at least until nearly the eve of signing. That's fair. The leading candidate might also be interviewed for cultural compatibility or personality fit by a professional, such as a psychologist.

This last step in diligence comes as a bit of a surprise to some board members. I admit that, even though my brother was a psychiatrist, I was a skeptic. How much could a shrink tell the board from a one-hour interview of the candidate? I became a believer when I observed a board decline to follow the recommendation of a psychologist ("do *not* hire this man!") and, in short order, realize that they had made a mistake. The face-saving escape was provided by an unsolicited offer to buy the company.

Whether the successor is from the inside or the outside, the physical health of the candidate is also relevant. It must be approached with some caution and likely in the post-offer period. A stark example of this is the 2017 hiring of Hunter Harrison as the new CEO of CSX as a result of the pressure from an activist shareholder. According to press reports, the board knew his health to be an issue, but it went ahead with the hiring and granted an $84 million signing bonus even after Harrison refused to allow an independent physician to review his medical records. He was hired on May 6, 2017, at the age of seventy-two, worked mostly from home using a portable oxygen tank, went on medical leave on December 14, 2017 (causing the stock to lose $4 billion in market value), and died a few days later.[5]

When succession is immediate, sudden, and unexpected, many boards today rely on the appointment of an interim CEO during the period of a search. Often the interim leader is a board member. In other instances, a member of the board becomes chairman (if there is not already a nonexecutive chair), and the interim CEO is a member of management (or a group comprising an "office of the president," with the occasionally telling abbreviation "OOPs!").

Disclosure is a relevant subject in any succession.

The securities laws, at first blush, create something of a hair trigger for disclosure about an impending retirement. SEC's Current Report on Form 8-K requires disclosure within four business days after the date on which a CEO (and certain other officers) "retires, resigns or is removed."[6] The SEC Staff has interpreted that item as being triggered by receipt of "a notice of a decision to retire . . . regardless of whether [it] is conditional." However, the interpretation goes on to say that "no disclosure is required solely by reason of . . . discussions or consideration of . . . retirement." So, the timing of obligatory disclosure is something that can be managed and, as appropriate, put off for a time.

Nevertheless, there can be times when a company (and its incumbent CEO) will want to make disclosure about a retirement even before it is absolutely compelled. Reaching out to external candidates can trigger rumors. Moreover, when a long-serving CEO is nearing what might be considered "normal" retirement age or the scheduled expiration of an employment agreement, he or she can expect inquiries about personal plans. Those inquiries can come in one-on-one discussions (watch out for Regulation FD) or in earnings calls with analysts (a safe non-answer might be "Someday I will retire, but it will be when the time is right for both me and the company.") Finally, it is often desirable to announce that the CEO will be stepping down at some specified time some months in the future or earlier, after a successor has been found by a search committee and selected by the board. It is highly desirable to avoid an "effective immediately" announcement, which can imply some sort of misconduct on the part of the departing CEO.

There is, of course, the other side of the disclosure—the selection of the new CEO. Form 8-K requires disclosure of the appointment of a new CEO (among others). While that is also subject to the requirement of four business days, the instruction to that item creates a huge exception—"If the registrant intends to make a public announcement of the appointment . . . the registrant may delay filing . . . until the day [of that public announcement]."[7]

Before a communication is issued about the new CEO, it is a very good idea to have reached agreement on the terms and conditions of his or her employment—if not the final contract, then at least a very detailed term sheet.

One of our clients had a vigorous negotiation with a CEO candidate (or at least his very aggressive lawyer). When it came time to sign, with the contract on the table and the pen in his hand, the would-be successor said to the director who was leading the search, "I just want you to know that I am being advised that I am leaving a lot on the table and would like you to consider improvements to my terms." The response of the director—who for many reasons had been given a great deal of authority over the process—was "Don't bother to sign . . . our offer is with-drawn." It would have been a real problem if there had been an announcement, at least in this case, simply on the basis of a term sheet.

The CEO contract is obviously an important document. The provisions delineating duties can be invoked in a discussion (or even dispute) about the allocation of roles and responsibilities between the board and management. The termination provisions amount to a prenuptial agreement. The definition of "for cause" termination should receive a great deal of attention. In the #MeToo era, some companies are including sexual misconduct at a prior employer in that definition.[8] The change-in-control provisions, including the definition of a termination by the CEO "for good reason," are also worth pausing over. Post-termination obligations of the CEO may be spelled out. These can include confidentiality and nondisparagement (although whistle-blowing must be carved out, per the decision in the SEC's *KBR* case[9]). A noncompetition provision of reasonable duration and scope is common. There may also be a standstill provision, largely to prevent a terminated CEO from joining forces with an activist or hostile bidder. Finally, because a board cannot remove a director, a CEO employment agreement should provide that upon any form of termination of employment, it is deemed that the CEO also has resigned from all boards within the corporate family.

The selection of a CEO is probably the most important decision a board can make. Directors should thoughtfully determine the attributes they are looking for in that person. In a ten-year study called the CEO Genome Project, the authors mined an extensive database. They state that, while "there is certainly no 'one size fits all' approach," there are nevertheless "key ingredients" to CEO success: "decisiveness, the ability to engage stakeholders, adaptability, and reliability."[10] Professor Steven Kaplan of Chicago Booth raised one note of caution: "Boards should focus on execution skills. . . . [They] overweight interpersonal skills in their hiring decisions."[11] Having said that, effective communication skills are critical for a leader. In addition to execution skills, boards are also being encouraged to give more weight to perhaps a surprising attribute when one thinks about CEOs—namely, humility. "Humility is a core quality of leaders who inspire close teamwork, rapid learning and high performance. . . . Humble leaders can also be highly competitive and ambitious."[12] Above all else, for the reasons expanded on in Part IV, boards should be looking for leaders, not just managers. (See chapter 7 for considerations relating to the role of the outgoing CEO as a board chair.)

Internal Investigations

Internal investigations are most often triggered by allegations of wrongdoing by members of management. These allegations can cover a broad range of activities: financial impropriety, improper financial reporting, and inappropriate behavior (including sexual misconduct). The allegations can come from a whistle-blower (anonymous or otherwise) or from the government (often after hearing from a whistle-blower).

While perhaps unusual, there are instances in which the commencement of an internal investigation can seem unwarranted for other than PR reasons, and perhaps not even then. For example, there was a report in 2017 that General Electric, on occasion, used backup aircraft to follow around CEO Jeff Immelt during his overseas trips that had "security risks and so-called business critical itineraries." That report led to an internal investigation that one hopes, but cannot be sure, cost less than the cost of operating the spare jet.[13]

It is absolutely critical that executives (and especially executives who may be implicated by a whistle-blower's allegation) understand that they cannot take any steps that could be construed to be retaliatory. Indeed, when the whistle-blower is anonymous, there should be no effort to determine the identity of that person. Most executives are aware of this requirement, but it is a service to them to provide a reminder in real time.[14]

Out of a misguided effort to show that the management team (or the law department) is on top of things, and to be able to present the problem and solution at the same time, there will sometimes be a preliminary investigation before the board is informed about the matter. If the allegation directly or indirectly implicates the C-suite, the allegation should be reported to the board before any steps are taken to investigate, so that it can decide how it is to be handled. Proper handling often involves the appointment of a special committee of independent directors who then hire independent counsel. It is best that the GC not participate in selecting that counsel, beyond advising which firms would not qualify as independent. Every effort should be made to protect the actuality and appearance of confidentiality. For example, for conference calls of the special committee, counsel should arrange the call-in numbers, not anyone at the company.

Because employees are likely to be interviewed, they will be given an "Upjohn warning" (sometimes referred to as a "corporate Miranda") to the effect that the lawyer doing the interview represents the company and not them.[15] To encourage candid responses and to mitigate adverse morale impact on employees, the committee overseeing the investigation should give consideration to employing counsel for the employees to be interviewed. This can be a single counsel for the entire group (referred to as "pool counsel") unless and until apparent conflicts arise.

About twenty-five years ago, the high-integrity CEO of a long-standing client called me to say that a former employee in his finance department had alleged that he overheard a conversation in which the CEO had told the CFO to "move revenues into the fourth quarter from the first quarter of the following year." The CEO asked us to do an investigation, effectively into his own behavior. I declined to do so, explaining that any report my firm might give about the matter might not be given credence because of our decades-long, close relationship with the CEO.

In another instance, I was hired to investigate allegations of racially insensitive remarks by a CEO directed at an employee. The very courageous general counsel advised the board of the allegations and recommended the hiring of independent counsel. Our report indicated that the CEO had violated the company's code of conduct. To my shock, one of the board members asked, "What code of conduct?" The CEO (a major shareholder) was simply reprimanded, and the GC subsequently left the company. If the remarks had been made in a more public setting, I expect the stock would have fallen and the CEO would have had the same fate as the founder of Papa John's.

More recently, I was hired to investigate a CEO's intimate, consensual relationship with a subordinate. In that case, there was a code-of-conduct violation, but it was not because of the relationship per se. Rather, the violation was his failure to report the relationship to the chair of the audit committee. He was admonished, and his bonus docked, as was that of the head of HR (who had been aware of the issue).

Sexual and other workplace misconduct has been around for a long time. The #MeToo movement has helped both men and women become more comfortable in speaking up about these matters, with the result that board-led investigations of misconduct have become increasingly commonplace. Even before the #MeToo movement, I advised a board about a very uncommon occurrence—an allegation of sexual harassment of a CEO's assistant by an independent director. The allegation involved inappropriate comments, repeatedly made by the director, that made the assistant understandably uncomfortable. This director was obviously ill-suited to exercise oversight regarding culture and risk management. The director was asked to resign. Fortunately, he agreed to do so. Even though his behavior violated the company's code of conduct (which, like most, applied to directors as well as officers and employees), recall that directors can be removed only by shareholders.

One of the first issues to be addressed at the outset of an investigation (and perhaps reassessed as the investigation proceeds) is whether there needs to be a public disclosure. Depending on the facts, under a strict legal analysis, disclosure may not be legally required at least at the outset. There can be practical considerations that will lead to an early disclosure, nevertheless. For example, it may be prudent to issue a "document hold notice" to protect the company against a later claim of obstruction or spoliation. If, to be effective, such a notice must go to a large number of individuals, then the risk of leak and rumor should be taken into account. A document hold to a large number of employees may be the equivalent of a public announcement.

In the case of an investigation that relates to alleged improper financial reporting or a material violation of law, even if there is not to be an early public disclosure, it may be appropriate to promptly advise the company's revolving credit banks. This is because most bank agreements have relevant representations and provide that every borrowing certificate "remakes" the representations. The issuance of a false borrowing certificate to a national bank puts the treasurer (or similarly situated executive) in a very bad position.[16] Finally, consideration should always be given to whether, when, and how to inform the company's outside auditor.

When the internal investigation relates to behavior that, if confirmed, represents a breach of the company's code of conduct on the part of its CEO, CFO, or principal accounting officer and the company "has granted a waiver, including an implicit waiver" of the code, then the company must make a disclosure of that waiver on Form 8-K.[17] So, if there has been a breach, the board must do something, and the most common action (other than a firing) is to dock the discretionary portion of a bonus. When this happens, it may obviate the need for an 8-K filing but also may lead to disclosure of some sort in the executive compensation section of the next proxy statement.

When it comes time to report to the board or special committee on the outcome of the investigation, careful thought should be given to whether the report is written or oral and how to protect privilege. Privilege (both attorney-client and work-product) is an issue because frequently the report (or its conclusions) will be shared with auditors, the government, or others outside of the umbrella of privilege.

If the internal investigation was not initiated by a governmental inquiry, the company will need to determine whether to self-report. This is a matter of significance that should be addressed at the board level. A decision to self-report may result in "credit" for full cooperation and thus mitigate punishment. In addition, there is always the risk that the government will learn about, or is already aware of, the issue being investigated.

Financial Distress

A corporation in financial distress clearly qualifies as a special situation deserving of close attention by, and often special meetings of, a board. Because of disclosure requirements and accounting rules, it is critical that a goal of budgeting and of routine financial risk management is to provide the board and management with significant advance notice of potential distress.

The centerpiece of SEC disclosure is the MD&A, which of course is included in periodic disclosure documents, including the Form 10-K. Among other things, the applicable rules mandate disclosure about "liquidity and capital resources." The disclosures are to give "a clear picture of the company's ability to generate cash and to meet existing known or reasonably likely future cash requirements" and whether "the registrant is, or is reasonably likely to be, in breach of debt covenants."[18]

An auditor's opinion on financial statements may include a "going concern" qualification if liquidity in the twelve months following the date of the financials raises a "substantial doubt" about the ability of the company to continue as a going concern. A related, slightly less troubling audit opinion qualification is called an "emphasis of matter," which draws attention to negative disclosure in a footnote to the financials.[19]

The purpose of all this, of course, is to warn investors against the kind of precipitous failure that Enron experienced. The reaction of most managements to conservative advice about MD&A disclosure along these lines is predictable—"if we say that, the trade will put us on COD [cash on delivery], the banks will not lend and a potential liquidity concern will become a self-fulfilling prophesy. . . . How is that good for our shareholders?" If management refuses to follow legal advice related to disclosure, counsel may be compelled to raise the issue directly with the board.[20] A related reaction will be for management (or even the chair of the audit committee) to argue with the auditors. Taken too far, there is a risk of being accused of seeking to exert "undue influence" (discussed in chapter 7). The thoughtful development of cash-flow projections and advance planning can do a great deal to prevent having the Hobson's choice of potentially damaging the company or violating the securities laws.

If the company files for bankruptcy protection under Chapter 11 and becomes the "debtor in possession," the board can operate the company in the "ordinary course" but must seek court approval for any transactions "outside" the ordinary course. The board also will authorize the exercise of special rights that arise under Chapter 11, such as the assumption or rejection of contracts and leases. Most importantly, the board approves the plan of reorganization within the "period of exclusivity."

When a company is in financial distress, either before or after a Chapter 11 filing, a board should consider whether the time has come to replace the CEO with a "turnaround" specialist or to supplement the current management team with specialized consultants.

"Friendly" Mergers and Acquisitions

A board considering a change-in-control transaction has additional duties. The clearest example of a change in control is a sale for cash. A merger in which shareholders receive both cash and stock can also be a change in control,[21] as can a merger in which shareholders receive only stock, if the combined company would have a controlling stockholder.[22]

In a change in control, under *Revlon* the board is obligated to follow a process that is reasonably designed to achieve the best deal (principally measured by price) for shareholders. In this instance law and market forces coincide nicely. If a board selects a second-best bid, the presence of a better bid will need to be disclosed and the shareholders will likely not accept the selected bid. Even in states that (unlike Delaware) have an "other constituencies" statute, many of the courts in those states have held that the requirement to pursue the best deal still applies.[23] About the only instance where "best deal" does not mean "best price" is where the highest-priced offer has serious impediments to consummation, such as antitrust or financing issues.

Fortunately, the courts have provided boards with significant latitude when it comes to pursuing the best deal in a change in control.

Boards can follow a single-bidder strategy so long as the merger agreement signed with the bidder does not contain "deal protections" (discussed at some length in the endnotes),[24] which effectively preclude a better deal from coming forward during the period between signing and the shareholder vote on the transaction. Even in a single-bidder process, it is unnecessary to provide for a "go-shop period," although it may be desirable to do so, especially if the single bidder is a private equity firm.[25] A common request from a single bidder is for a period of presigning "exclusivity"—that is, an agreement not to place outbound calls to potential competitive bidders and, also, not to respond to any inbound calls. If anything along these lines is given, it should be based on a strong rationale. Moreover, it is far preferable for it to be limited only to no outbound calls for a limited period of time. At the other end of the continuum, a board could publicly announce that it has hired a banker to help it pursue strategic alternatives—code for "we are for sale." Many deals are done in the middle. That is, a banker is hired to contact potential bidders on a confidential basis and a "quiet auction" takes place.

There are other obligations of a board in any M&A transaction (even if it does not qualify as a change in control) where the company is not going to "survive" as a public company. The courts expect that the board will take "an active and direct role."[26] The board should be able to show that it "was closely engaged at all relevant times in making decisions about how to handle the negotiations."[27] This does not mean that the board will be on the front lines of negotiations, but it does mean that the board will function on all critical decisions. The first decision is, of course, whether to explore a possible transaction—what is the business case for doing so, and is this the right time in the company's life cycle and in the economic cycle for the company's industry sector—and, if so, the next decision is which process described above to follow.

An issue to be understood early in the process is disclosure: when in the process a public disclosure must be made and how detailed it must ultimately be. First, the full board should receive advice about whether discussions have progressed to the point that the potential of a transaction taking place in the future is "material" today. If it is, then the company must either make a disclosure or it (and its "insiders") must abstain from securities transactions. The U.S. Supreme Court provided guidance about this in *Basic v. Levinson*. It rejected a relatively objective test—that is, whether there had been an agreement in principle as to price and terms. Instead, it imposed a somewhat more subjective test—namely, an assessment of "the probability that the event will occur" and "the magnitude of the transaction." In addressing probability, the Court called out a nonexhaustive list of examples—"board resolutions, instructions to investment bankers, and actual negotiation."[28] (Incidentally, where there is no counterparty to negotiate with, as is the case in a spinoff, probability may become high early on.) For a company being sold, magnitude is huge; for an acquirer, magnitude depends on relative size but also may be a function of whether the transaction represents a significant change in strategic direction or capital structure.

If it is determined that discussions have not progressed to the point of reaching materiality, then even directors and others "in the know" can trade the company's stock (assuming the trading window is otherwise open), and the company can proceed with issuing equity and debt. A word of caution, however—cases involving disclosure and insider trading are always litigated in hindsight, and as a result, a degree of conservatism about cessation of trading by directors and officers (even when windows remain open for employees) seems appropriate. If the analysis suggests that discussions have risen to the level of materiality, there is nevertheless not an affirmative duty to make a disclosure about those discussions, unless (a) there is trading by insiders or issuances or purchases by the company itself, (b) rumors about a possible transaction have emanated from the company, or (c) there is a prior disclosure that needs to be corrected. If there are rumors that have not emanated from the company, then, in response to inquiries about those rumors or about unusual market activity, the company can stand behind a "no comment" policy. (Another caution: a statement to the effect that "there are no corporate developments" is not the same thing as "no comment.")[29] If things are handled correctly, the first disclosure about a transaction is the announcement of the signing of a definitive agreement.

Second, there is a notion that has been labeled "the partial disclosure-materiality issue." Simply put, when disclosure is made about a subject that may or may not be material, if that disclosure is not complete, there may be a breach of the duty of candor. As the Delaware Supreme Court stated, "Once defendants traveled down the road of partial disclosure of the history leading up to the Merger and used the vague language described, they had an obligation to provide the stockholders with an accurate, full, and fair characterization of those historic events"[30] As a result, the disclosure contained in the background section of a proxy statement soliciting votes can best be described as "granular." When a transaction is subject to the enhanced disclosure requirements of SEC Rule 13e-3 (pertaining to going private transactions with an affiliate), the disclosure becomes even more extensive.

If the decision is to explore, a board should quickly turn to hiring financial advisors. Having experienced advisors will lead to a better outcome and will provide protection to the board (see chapter 6).

Boards often ask whether there should be separate advisors for independent board members. (A related question is whether there should be a special committee of independent directors.) My invariable advice is that there should be separate advisors (and/or a special committee) *only* when necessary to address a conflict of interest. In the M&A context, such a conflict will arise mostly when the management director is a bidder. (It can also arise if there is a dual-class common stock capital structure if the certificate of incorporation does not provide for equal treatment in a merger.) Having the separate counsel or establishing a committee creates a strong inference that there is a conflict to be addressed. I was once asked to represent the independent directors of a board exploring a possible sale. Because there was no conflict, I argued against being hired. I did not prevail, took on the assignment, and when the deal was announced, the LID was asked in his deposition, "What was the conflict that led you to hire separate counsel for the independent directors?" However, if the directors seek additional counsel because they feel that the company's regular counsel is not up to the task, the additional counsel should be designated as co-counsel and serve alongside the regular counsel.

There are times when a conflict does warrant the appointment of a special committee. On one such occasion, I recall a director being asked in the board meeting, after this advice was given, if he would be willing to chair such a committee. He was the CEO of a manufacturing company who had come up through the ranks in factory operations. He declined the invitation, saying, "I abhor spending that much time with lawyers and bankers." While I personally think spending time with lawyers (if not bankers) is lots of fun, he was correct in noting that members, and especially chairs, of a special committee have significant demands placed on their time.

The advisors should be selected with care but also in a manner that does not run the risk of triggering rumors about a possible transaction. For example, interviewing multiple investment banks means that one (or possibly two) bank is hired, and the rest that were interviewed are aware that the company may be "in play." The banks not hired may not be able to resist mentioning to other companies in the industry or private equity firms that this might be a good time to approach the company.

There is another consideration relevant to hiring the financial advisor. Based on a handful of cases beginning in 2015, it is critical to do due diligence on potential banker conflicts.[31] The issue is not "plain vanilla" conflicts (e.g., that the bank's commercial arm finances some of the possible bidders; that the standard "success fee" arrangement creates a strong incentive for the bank to issue a favorable fairness opinion). Rather, it is with conflicts that may cause the bank, or even the individual banker, to favor one bidder over another. If there is an undisclosed conflict or a disclosed conflict that is not handled well, it is the board that can be determined to have breached its duty of care— an ironic outcome, as the board can also be viewed as "victim." A conflict can also adversely affect the ability of directors to be protected in relying on the advice given to them by the bankers.

If the board is both satisfied with the expertise of the proposed financial advisor and believes that there are either no conflicts or that any conflicts are manageable, then the retention of the advisor is formalized with an engagement letter. The board can clearly delegate the negotiation of the engagement letter to management and counsel, but in the course of approving the terms thereof, the board should ask (or be advised of) at least the following:

- Does the board have the latitude to add another advisor if it wishes to? (This question is relevant because advisors' standard first drafts include the word "exclusive.")
- Has management reviewed fees paid in precedent transactions to determine that the financial terms are appropriate?
- Is the company committing to use the financial advisor in subsequent transactions? (Again, a common first-draft provision.)
- What is the duration of the "tail"? This is the provision that indicates that, if the transaction for which the advisor is engaged does not proceed, but there is a similar transaction within a specified time in the future, then the advisor is entitled to its fee even if not retained for that future transaction. A related question is whether the tail runs for a specified period after the engagement letter is (a) terminated by the company (which companies often forget to do) or (b) terminated automatically after a date specified in the letter (a good fail-safe against forgetfulness).

Another conflict that can be created during the process of exploring a transaction is on the part of the CEO. Especially when the potential bidders are financial sponsors (i.e., private equity firms), but even if the bidders are "strategics," there is always the possibility that a bidder will want to speak to the CEO about what his or her role might be post-transaction. This has the potential to create the impression that a CEO has a favorite bidder. Courts have worried that a CEO playing favorites can tilt the playing field in subtle ways, such as how management presentations are made or questions answered during due diligence. The antidote for this is to have a board direct management not to have any discussions about personal arrangements without permission from the board, which will not be granted until at least all material terms pertinent to the shareholders have been agreed to in principle. Because it can be hard to prove a negative (i.e., that there were no such discussions), some boards require that the CEO have no unchaperoned meetings with representatives of the bidders.[32] At a minimum, a failure to insulate the CEO in this way could require that he or she be recused from board deliberations.

Another decision for the board from the very outset of an exploration relates to projections. Projections are among the very first pieces of information to be supplied to potential bidders. Projections are the raw materials for a valuation analysis and support for a fairness opinion. They are relevant to price negotiations. Projections supplied to bidders and bankers will also be included in a merger proxy statement in one form or another.

A board should be satisfied that the company's current set of projections represents the best current thinking. Where that is not the case and an updated set is to be developed, the board should be provided with a bridge between the prior and the new set of projections and should understand the process by which the projections were developed. While the company will not be giving representations and warranties with respect to the projections, the temptation to "boost" the numbers should be resisted. Even in the absence of a contract claim, projections that are not prepared in good faith and with a reasonable basis can support a fraud claim.[33]

The company's projections are a critical input into an analysis of what the company is worth on a stand-alone basis. That analysis provides support for the fairness opinion that is delivered at the approval meeting (discussed later).

Projections, and resulting fairness opinions, can be tricky for a company in transition, either on a micro level or a macro level. The micro-level issue arose when I sold a company that was pursuing a promising but somewhat untested new technology that had the potential to double the company's revenue and profit growth. To address the uncertainties of the new business, the board instructed the financial advisor in preparing its fairness opinion to assume a 50 percent probability of achieving the projected results for the new business during the projection period. (An intuitively appealing alternative would have been to apply a deeper discount to the unadjusted new business projections in preparing the DCF for the overall enterprise. The financial advisor indicated that such an approach would be problematic, because the discount rate needed to be formally derived from the weighted average cost of capital, or WACC, for the company.) The macro-level issue arose in the context of selling a retailer that was contending with the uncertainties created by the disruptive influence of online sales. In that instance, the board sought advice from a leading strategy consulting firm about the prospects for the overall industry and applied those insights and board members' own perspectives in assessing the projections prepared by management.

There is another set of projections that, together with the company's projections, is relevant to price negotiations with strategic bidders—namely, the projected synergies resulting from the combination. There are two types—cost (often called "hard") and revenue (or "soft"). Cost synergies are often thought to be more reliably estimated and more likely to be attained. Indeed, there can be rules of thumb about what percentage of the target's selling, general and administrative (SG&A) costs can be eliminated. Revenue synergies need to be approached with caution. Those resulting from access to a better distribution network are fine. Those resulting from an anticipated decrease in competition or increase in market power that lead to the ability to raise prices will attract the attention of regulators. Whatever is written down and presented to a board or executive officers may need to be delivered to the antitrust authorities and can be subject to discovery in litigation.[34] Statements defining relevant markets should be carefully considered. The word "dominant" should never be used!

The board will obviously be focused heavily on the terms of the merger agreement—not just understanding the terms of the finally negotiated document before approving it, but giving guidance on the company's position on critical terms throughout the period of negotiations. "Deal protections" were mentioned earlier (and discussed in the endnote there).

Another set of terms that receives a great deal of focus pertains to "social issues." Those provisions address critical governance matters such as who will be CEO of the combined company and what the makeup of its board of directors will be. They can also cover the corporate name, where headquarters will be located, and so on. Social issues are very appropriately addressed in a merger agreement when the target company's shareholders are to receive stock in the combined company as all or part of the consideration being paid in the deal. Because the resolution of those issues can have an impact on the value of the stock to be held by the target company's shareholders, that fact provides legitimacy to the target company's demands for provisions that are also of great personal interest to its CEO and directors. When the target company's shareholders are being entirely cashed out, that legitimacy is absent; therefore, that kind of merger agreement is silent on social issues, with two exceptions. It is common, in both an all-cash deal and in a deal providing for some stock as all or part of the consideration, to have provisions relating to compensation, benefits, and sometimes retention bonuses for employees of the target company. The rationale for such provisions is that those people need to be engaged between signing and closing, or else there is a risk that they will leave and heighten the risk of nonconsummation. Another provision that is common to all deals requires continuing indemnification and obtaining D&O insurance "tail coverage" for the benefit of the target company D&Os. This is simply "market."

The negotiation of the makeup of the board of directors in a deal in which target shareholders receive stock can be a very sensitive matter, especially in a "merger of equals" (MOE)—an all-stock deal between two roughly equally valued companies. In an MOE, the combined company board will sometimes comprise an equal or nearly equal number of incumbent directors from each constituent company. The identities of the directors are sometimes agreed to at the time of the signing and, thus, spelled out in the merger agreement. Alternatively (and to keep not being selected from entering into the thinking of an individual director), it can be agreed that each company will designate its directors between signing and closing and will be disclosed for the first time in the proxy statement relating to the merger. When there is to be an equal number of directors, there may be an agreement to select one or two more directors with no past affiliation with either company—a "yours, mine, and ours" board. There may be further stipulation about the makeup of the critical committees and who will be the chairs. It may be agreed that the one company supplies the CEO and the other selects the board chair. On rare occasions, the agreement will provide for co-CEOs, which is generally a terrible idea. Co-CEOs work best, if at all, when the individuals have been colleagues for years.

A board that has negotiated for its CEO to be the CEO of the combined company may wish to consider how to make that decision stick, post-closing. At one point, lawyers went to great lengths to "hardwire" that decision. For example, when the combined company board is to be made up of a roughly equal number of directors from each side, there might be a provision requiring that a termination of the CEO be approved by a supermajority of the board, at least for some time. There was then a period where the parties became a bit more relaxed about this. Then came the Duke–Progress Energy deal, in which the agreed-on individual from Progress was made CEO (in keeping with the agreement) but was terminated by the board (which had a majority of its directors from the Duke side of the transaction) on the very same day as the consummation of the merger.[35] At least for now, attention is again being given to some form of hardwiring.

The operation of a board after closing an MOE can be challenging. I was once invited to a board meeting of a client company that resulted from an MOE. To my surprise, only half the board members were there—"legacy directors" from one of the companies in the merger. They were seeking legal advice about how to deal with the other half of the board and the CEO of the combined company (who had come from the "other side"). I had to tell them that, despite the fact that "their company" had been our client in the merger, because the combined company was now our client we had responsibilities toward the full board. As a result, I was not in a position to counsel them on the matter.

What a board typically goes through during the course of initiating, overseeing, and finally approving an M&A deal has become quite elaborate. Good examples can be found in merger proxy statements and tender-offer documents in the section titled "Background of the Transaction."

Among the most important items on an approval meeting agenda is the final presentation by the financial advisors—the delivery of the fairness opinion and supporting analysis. That analysis includes the "football field" summarizing various valuation methodologies. (There will be earlier versions of the football field presented to directors; it is important that the directors are shown a "bridge" between each version and the current one.) Appendix 4 to this book includes a primer on valuation methodologies. It is important to note that an opinion about "fair price" is not an opinion that the "best price," for *Revlon* purposes, has been achieved. Also, a fairness opinion is formulated with the same words whether the price is "just fair" or "exorbitant." The premium that a deal price represents to an unaffected trading price is essentially irrelevant to intrinsic value. Nevertheless, most boards, and even judges, will take notice of the premium and how a deal price relates to the fifty-two-week trading range. Clearly, the market notices and a great deal of thought goes into whether the press release refers to a one-day, thirty-day, and/or ninety-day volume-weighted average price (VWAP) for purposes of calculating the premium.

If the sale is to a financial sponsor in an LBO, there is another opinion that might be provided to the board. Under various theories (illegal dividend or fraudulent transfer), directors have been threatened with liability when they approved an LBO and the company entered into bankruptcy within a few years thereafter.[36] To protect the directors, they might be provided with a "solvency opinion" from a firm of outside experts, which is probative but not dispositive. The critical inputs to such an opinion are the company's financial projections, the anticipated post-LBO capital structure, and terms of the acquisition financing. A solvency opinion is different from a "fairness opinion." In fact, many fairness opinions expressly state that they are not commenting on solvency. At a minimum, the solvency opinion (if provided for) and the underlying analysis would be delivered to the board at the time it approved the deal. Because there is typically several months' lag between board approval and consummation of a public company deal, there can be a vigorous negotiation over whether the solvency opinion is to be "brought down" as a contractual condition to closing. Alternatives to a third-party solvency opinion are reliance on officers' certificates and/or reliance on a representation and warranty from the LBO buyer. Because the financing banks often do not hold onto the loans, there is less of a basis for relying on the fact that the lenders would do their own diligence and not want to see the company fail after the LBO.

Appendix 3 provides templates of agendas that I have used for the first and last meetings of a board that is considering a sale of the company. As indicated in proxy statement background sections, there will be many meetings in between. The agenda for the last meeting is designed to "put a bow on" the record of the directors' discharge of their duty of care.

One item in the approval meeting agenda warrants a bit of explanation. The review of "factors considered" serves two purposes. First, because there will be a section with that title in a merger proxy statement, actually reviewing with the board a summary of those factors is good evidence of the accuracy of the proxy statement disclosure. In addition, the summary brings "top of mind" for the directors all of the important considerations that will go into their vote. It is good for the record when directors suggest edits (especially additions) to the draft factors.

Most merger approvals garner a unanimous vote of the directors. It is highly unusual, but on occasion there will be a negative vote. (I once had a director vote against a deal with a 100 percent premium to the unaffected trading price—which was, by the way, also well above the fairness range.) In the old days, there would be peer pressure placed on the naysaying director, using an argument that the no vote would put all of the other directors at risk. In fact, it usually just put the director who voted no at risk for a long deposition. In current practice, if a director votes no, that fact and his or her reasons are simply noted in the proxy statement.

An Unsolicited Takeover Proposal

Not all M&A deals are initiated by the board of the target company, of course. So, as described in chapter 7, as a matter of routine, a CEO and board need to be prepared for the possibility of an unsolicited approach. Just because an approach is unsolicited doesn't make it hostile. Many "friendly" deals start that way. Similar to CEO succession, advance planning is one thing—actually dealing with an unsolicited approach is another.

The approach is most likely to come by way of a call to the CEO from the other company's CEO. At the time of the first approach, the target CEO should be thinking about these five things:

- Not all unsolicited proposals that are rejected go hostile.
- But if this one does, anything I say could be used against us; so, I should be largely in "listen-only mode."
- I cannot preempt my board on a matter of this magnitude (and relatedly, I should not offer a "personal view" one way or the other).
- I should decline an offer to put the proposal in writing.
- The best way to end the call is with something like "Thanks for your call . . . I will convey all of this to our board in due course. If there is any interest in pursuing your idea, we will get back to you" (note that this does not promise any call back or set the time for any response).

The approach might also be initiated in writing, or the call followed up by a letter. Any writing should be shared with the board in a manner that will keep it confidential.

The target company's board should be immediately advised of the call and/or letter. With the benefit of advisors, the board should early on consider a number of issues, including the following:

- Even though we did not initiate the approach, should we nevertheless explore a possible transaction? In this regard, it is important to note that there is no obligation to respond positively to an unsolicited approach, even if the other side says something like, "We are prepared to offer a substantial premium." If the decision is not to explore, the board's reasoning should be articulated and memorialized in an appropriate fashion. Reasons may include:

  - This is the wrong time for us (e.g., bottom of the cycle, working on something big) or the wrong time for other possible bidders who could set up a competition (e.g., they are working on other deals)
  - We don't think the caller can do a deal at a price we would find attractive financially and/or as a matter of antitrust clearances

- If we decide to explore a transaction, should we follow a single-bidder strategy or start a process? If the latter, who should we contact?
- If we turn the caller down, what is the likelihood the caller will go hostile? What is the caller's track record, and what language did the caller use around this (e.g., we *prefer* to do this on a friendly basis)?
- If the caller goes hostile, what is the chance we can remain independent? What is the status of our structural defenses, and are there active defenses available? Who owns our stock (e.g., could an activist have encouraged this approach)? Do we have the will and resources we would need to resist?
- Even if we think they will go hostile and we will not be successful in remaining independent, should we rebuff this first overture as a tactical matter to get the best price and other terms? As many believe, saying no is a form of negotiation. A variant on that is this: "The number you propose is not a legitimate starting point for a discussion."

When I advise boards that have just received an unsolicited takeover bid, I often start with a shorthand: "You can just say no, but you can't just say yes." This glib summary of *Unocal* (on the one hand) and *Revlon* (on the other hand), of course requires a good bit of elaboration, but it's a good start.

Of course, under *Newmont Mining*, if the bid is inadequate, the board has an obligation to resist. Inadequacy is sometimes memorialized in an "inadequacy opinion" by an investment bank. This is the flip side of a "fairness opinion" but obviously stronger than simply a statement from the bank that is it unable to issue a fairness opinion. I was on a panel that included a prominent Delaware Vice Chancellor shortly after the Air Products/Airgas case came down (see chapter 11). I mentioned that, on defense, I would sometimes advise a board not ask for an inadequacy opinion, because if the bid was raised, the opinion might have to be withdrawn, potentially undermining the basis for resistance (although the "not the right time" rationale may still apply). The Vice Chancellor was revealingly incredulous; he thought (errone-ously) that to get an inadequacy opinion from a bank, all that a board needed to do was ask.

I also tell boards that, when an unsolicited bid goes "hostile," it can live up to that label. Hostilities can start with the nearly simultaneous launching of a bid, a proxy contest, litigation, and a PR campaign—and all before lunch! And the launch can be timed to inflict maximum disruption. I have defended against bids begun on Christmas Eve and on the Friday after Thanksgiv-ing (a truly black Friday). For this reason, a board's will to resist is an important consideration.

Other Material Transactions

The robust approach followed by a board in discharging its duty of care when deciding on a sale of the company can be utilized in the consideration of other material transactions, such as a major acquisition or other major capital expenditures.

For example, in deciding on a major acquisition, among other things, the board should consider the following over the course of an appropriate number of meetings:

- the strategic case for the acquisition, and if it is not consistent with the strategic plan, whether it is nevertheless a compelling opportunity

- the alternative to this acquisition (e.g., other targets, build rather than buy)
- the financial case for the acquisition and source of funds
- the estimated synergies, their cost and time to achieve
- the fairness to the acquiring company of the price being paid
- the scope, quality and results of the due diligence review of the target
- the accounting treatment for the acquisition (including making sure that no "cookie-jar" reserves[37] are being contemplated)
- the impact of an announcement on the company's share price (e.g., will there be a risk of a multiple contraction?)
- the ability of the current management, either alone or with the management being "acquired," to integrate the businesses and run the larger combined company
- risks of nonconsummation
- whether an announcement will trigger a possible bid for the acquiring company by a competitor that believes that, if the acquisition is consummated, it would make the acquiring company difficult to take over due to antitrust concerns; if so, is the company ready for that eventuality?
- whether consummation of the deal will foreclose other opportunities because of financial, antitrust, or other considerations

---

Trying to understand the potential impact of an announcement on share price is worthwhile but challenging. It is significantly affected by strategic implications, financial terms, and quality of communications about the deal (both the formal announcement and the Q&A). Further, there can be a short-term reaction followed by a recovery. One of my favorite answers from an investment banker to the question, "What will happen to the share price?" was a joke from the banker: Albert Einstein checked into a hotel late at night and was told by the clerk that the only room available was one of the four bedrooms in a suite that had a large living room. Dr. Einstein took the room. When he went upstairs, he was greeted by the three other occupants of the suite who were enjoying a beer and conversation. He went to the first and asked, "What is your name and what is your IQ?" The first person gave his name and said, "My IQ is 160." Einstein said,

"Wonderful, we can discuss nuclear physics." The second person announced that his IQ was 120. Einstein replied, "Wonderful, we can discuss teaching physics to high school students." When the third replied that his IQ was 80, Einstein asked, "What's going to happen to the stock market?"

While the acquiring company's board should consider whether the price it is agreeing to pay is "fair" to their own company, this is not to suggest that the board should always obtain a fairness opinion. They should be made aware, however, if their financial advisor has concluded that it could not deliver such an opinion, if asked. This is especially important as a practical matter if the engagement letter that the company entered into with its financial advisor contemplated that it would issue an opinion, if asked. A board could, under the right circumstances, authorize paying more than the intrinsic value of the target company, or even intrinsic value plus the value of synergies. There could be strategic reasons for doing so. The important thing is that the acquiring company's board consider what fair value is, have a rational basis for any decision to pay a price in excess of fair value, and be able to articulate that rationale. The board should also be aware that paying far in excess of fair value and any communication to shareholders (or even notations in board minutes) explaining the board's reasons for doing so might arouse the suspicions of antitrust authorities.

One of the most interesting questions I ever received while advising a board about a major acquisition came from a very intelligent and highly analytical director. He first calculated the aggregate premium his company (our client) was going to be paying to the selling shareholders. He then asked for a calculation of the net present value of the anticipated synergies from the deal. When he observed that the two numbers were nearly identical, he asked, "Doesn't this mean that we are giving away all of the synergies created by the merger and that our shareholders are essentially getting nothing out of doing the deal, but taking all of the risk?" The answer started with an understanding that the aggregate market value of a company's outstanding shares before the deal is the product of the per-share stock price times the number of outstanding shares. That number is not the intrinsic value of the entire company—which includes the value of control—best understood from the DCF valuation. In responding to the director's question, we compared the DCF valuation of the target company to the price (including premium) being paid, and it led to a very different conclusion. That conclusion was that the acquiring company was capturing the entire net present value of the synergies for the benefit of its shareholders.

One director of a company that I represented in a transformative acquisition inquired about risk in a very comprehensive way. He asked, "What are the risks (and costs) of nonconsummation? What are the risks to the company of not doing this deal? What are the risks that we are bearing by doing the deal?" As to the last point, a very self-confident CEO of another client company tasked a "challenge team" to present to his board all of the reasons for not doing an acquisition. Similarly, some advocate engaging in a "pre-mortem"—a hypothetical exercise designed to assess the most likely cause of failure and how that outcome might be mitigated.[38]

When considering a major capital expenditure, the board should be given a thorough briefing. For example, if the proposal is to build a new plant to expand production capacity for a key product, the board might consider the following:

- What is the estimated cost (including contingencies) and how confident is management in the accuracy of that estimate?
- How will the cost be financed? If existing cash balances are to be used, will that limit our flexibility to pursue other opportunities? If borrowings are to be made, will additional leverage create financial risk in a down cycle and/or have an impact on our credit rating?
- What is the future need and pricing potential for the product? What do our marketing surveys tell us? That is, are competitive products now or

in the future threatening to take market share because the company is losing patent protection or because of other innovations?

- If the new plant is to use new technology, has that been tested?
- When making siting decisions, will there be a sufficient number of skilled personnel available, and what are the logistical issues (if any) associated with the new location in terms of access to raw materials and the cost of distributing the finished product? Has the company taken full advantage of tax incentives? If the plant is outside the United States, what is the political and FCPA risk? Does management have the bandwidth to oversee a major operation from afar?
- Is there an alternative to adding our own production capacity? If so, would there be risks in contracting that out?

In the 1980s, I was hired as outside counsel to the independent directors of a company that had made a major bet on a new cement plant. The flaw in the planning was that the manufacturing method selected for the new plant did not work with the limestone in the area. The company had three theoretical bad choices—change the manufacturing design and machinery, import limestone, or further process the local limestone before it was used in the plant. The third alternative was the least expensive and was the one ultimately selected. The plant had been named for a late chairman and CEO. The plant's issues began to weigh heavily on the company's finances, and frequent headlines in the local business section read something like "[Name of former CEO] Plant Drags Down [Company Name]." Before long, the family of the departed CEO asked the company to change the name of the plant.

Attack by a Financial Activist

This a *very* special situation and is covered in chapter 10.

9

A Digression on Private Companies, Not-for-Profits, and Congress

Boards of private companies and of not-for-profits have a number of similarities to those of public companies. The boards of all three types of entities play similar roles, should be assembled using the same kinds of considerations (including utilizing a skills matrix), should be focused on complying with applicable standards of conduct, should address many of the same issues on a routine basis (including self-evaluation), and should be prepared to step up in the case of some of the special situations identified in chapter 8.

In some ways, Congress is the analog of a board of directors. We can dream about how our federal government, and thus all of our citizens, might benefit by having some directorlike responsibilities applied to the members of Congress.

Private Companies

In terms of private companies in the corporate form, the fiduciary concepts discussed earlier in this Part II are equally applicable to their directors. (Private companies that are limited liability companies (LLCs), limited liability partnerships (LLPs), or other alternative forms have more latitude to address responsibilities and accountability by way of contract.)

A private company may still be in the hands of a single shareholder-founder and CEO. In that instance, the board is really an advisory group, and there is very little in the way of potential exposure for the directors. To the extent that such a company has been passed down to the next generation of the founder's family, there may still be little exposure. Having said that, there may be family members who are inside the company and others who are not. There may also be shareholders who are trustees who must look out for the interests of other family members. Especially when the company is operated by family members who are several generations removed from the founder, this creates the potential for personal conflict and resentment that can be manifested in fiduciary duty claims. There are some celebrated instances of this having come to pass.[1]

A private company may be the brainchild of an entrepreneur who has gotten the backing of venture capital funds. The board may comprise the founder and individuals affiliated with each of the funding sources. Some of the funding sources may ask for "visitation rights" in addition to, or in lieu of, board seats. (Again, be careful about having counsel review privileged matters in front of "visitors.") The challenge for the directors is to understand that they have duties to all of the shareholders, and not just to the shareholder that literally brought them to the table.

Those directors have a further issue under the corporate opportunity doctrine. Under that doctrine, when there is a transaction brought to the attention of a director, the duty of loyalty requires that he or she present that opportunity to the company and give it the option to pursue the opportunity. This can be a challenge for the venture capital director whose fund may have other portfolio companies in an adjacent industrial sector or whose fund might simply be interested in taking the opportunity for itself. The Delaware statute has a solution—the certificate of incorporation can negate any fiduciary duty of this type.[2]

The conduct of private company board meetings often has attributes of a staff meeting, where the discussion can truly get into the weeds and people can talk over one another. After the company has gone public, if the entrepreneurial founder is still the CEO or is on the board, that attribute can continue into the operations of the public company board. A challenge for a CEO who succeeds the founder is to help the board break that habit. One such successor who I observed literally had to impose a rule in board meetings he called the "talking stick." Analogous to the conch shell in *Lord of the Flies*, only the person holding the CEO's pen was supposed to be speaking.

As noted in chapter 1, there are some who believe that the current state of affairs in the New Era in Corporate Governance has contributed to the decline in the number of public companies. In 2018, the number of public companies was only about half of what it was some twenty years earlier.[3] Ironically, the Wilshire 5000 Total Market Index contained only 3,492 companies at the end of 2017. While the decline can be attributed to a variety of factors (including a robust M&A market), one explanation is that, because public companies have regulatory demands and shareholder pressures for short-term results, emerging growth companies are choosing to forgo IPOs. Some commentators are concerned that this means that the opportunity to invest in companies with great growth prospects is now out of reach for the typical retail investor. SIFMA (the Securities Industry and Financial Markets Association) and others are so concerned about this trend that they issued a 2018 report with recommendations for "helping more companies go and stay public."[4]

When a founder is, nevertheless, convinced to go public, there is a school of thought that—especially in the tech world—"idolatry of founder-CEOs" can lead to mistakes in structuring governance arrangements. For example, to induce the founder to agree to an IPO, the company may implement a "high vote, low vote" capital structure of the type described in chapter 5. This, in turn, gives the founder absolute power over selecting board members and reduces the likelihood of meaningful oversight.[5] It may be that the founder is perfectly able to lead the company during the early period of being public, but not all founder-CEOs are able to give up the reins of power even when the company has grown to a size or complexity that exceeds their ability to lead or manage.

Finally, as perhaps exemplified by Elon Musk's performance at Tesla, not all entrepreneurs have the right temperament to be a public company CEO. And this can present problems for the boards of their companies. Shortly after the resolution of the SEC case arising out of Musk's infamous "going private" tweet, the board of Tesla was served with a shareholder derivative case alleging that "despite being put on notice of E. Musk's propensity for erratic public communications . . . the board consciously disregarded his actions and failed to do anything . . . put[ting] their loyalties to E. Musk ahead of their fiduciary duties to the company and its shareholders."[6] The disloyalty characterization was, of course, designed to get around the protection afforded by the exculpatory charter provision. Short of removing Musk from the company—likely unattainable given his ownership position and perhaps even unwise—one wonders what the board could have actually done.

One of my heroes in business is Michael Krasny, the founder of CDW, the largest computer reseller in the United States. Michael was a used-car salesman who was intrigued by how easy it was to sell his used laptop by placing a classified ad. He turned that intrigue into a private company that then went public. When the company reached annual sales of $4 billion, he concluded that it was time to bring in a "professional manager" to be CEO. While it was sometimes hard to fully hand over leadership to his successor (and as the largest shareholder, there was significant legitimacy to his making his voice heard), Michael did the right thing and the company continued to prosper. CDW was sold to private equity in the 2007 surge of LBOs and was taken public again in 2013.

Not-for-Profits

Not-for-profit board members have very little exposure to financial liability. A typical statute for not-for-profit corporations provides significant protection for other than "willful or wanton conduct" for directors who serve without compensation.[7] (In truth, given the philanthropic expectations of not-for-profit directors, most such directors work for negative compensation.) Those statutes often provide as well that the state attorney general has standing to bring suit, although that authority is used more for addressing fund-raising abuses than for imposing accountability on board members.[8]

Nevertheless, the boards of large, prominent not-for-profits often operate in ways that make them difficult to distinguish from the operations of public companies. This is for three reasons: many of the directors are also involved in public companies and see no reason to operate differently; there can be significant reputational exposure to board members in the event of a financial failure or misstep of a not-for-profit enterprise,[9] and a not-for-profit that is poorly managed (e.g., with too-high nonprogrammatic expenditures) will have great difficulty raising funds.

One big difference between public company boards and boards of not-for-profits is size and activity level. Largely because of fund-raising imperatives, a typical not-for-profit board can be extremely large. It might meet only a few times a year. A university or hospital board might have fifty members and meet only three or four times a year. Even when such a board does a good bit of its work in committees, a very large board that meets infrequently leads to the risk of "social loafing" (described in chapter 5) and not providing meaningful oversight to management. The ultimate example of social loafing may be the individual who accepts the title and responsibility of director or trustee but feels that his or her commitment is fully discharged by writing large checks.

There are a number of structural solutions to this problem. First, there can be an executive committee that comprises a smaller group that meets monthly and effectively operates as the "real" board. Or, a large number of the directors or trustees can be spun off into the board of a foundation or an advisory group, where their clear, and limited, mission is philanthropy. Finally, there can be ways to honor and show respect to life trustees in ways other than inviting them to the business meetings of a board. One should not underestimate the difficulty of effecting the latter two structural solutions.

Even when a not-for-profit is thriving, its board can have reputational damage if it is not disciplined about executive compensation and perquisites. The experience of the NYSE (before it became a public company in 2006 with its merger with ArcaEx) tells a cautionary tale. Richard Grasso was the CEO and by all accounts did a terrific job leading the Exchange. The compensation committee of the board of the NYSE rewarded Grasso handsomely, including a $140 million lumpsum payment. At the time he was CEO, the NYSE was a mutual company owned by its member brokers, and for purposes of New York law was a not-for-profit. That status gave the New York attorney general standing, and he sued, challenging the payout as excessive. While the suit was ultimately dropped,[10] following a court's decision that it could not continue after the NYSE was no longer a not-for-profit, the members of the compensation committee faced considerable criticism over a number of years. Another consequence of excessive compensation at a not-for-profit can be adverse tax consequences under the Internal Revenue Code.[11] In the 1990s, the United Way of America had to contend with fallout from revelations that its CEO had lived a lavish lifestyle based on perks from the charity.

One can speculate about how these kinds of things happen—board members tend to be successful businesspeople who think of the CEO as a peer and forget that he or she has selected a public service occupation. There is also inattentiveness or, worse, a belief that "no one will ever know." This last item is simply incorrect. Not-for-profits must file financial information on IRS Form 990, and that information is made public.[12]

Even beyond executive compensation and Form 990, the IRS has expressed views about not-for-profit corporate governance.[13]

Not-for-profits are not immune from the kind of behavior that has embarrassed public companies and their boards. In 2018, one of the largest not-for-profits, the Silicon Valley Community Foundation, with $13.5 billion in assets, parted ways with its top fund-raiser amid complaints about bullying and even worse. Further, there were allegations that the CEO had ignored complaints, because the fund-raiser was so effective at her job. As a result, the CEO was put on leave.[14] Sexual misconduct at Penn State and Michigan State has been even more infamous and problematic for their boards. A not-for-profit board should be as attuned to organizational culture and compliance as its for-profit counterparts.

Congress

It is an imperfect analogy, but think about our federal government as a corporation: The president is the CEO, with the executive branch as the rest of the management team; the Congress is the board; citizens, or at least those who are eligible to vote, are the shareholders. All the shareholders are "retail" investors, other than those who fund election campaigns and political action committees and have influence more like the institutional shareholders. With the trend toward the increasing power of the executive branch, our political governance is going in the opposite direction of board-centricity manifest in corporate governance.[15] Depending on one's view of the individual occupying the White House, this may or may not be a problem. Even a weakened Congress, however, should exercise oversight, and its individual members should discharge their role responsibly. The leadership of the House and the Senate should facilitate all of that.

Imagine, if you will, that members of Congress were held to even just one of the fundamental standards of conduct applicable to public company directors. It is too much to hope for to require behavior consistent with the duty of loyalty (which among other things requires that "entrenchment"—in this case, reelection—not be a primary motivation) or that any politicians actually comport themselves with candor. Nevertheless, it seems fair to ask for behavior consistent with the duty of care.

The duty of care would require that members not act on a piece of legislation until they receive and understand the analysis from the Government Accountability Office and otherwise hear from reliable experts. The same duty would require that members read at least a fair summary of legislation before voting. It would require members of one party to supply all pertinent information about a bill (including a copy) to members of the other party a reasonable period of time before bringing the matter to a vote. There is no doubt that both political parties have violated these well-established procedures from the corporate world.

PART III

Activism and the Threat of Shareholder-Centricity

Another outcome of the factors described in Part I is the growth of shareholder activism. It is critical that managements and boards have a good understanding about what activism is about, how to prepare for it, and when and how to resist. While the movement from management-centricity to director-centricity has been a generally positive development and there are some benefits from shareholder activism, a push toward shareholder-centricity is troubling for a variety of reasons.

10

Activists and Their Goals and Tools

While most boards think of hedge funds when they hear the word "activist," it is important to understand that there are several interrelated categories. They all have specific goals and use different tools to achieve those goals.

A Taxonomy of Activism

Activists tend to fall into three categories: governance, CSR, and financial.

Governance activists seek changes in a company's governance structure in ways that they believe will make boards more accountable. So, for example, governance activists have been the initiating force behind the trends to eliminate staggered boards, to allow shareholders to call special meetings of shareholders, for separation of board chair and CEO, and for majority voting and proxy access. They have enjoyed considerable success in these endeavors. Among the most prominent governance activists are union and public employee pension funds and related parties (e.g., CalPERS, AFSCME, New York City controller). Index funds are significant governance activists. Despite, or perhaps because of, the fact that they follow a passive investment strategy, they can be at the forefront of governance activism. As the CEO of Vanguard stated in his 2015 letter to CEOs of investees: "Some have mistakenly assumed that our predominantly passive management style suggests a passive attitude with respect to corporate governance. Nothing could be further from the truth."

CSR activists are interested in, among other things, workers' rights, as well as environmental and sustainability issues. Perhaps surprisingly, some hedge funds are calling for CSR.[1]

For some issues, it is difficult to determine whether the goal is related to governance or CSR. Indeed, this gives rise to a different label—ESG, which stands for "environmental, social, and governance." A good example of such an issue is corporate political activity, where activists are interested in both board oversight and public disclosure.[2]

A principal tool for both governance and CSR activists is the SEC's shareholder proposal process under Rule 14a-8. That rule allows any shareholder who "has continuously held at least $2000 in market value, or 1 percent, of the company's securities entitled to vote . . . for at least one year" to submit one proposal for any shareholders' meeting. The deadline for submission is typically 120 days before the anniversary of the date of the proxy statement for the previous annual meeting. The proposal is a "recommendation or requirement that the company and/ or its board of directors take action." If properly submitted (and not permitted to be excluded by the rule or withdrawn following negotiation), both the proposal and a supporting statement must be included in the company's proxy statement and an opportunity to vote on the proposal must be included on the company's proxy card.[3] A company can include a statement in rebuttal in the proxy statement.

The SEC allows companies to exclude a shareholder proposal on a number of bases, including its being improper under state law, a personal grievance, "a matter relating to the company's ordinary business operations," or conflict with a company's own proposal. Over the years, the trend has been for the SEC to become more reluctant to allow exclusions. In one remarkable instance, the SEC first agreed with a company that an item could be excluded, and then reversed course some months later.[4] While most shareholder proposals are "precatory" (i.e., advisory only), they are made less so as a result of the combination of ISS's "responsiveness" guidelines,[5] and also the related potential for a withhold vote the following year coupled with the operation of majority voting. The combination of these two factors leads some companies to seek to negotiate a withdrawal of proposals.

Financial activists (typically hedge funds) are the third category. Financial activists "punch above their weight." Compare the assets under management of BlackRock, $6.8 trillion at the end of 2017, to the "mere" $35 billion (at the same time) of assets under management of the largest activist hedge fund, Elliot Management, or the $10 billion held by Pershing Square. The influence of a hedge fund over a company can be a function of its ability to concentrate its holdings. For example, in mid-2017 BlackRock owned 5.8 percent of Mondelez, but Pershing Square owned 6.5 percent. It can also result from reputation. What CEO and board don't shudder on receiving the call from one of the SharkWatch 50 announcing that its fund owns 3 percent of the company and may soon be filing a 13D?

Within the financial activist category there are three basic orientations:

- Transactional—those who seek to force (or block or increase the price in) a sale of the company, or those who advocate a spinoff.
- Balance sheet—those who wish to influence the capital structure of the company and most typically seek to cause the company to lever up and buy back shares to create a "more efficient" balance sheet. (Some institutional shareholders have expressed concerns that managements are too quick to recommend that a board accede to calls for significant share repurchases; they note that a predicted increase in earnings per share favorably affects those bonuses based on a formula that includes EPS.)
- Operational—those who believe that the company is being mismanaged and who often call for a change at the top or greater oversight by the board. This group tends to specialize in particular industry sectors.

Regardless of orientation, financial activists all have the same goal—making money for their fund. Virtually all have a short-term investment horizon, although some of the operationally oriented financial activists claim a longer-term horizon and can back that up with evidence of their holding periods. A second goal is to gain the notoriety that will allow them to raise money for their next fund and make money for the fund managers. There is a traditional "2 and 20" compensation structure for hedge funds: fund managers receive an annual fee of 2 percent of assets under management and an additional 20 percent of the appreciation of the portfolio investments. As a result, the fund-raising boost from a successful activist campaign is critically important, especially for newer, smaller hedge funds, which are often the progeny of more established funds.[6]

In addition to utilizing the three basic orientations described here, a financial activist might seek to make money by evoking the historical origin of hedge funds—taking a "short" position in a company's stock and then publishing information that will cause the stock to decline. This approach, sometimes called a "bear raid," is not typically associated with the leading financially oriented activists. Pershing Square's attack on Herbalife stands out as an exception. The attack began in 2012 with a 342-slide presentation by Bill Ackman claiming that Herbalife was a "pyramid scheme." In that situation, which played out for five years, Pershing Square was countered by Carl Icahn's "long" position. Corporate America couldn't decide whom to root for. Although Herbalife ultimately agreed to a settlement with the Federal Trade Commission that involved a $200 million fine and an agreement to restructure its business, the winner from an investment point of view was Icahn. It has been reported that Pershing Square closed out its position "deep in the red" and that Icahn gained about $1 billion on his investment in Herbalife.[7]

In the 1980s, I worked with a client that thought it was the target of a bear raid, as the client felt that inaccurate, negative information about the company was being disseminated anonymously by a group of "shorts" to drive the price of its stock down. We did some sleuthing and put together a binder of information that I hand-delivered to the head of enforcement at the SEC. His reaction was memorably dismissive: "We don't typically pursue these matters, because we have so often found that the 'shorts' are correct."

Governance and financial activists play off of each other. The successes of governance activists have made companies more vulnerable to attacks by financial activists. For example, a company that no longer has a staggered board has directors who can be removed without cause, and if some small percentage of shares can call a special meeting, directors are more vulnerable. Traditional institutional investors who are usually thought of in terms of governance activism are rumored to encourage financial activists to attack a company. (This is the so-called RFA, for "request for activism.") Operationally oriented financial activists have been heard to assert that they are closer to fund portfolio managers who share their interest in a particular sector than are the senior executives of the companies in that sector.

Being Approached by a Financial Activist

A financial activist will typically have two distinct phases in its approach to a company—private and then public. Hopefully, the company has done a good job of advance preparation (see chapter 7).

During the private phase, the activist will contact the company, state something to the effect that it is the holder of less than 5 percent of the stock, believe the company is undervalued, and want to share some ideas with management and the board. Unlike a call from a potential hostile bidder for the whole company, this request for a visit with management can be hard to decline; the activist is, after all, a shareholder. And the ideas the activist wishes to share may have merit. A CEO who is asked to allow the activist to make a presentation to the board can, however, defer an answer, stating that it will be up to the board.

In preparation for such a visit, the management should do the following: inform the board (or the chair or LID); do some research into the activist and its modus operandi (e.g., call up the sharkrepellent. net report on the activist); get a refresher on Regulation FD; check the shareholder list for any evidence of a wolf pack of activists (discussed at some length in the endnotes).[8] The members of the defense team should also be rallied. The sharing of ideas by the activist may be in writing or orally. The ideas often include adding individuals to the board. Whatever the format in which the ideas are shared, the activist's interest and perspective should be reported to the board.

The activist may wish to keep its interest private as a means of pressuring management and the board. It knows that the threat of going public provides it with leverage for a possible early settlement with the company. The activist will have no choice, however, and will need to go public by way of an SEC filing on Schedule 13D within ten days following the date on which its ownership of the company's stock exceeds 5 percent. The filing will provide detail about its ownership but will also include a disclosure under Item 4 about its plans and proposals with respect to the company. After the initial filing, the activist will need to amend its filing promptly (within one day) with each 1 percent increase in its ownership and following any change in its declared plans or proposals.

Aside from the 5 percent threshold for filing a 13D, an activist will be thinking about other percentages in deciding how much of a target company to buy. It may not want to exceed 9.9 percent, because going to 10 percent would subject it to the short-swing profit recapture under Section 16(b) of the 1934 Act. It might also consider 10 percent as a stopping point under the "solely for investment" exemption under HSR. (It will, however, be concerned about the views of the antitrust regulators to the effect that seeking to influence management creates a disqualification from using that exemption.[9]) An activist might consider the 15 percent limit under the Delaware anti-takeover statute (or similar limits applicable to non-Delaware corporations), but most activists are not considering the types of actions that make that statute a cause for concern. Finally, there may be a relevant threshold if the company adopts a poison pill. A summary of key percentage is included in appendix 5.

One of the biggest regulatory gaps when it comes to activism is this ten-day gap before the initial filing of a 13D is required. In the information age, the presence of the gap clearly has no practical justification. Moreover, in another context, the SEC has stated, "Investors are entitled to current and accurate information about the plans of large shareholders."[10] I moderated a panel including the cofounder of a major activist hedge fund and asked him what the regulatory rationale could possibly be for the ten-day gap. His response was to the effect that the ten-day gap allows for activists to make more money (because they can buy more stock before the market knows they are involved);

thus, he said, if you think that activists play an important macroeconomic role, then the ten-day gap (and the activists' path
to riches) should not be closed. Paul Singer of Elliott made a
similar point in a presentation at the June 7, 2018, Corporate
Governance Conference sponsored by The Deal.

When an activist goes public, the center of attention is on the threat
or actuality of a proxy contest in which the activist puts forth its campaign platform and its candidates. This second phase will often feel like
an attack. The activist's platform is initially put forth in a white paper and
embellished in a series of "fight letters" issued during an actual contest.
In addition to business and financial issues, the activist will comment
on governance "flaws" to appeal to some of the institutional holders.

It can be a source of frustration for a board if an activist comes
out publicly advocating corporate actions that the board is already actively considering on its own. I advised a company
whose board was already actively considering separating out its
businesses through sale and spinoff when Pershing Square came
forward with essentially that proposal. The effect of the attention
from Pershing Square was to modestly accelerate the board's
decision making. The dilemma was what to say about Pershing
Square in the press release. The CEO's quote in the announcement included this: "Our Board considered the interests of all
of our shareholders, including the views of our long-term shareholders and our largest current shareholder, Pershing Square."
Not all companies can advance the time of such an announcement so easily and can be faced with a difficult judgment call.
Should it inform the activist about what it is considering (under
a short-term nondisclosure agreement) or make a premature announcement about a possible transaction (and put the success
of the transaction in peril) to defend against a proxy contest?

While, in theory, an activist might avail itself of proxy access to put forward its candidates, this has not been the case so far. (Most activists may not meet the holding period requirements and, in any event, will want to strike a more aggressive posture.) In a proxy contest, the activist's candidates are nominated in accordance with the requirements of the company's bylaws, which set forth the requirements for timing and for information about the candidates. The candidates will sometimes be affiliated with the fund. Hedge funds will often seek board seats for their own people, despite the potential loss of liquidity associated with taking a board seat (because of frequent closing of trading windows when there is material nonpublic information). Unlike an open-end mutual fund, hedge funds do not need to be constantly prepared for redemptions by their investors.

Alternatively, an activist's candidates may be "professional directors" who are friends of the fund. There now seems to be less reluctance for "establishment" directors to agree to serve on an activist's slate. Things can get very interesting when the candidates include a disgruntled former CEO of the company.[11] That person may be highly regarded by some of the long-term shareholders and a real asset to the activist. For this reason, CEO severance agreements often include a "standstill" provision.

Typically, an activist will nominate only a "short slate," that is, seek less than a majority of the board. (There have been a few notable exceptions of an activist seeking to replace an entire board.[12]) There are two reasons for this. First, it is too easy for a company to defend against turning over the entire board with the argument, "Don't give away control without getting a control premium." The second reason has to do with ISS policy. ISS has stated that when an activist seeks a minority of the board, it simply has to make a case that some change would be beneficial. Conversely, when the activist is seeking the entire board, ISS states that the activist must come forward with an entire business plan and prove that it is superior.[13] By definition, if the board is still staggered, the activist will be seeking to replace a minority of the board.

When coming up with a short slate, the mechanics of proxy voting will usually lead the activist to target specific directors for replacement with its candidates. (Targeting is, in some ways, a natural result of the current practice of competing proxy cards, but it may continue even if "universal proxies" are adopted.[14]) Among the most targeted incumbent directors are those with very long tenures. Those directors can be argued to have lost their independence and also to be most responsible for the issues that the activist identifies in its substantive platform. The activist needs to think carefully about whether it wishes to seek to replace diverse members of the board. It is hard to predict whether the targeted directors will be hawks ("let's fight") or doves ("let's settle"). A targeted director will sometimes ask, "Even if I am voted off by the shareholders, can't the board simply vote to expand the board and put me back on?" The best answer is, "We shouldn't do that." Other than possibly in the case of reinstating the CEO, this would be a perilous move.

Both sides in a proxy contest plead their case directly to the shareholders (by way of fight letters and a road show of one-on-one visits with major institutions) and indirectly through the proxy advisory firms. In the case of ISS, this is done by an in-person visit about four weeks before the shareholders meeting. Who goes to the meeting at ISS is a critical decision. There is an obvious benefit to taking any targeted director and the LID, but only if he or she will take the time to prepare and will otherwise leave the right impression.

Very little attention is given to "retail" investors, because they own so little of most companies. So, the full-page ads with fight-letter messages in the *Wall Street Journal* are, for the most part, a thing of the past. The exceptions that prove the rule are Trian's fights with DuPont in 2016 and with Procter & Gamble in 2017.

In defending against a proxy contest, a company needs to be cognizant of three legal considerations with respect to timing. It is sometimes desirable to set a date for an annual meeting that is later than usual—to allow more time to tell the company's story, or to pursue a transaction that would not be ripe for disclosure by the time proxies would normally be solicited. If the date to be set is more than thirteen months after the annual meeting in the prior year, under Delaware law any shareholder can go to court and, in a summary and expedited proceeding, force the holding of the meeting.[15] Moreover, if the date is deferred significantly, it may require a reopening of the nomination window under the company's advance notice bylaws and the Rule 14a-8 window for shareholder proposals. Finally, if the meeting date is set, it can be problematic to postpone the meeting. A postponement can be attacked as an interference with the shareholder franchise that must meet the compelling-justification standard under the *Blasius* case (discussed in chapter 6).

A threatened or actual proxy contest can be settled at any time, even just before the time of the vote (or more likely just after the receipt of the ISS recommendation preceding the vote). The most relevant consideration in terms of timing of settlement is whether the company is prepared to absorb the expense and disruption associated with a proxy contest. Also, a later settlement may come at a higher price, if *later* connotes vulnerability to losing.

The board should consider a number of factors in deciding whether to settle:

- Company vulnerability (e.g., stock price, operating performance, possible governance issues).
- Quality and vulnerability of targeted directors—a settlement will sometimes allow them to remain on the board despite vulnerability if they are valuable as directors.
- Quality of the activist candidates (sometimes based on opposition research by a private investigator)—it is generally a bad idea to use ad hominem arguments even though an activist will engage in personal attacks on incumbents.
- Feedback from shareholders, although they will often be saying supportive things to both sides.
- The risk of a follow-on activist attack—remember that a settlement with one activist does not foreclose (and might even encourage) another, but a settlement with a substantial activist can *sometimes* help defeat a second activist.[16]
- The terms of the settlement: how many seats (and will the number of new directors and the context of their election trip the definition of "change in control" under various HR provisions), who the new directors are, scope and duration of a "standstill," whether the activist is seek-

ing reimbursement of expenses, whether the activist is seeking seats on the compensation committee to maximize control over management, and what the confidentiality obligations are.

Finally, before settling, a board should understand that new directors who are affiliated with the activist fund will often have something of an outsized influence in the boardroom. This goes beyond simply an aggressive personality. Unlike most directors, they carry the imprimatur of representing a large shareholder. Moreover, they will have analysts at the fund who will help them prepare extremely well for the board meetings.

This last point about directors who are affiliated with the fund warrants a bit of expansion. I have witnessed a continuum of personality types among activists. Some like to call themselves "constructivists" or even "reluctivists." The like to say, "We are here to help," and some actually mean it and can make a positive contribution in the boardroom. They do not need coaching on boardroom etiquette. Others can change the whole dynamic in the boardroom by cursing, bullying, and threatening; they are clearly there to serve only one shareholder.

There are multiple sources of statistics, and the sources appear to apply different criteria or categories. That said, the following seems to be a fair summary from recent years:

- Each year, there are between two hundred and three hundred "campaigns," about half of which result in actual or threatened proxy fights.
- The vast majority of proxy fights are seeking board seats, and the vast majority of those are for a short slate. Other proxy fights relate principally to a merger or other management proposals. When an activist opposes a merger and is seeking better financial terms, that is called "bumpitrage."
- A majority of proxy fights are settled before a vote; only 30 percent to 40 percent of proxy fights go all the way to a vote.

Such outcomes of this include the following:

- Over half the time, activists seeking board seats achieve at least one board seat.
- Most of the seats result from a negotiated settlement rather than a vote. In a settlement, negotiations cover, among other things, the number and identity of the activist's candidates.
- Between 20 percent and 30 percent of activists' seats are won as a result of a vote. Boards achieve a complete victory a little more than half the time that a contest goes all the way to a vote.
- Importantly, employees of the activist fund become board members only about 30 percent of the time.
- Results are highly contextual and idiosyncratic.

When a candidate put forward by an activist is elected (as a result of a settlement or otherwise), it is critical to treat that director like any other director. There is no varsity and junior varsity on the board. It would be hypocritical to expect the new director to act like all the other directors if he or she is not treated like all the others. And the new director will have the robust information rights of any director.

When a shareholder misses the "window" for nominations under advance notice bylaws (described in chapter 7), it has two alternatives. First, if it can credibly allege that there have been material changes since the date the window closed, it can bring suit to reopen the window, citing the Delaware Chancery Court decision in *Amylin*.[17] Alternatively, it can mount a withhold or vote-against campaign to urge shareholders (directly and through appeals to ISS and the other proxy advisors) to reject one or more directors who are up for election at the meeting. A successful campaign, when coupled with a majority voting provision and ISS standards for responsiveness, can put significant pressure on a board.[18]

11

The Case against Shareholder-Centricity

In the New Era in Corporate Governance, financially oriented activism has replaced hostile takeovers as the principal vehicle for holding CEOs and boards accountable. Put another way, in recent years CEOs and boards seem much more concerned with activism than with hostile takeovers. Why is that?

To begin with, in the past decade attacks by activists have been much more common than unsolicited takeover bids that actually go fully hostile.[1] Even though hostile bids have become more socially acceptable in the corporate world, they may be in decline because they are easier to defend against than a proxy contest. If a bidder is seeking to take control through a tender offer at an inadequate price or at an opportunistic time, the board will be able to resist by implementing a poison-pill defense (see note 8 to chapter 4) that a court will likely allow to remain in place even if a majority of the outstanding shares have been tendered. The Airgas saga is instructive in this regard, where the efficacy of the pill was enhanced by the fact that the target company had a staggered board. In 2009, Air Products launched a hostile bid for Airgas for $5.9 billion, coupled with a proxy contest. Airgas put in a poison pill to forestall the bid. The Delaware courts declined to force the board to redeem the pill, despite the fact that a majority of the outstanding shares were tendered into the offer. Critical evidence in defense of the pill was an "inadequacy opinion" and the fact that the directors elected as Air Products candidates were "turned" and joined in rejecting its bid. Moreover, arbitrageurs indicated that they did not care about whether the price was fair; they wanted only a price that was higher than their basis in the stock.[2] Airgas remained independent and, in 2015, was sold to Air Liquide for $10.3 billion, proving the legitimacy of the 2009 defense.

In addition, hostile takeovers may be less concerning because, if a hostile bidder has success (or if the outcome is a sale to a "white knight"), the CEO will receive significant benefits under golden-parachute severance provisions and also receive the value of the premium on stock owned directly and on equity-based compensation that accelerates upon the change in control. In contrast, the provisions that convey those benefits in a change in control do not always apply in the event of a loss or settlement of a proxy contest, which can be the beginning the end of a CEO's tenure.

Of course, there can be some benefits from financially oriented activism. Walter Frick, in "The Case for Activist Investors" asserts that "they're helping to drive strategy" and cites research that "shows that activists apparently make companies more profitable and productive, on average—not just in the next quarter but three years after the fact."[3] There may be additional benefits, as well. The mere threat of activism should lead to the advance planning described in chapter 10. Advance planning can result in a closer relationship with major shareholders and consideration of actions identified in a mock attack that will benefit the company and its shareholders. And, there are some activists (the "constructivists") who make good board members. Whether activists are "capitalism's unlikely heroes," as an issue of the *Economist* suggests, is clearly open to debate, however.[4]

A superficially balanced perspective was put forth by Jeff Gramm in his book *Dear Chairman*, which included case studies of eight activist campaigns stretching from 1927 to 2005. Gramm states: "Shareholder activism can be put to good use and bad. It challenges inefficient corporations that waste valuable assets, but it can also foster destructive and destabilizing short-term strategic decisions." He reveals his bias (Gramm is a hedge-fund manager), however, with the very next sentence: "The key issue in an activist campaign often boils down to who will do a better job running the company—a professional management team and board with little accountability, or a financial investor looking out for his or her own interests."[5] It is a rare board and management that do not feel highly accountable. It is a rare activist that is highly competent, or even interested, in "running" a company. Moreover, an activist "looking out for his or her own interests" may not have interests that align with those of all shareholders.

A good case can be made that financially oriented activism represents a movement toward shareholder-centric decision making. What else can you call it when pressure from a relatively small and transitory shareholder causes a board to commit to something like a share buyback program of a size that the board might not otherwise consider to be prudent? This appears to have been the case when the board of GM—a company in a notoriously cyclical industry that had earlier been in bankruptcy—acceded to pressure in 2015 from an activist owning about 2 percent of the company's stock.[6]

The movement to board-centric decision making on the right issues has yielded benefits. There are a number of reasons to argue that shareholder-centric decision making will *not* do the same.

First, other than controlling shareholders who own more than 50 percent, or who own less but exercise actual dominance over the board,[7] shareholders do not have fiduciary duties to the company or to other shareholders. They are permitted to, and in the case of financially oriented activists will, act in their own selfish best interests. It should be remembered that the actions of a board that succumbs to activist pressure and authorizes a particular corporate action will need to comport with its own fiduciary duties in doing so. "The devil [activist] made me do it" will not be a defense! Worse, if it can be credibly asserted that an ill-advised action was undertaken to preserve a board seat, that could be alleged to be a breach of the duty of loyalty (not eligible for exculpation).

Second, with some rare exceptions, financial activists' self-interests have a decidedly short-term orientation. In a situation where an activist pressures the board to boost its share buyback, the activist can cash out at a stock price that may be enhanced in the short term because of the buyback, long before any negative impact of a buyback is experienced. The potential negative impact is not limited to possible future liquidity issues. Using funds for a buyback may mean delaying or even canceling R&D or M&A activity with the potential for long-term value creation.

Chief Justice Strine has made the argument that "stockholders who propose long-lasting governance changes should have a substantial long-term interest that gives them a motive to want the corporation to prosper." He suggests that when "stockholders . . . make substantive proposals with long-term effects . . . the corporate electorate should receive full disclosure of the economic interest of proponents of such action."[8] Strine's focus was principally on governance matters. His suggestion that activists should be around to "eat their own cooking" has merit, but disclosure about the duration and other aspects of a shareholder's historical ownership position does not ensure that the shareholder will have an interest in the company's future.

To digress a moment on the debate about short-termism, one of the most interesting policy issues in all of corporate governance. In the aftermath of World War II, a perceived benefit of the advent of large corporations was that "bigness can contribute to social stability because a big business can subordinate temporary gains to long-term policies."[9] As noted in chapter 2, Chancellor Allen noted that the blessing of the courts for directors to focus on the long-term interests of shareholders allows a board to take actions that benefit the other constituencies. Rather than focusing on the impact on CSR, however, most commentators criticize short-termism as bad in economic terms for both a company and for the overall economy. A study issued by McKinsey notes that companies with a long-term orientation perform best.[10] And many strongly advocate for a long-term orientation.[11]

Short-termism carries with it a number of costs, the most obvious of which is a reduction in investment that has potential long-term benefits but will burden reported earnings in the short term. Equally concerning is the potential that "short-termism invites corruption,"[12] or at least aggressive (or worse) accounting and sales practices. "Channel stuffing" and other techniques might be relied on by an executive desperate to "make the numbers" on a quarterly basis. The SEC has ever more sophisticated techniques to ferret out this kind of misbehavior,[13] and this is fertile territory for whistle-blowers. Nevertheless, such behaviors continue.

There is a considerable range of thought about the causes of short-termism. Certainly some point to the impact of financially oriented activists. Professor Coffee of Columbia and his coauthor noted, "Some empirical evidence strongly suggests that . . . a strong correlation exists between 'short-termism' within firms and a high ownership level on the part of 'activist' hedge funds." They state further that "the more stock that the 'wolf pack' of hedge funds acquires in a firm, the greater the likely underweighting of the firm's longer-term investments in R&D."[14]

Other explanations include the following:

- the "myopic concern [of institutional investors] for short-term performance" of their own funds, which is asserted to be "fundamentally inconsistent with the objectives of most of their end-user investors"[15]
- the obsession of managements and boards with meeting quarterly earnings expectations—set either by their own expression of "outlook" or by the "Street consensus"[16]
- other sources inside the corporation—the short tenure of CEOs, some of whom are looking to establish a good record to support their next job search, or the design of executive compensation programs[17]
- the annual election of directors[18]

Assuming that short-termism deserves to be a pejorative term, from a governance standpoint what should be done about it? Professor Roe of Harvard asks, "Should it become a basic consideration in making corporate law, from the bench or in the legislature?" He notes that "important and influential lawmakers have seen short-termism as costly and in need of correction." He nevertheless argues that "courts are not well equipped to evaluate this kind of economic policy." He also would oppose solutions that involve insulating directors and officers from the demands of financial markets.[19]

Assuming that Professor Roe is correct in his assessment, or that insulating directors and officers is unattainable, there may nevertheless be ways for companies to mitigate short-termism. First, companies can make sure that they have best-in-class communications functions that can effectively and credibly convey what is being done in the service of the long-term and what the anticipated or hoped-for benefits will be. Second, when activists press for actions that will benefit the price of the stock in the short term at the cost of investments for the long term, boards should have the tools, and have the will, to stand up to those demands. End of digression.

The third reason for resisting shareholder-centric decision making is captured by the term "empty voting." This is a shorthand way of stating that, through the use of derivatives and otherwise, there can be a separation of economic interest and voting power. (A related concern is "vote buying" when there is not an alignment between voting power and economic interests.[20]) Professors Hu and Black have written extensively about this,[21] and the SEC raised it as an issue.[22] This is not simply the case of a party with the right to vote not having an interest in the success of the company. Worse, in some cases, the voter that is short the stock might actually benefit from the failure of the company. In some ways, the influence of ISS is the ultimate example of empty voting.

Fourth, there can be an information gap. While public companies are obligated to make extensive disclosures under the securities laws, there can be times when material nonpublic information is properly withheld from disclosure.[23] Moreover, information about prospects and plans may not have attained the level of probability that causes them to rise to the level of materiality, but those with a responsibility to manage the company will certainly regard those prospects and plans to be pertinent in making decisions.

Fifth, there can be an expertise gap. A well-constructed board includes directors with relevant experience and expertise. A successful career as an investor does not necessarily qualify a person to help with critical business decisions that a board must make or to be an expert in corporate governance.[24]

Finally, shareholder-centric decision making can clearly involve a challenge to the ability of a CEO to be the leader of the business.

PART IV

Challenges to CEO Leadership

There is a critical difference between leadership and management, between a long-term and a short-term orientation. Boards that cross the line and pressures from financial activists can impede the ability of CEOs to lead and to focus on the long term.

Herein, a statement of the problem and some thoughts about a solution.

12

The Problem

To state the obvious, to be the kind of corporate leader capable of withstanding the challenges to leadership in the New Era in Corporate Governance, a CEO must first have the attributes of a strong leader.

There is an endless supply of books, articles, seminars, and blogs about CEO leadership—attributes, styles, and so on. One of the best books about leadership in general is the classic *On Leadership*, by John Gardner. Among his greatest contributions is delineating all the things that leadership is *not*. He states that "we must not confuse leadership with status . . . with power," and he notes that "many people with power are without leadership gifts."[1] Gardner lists six ways in which leaders "distinguish themselves from the general run of managers":

- "They think longer term—beyond the day's crises, beyond the quarterly report, beyond the horizon."
- "In thinking about the unit they are heading, they grasp its relationship to larger realities—the larger organization of which they are a part, conditions external to the organization, global trends."
- "They reach and influence constituents beyond their jurisdictions, beyond boundaries."
- "They put heavy emphasis on the intangibles of vision, values, and motivation and understand intuitively the nonrational and unconscious elements in leader-constituent interaction."
- "They have the political skill to cope with the conflicting requirements of multiple constituencies."

- "They think in terms of renewal. The routine manager tends to accept organizational structure and process as it exists. The leader or leader/ manager seeks the revisions of process and structure required by ever-changing reality."[2]

Finally, Gardner states that perhaps the most important attribute of a leader is "the capacity to move people to action, to communicate persuasively, to strengthen confidence."[3]

Much has been written about various styles of leadership. Daniel Goleman describes six leadership styles—commanding, visionary, affiliative, democratic, pacesetting, and coaching—and suggests that the different styles work best in different contexts. For example, the commanding style works best in a time of crisis, and a visionary style works best during a period of change.[4] All of this suggests that a strong leader must have the ability to vary his or her style depending on the situation. There may also be a need for different styles depending on whether the followers are baby boomers or millennials or Generation Z. Styles may differ depending on the business of the corporation. The appropriate leadership style for a manufacturer, for example, is likely different from what is appropriate for a professional services firm.

There are many public companies that are professional services firms. They are engaged in advertising, investment banking, executive recruiting, engineering, insurance brokerage, and so on. While U.S. law firms are not able to take on nonlawyer investors and therefore will not be publicly held, such firms can be large, complex, and global. They will often have a "board" or other governing body providing oversight and participating in the big decisions. Therefore, leadership of such a firm is not unlike leading a publicly traded corporation that provides professional services. Shortly after I became chair of my firm's executive committee, I hosted a dinner for a law school dean and the CEO of a preeminent management consulting firm. The thought was that we were not competitors and that we might benefit from the exchange of ideas about how to lead our respective enterprises. The dinner started with some small talk, and with the dean asking, "What's it like to run a big law firm?" My response was a bit cheeky, but I blurted out in reply, "What's it like to 'run' a faculty?" Another subject that is relevant to leading a professional services firm is to what extent the head of the firm continues to provide professional services or becomes a full-time manager. My own view is that it is much easier to be a leader—to be respected as such and to really understand the business of the firm and how to best advance the professional lives of colleagues—if the head of a professional services firm keeps a hand in direct client service.

A strong leader must also be sufficiently self-aware to recognize how he or she changes, personally, over time. A wag once quipped that "CEO is a progressive disease."[5] A perhaps more scientific observation leading to the same conclusion is found in a 2012 study by Xueming Luo and others, who observed that "CEOs are most effective in the initial years because they are more open to outside opinions and less risk-averse" and concluded that the "optimal tenure length" is 4.8 years.[6] (Perhaps by coincidence, by 2017 the median CEO tenure for large companies had fallen to 5.0 years.[7]) That may be the case, but there have been some spectacularly successful long-tenured CEOs. Moreover, a common thread from the "Corner Office" columns in the *New York Times* is that the interviewed CEOs claim that they became better listeners over time.[8]

One of the symptoms of a CEO succumbing to the progressive disease is an unwillingness to take advice from subordinates or admit when they are correct in disagreeing with a course of action proposed by the CEO. In contrast, successful CEOs often display open-mindedness and humility. Shortly after the law firm Dewey Leboeuf imploded, I was at a dinner for the board of a client. One of the board members, the retired CEO of a very large pharma company, upon learning the role I played in my own law firm, buttonholed me. He was interested in my views about what had happened to Dewey, which I shared with him. The most interesting part of the conversation, however, was when he said that, whenever he came up with a really dumb idea, his colleagues in the C-suite would not relent until they had talked him out of it and that he was grateful for that. He clearly was not inflicted with the "disease," despite the extraordinary success of his company during his thirteen-year tenure.

A strong leader has a vision for the organization and can articulate the company's mission, and, with the help of others, develops a strategy for achieving that vision and mission that is realistic in light of available resources. Of all the resources available to the leader to help execute on the strategy, perhaps the most important is the human capital represented by the leader's team. The ability to get the most out of the team and to attain "followership" is a keystone of strong leadership.[9]

A board can tell a great deal about the quality of a leader by the quality of the team that he or she is able to recruit and retain. Quality is more important than stability. A highly stable team that is of low quality can be evidence of excessive loyalty or insecurity on the part of the CEO. That kind of team foreshadows an organization that will not do well under stress. On the other hand, a CEO with a high-quality team that is subject to periodic successful raids by the competition, but who is able to replace the departing executives with ones of equal quality, is probably an excellent leader.

In four decades of practice and working closely with CEOs, there was only one time that I approached a CEO to suggest that he needed to upgrade his team. The CEO was a founder-entrepreneur whose team included a couple of people in critical positions who had been with the CEO from the beginning but had not grown along with the company. His reluctance to improve the quality of his team was based on loyalty, not insecurity. The company was under considerable stress with a potential for existential crisis. While the conversation I initiated was not typically within the purview of an outside lawyer, I felt a personal and professional obligation to the CEO, borne of a couple of decades of working closely together. For all I know, his board was telling him the same thing. Or, perhaps the nudge I gave him was something he welcomed. Fortunately, he made the needed changes, and with the upgrades, the company was able to recover and prosper.

I observed another CEO who lost four key members of his team to be CEOs themselves. That was not at all evidence of weak leadership on his part. Rather, it showed that his "lieutenants" were learning a great deal under him, and their recruitments actually enhanced the reputation of the organization. Those factors contributed to his ability to recruit or promote individuals of like quality to step into the vacancies.

A group of high-quality individuals needs the guiding hand of the leader to become a high-quality team. A strong leader gives a good bit of thought to how the human capital of the enterprise is organized. A leader who pigeonholes his or her team members—asking for the views of individuals only about issues within their respective areas of expertise and not encouraging the entire, cross-disciplinary team to deliberate together—will stifle their growth and, worse, establish silos that can put an organization at risk. For example, silos in financial institutions were thought to have been a cause of the global financial crisis.[10] One technique for "silo busting" as part of leading change is the careful use of multidisciplinary task forces.[11] Another organizational issue is whether to centralize or decentralize decision making. While decentralization can facilitate faster decision making, for some issues it can lead to cutting corners. Decentralization of responsibility for safety, for example, was identified as a cause of BP's Deepwater Horizon disaster.[12]

As discussed in chapter 2, as a legal matter, corporations are to be governed for the benefit of the shareholders (while board and managements must also faithfully discharge more specific duties to other constituencies and are given the broad latitude to take actions that will ultimately benefit shareholders). Nevertheless, as a business matter, the reality for a CEO is that he or she operates in a "multiconstituent world." Satya Nadella, the CEO of Microsoft, in response to the question, "What was the biggest thing you didn't expect about being a CEO?", answered "I was not exposed to how multi-constituency the world really is. It's about the shareholders. It's about your team members and employees. It's about customers. It's about governments, and it's about much much more."[13]

Finally, a strong leader recognizes the need to set a proper "tone." This is not just about tone at the top for purposes of compliance. Tone in a broader sense is about treating people fairly, giving credit to those who deserve it, and accepting (not deflecting) blame when appropriate. Dwight Eisenhower had this to say along those lines: "Every leader should have enough humility to accept, publicly, the responsibility for the mistakes of subordinates he has himself selected and, likewise, to give them credit, publicly, for their triumphs."[14] An element of good tone includes not being personally (or, at least, visibly) obsessed with compensation. An inspiring leader exudes "selfless ambition."

Even an individual who has all the characteristics and attributes that would make him or her an effective corporate leader must, in the new era, contend with a number of major challenges—the potential for inappropriate board encroachment into the leadership role, pressure from financially oriented shareholder activists, potentially excessive time demands for dealing with governance issues. Others have observed these challenges as well. As to activists, John Simons wrote in the *Wall Street Journal* that "influential outsiders like Nelson Peltz are challenging the notion of a CEO as chief decision maker and lead strategist."[15]

To supplement my own observations and comments that I have heard over the years from CEOs about these challenges, as part of my research for this book, I undertook a nonscientific, but I think reliable, survey of a dozen or so CEOs. I say "nonscientific" because, compared to myriad CEO surveys (which often focus heavily on long term and short term), I no doubt have failed to comport with the requirements and techniques of good polling. Nevertheless, I believe my results are reliable and reasonably instructive. The CEOs I surveyed were all people I have known for some time and who, because of that relationship, I believe accepted my assurances that their responses will be kept anonymous. This led to candid responses. Moreover, they are all currently or in the relatively recent past were successful CEOs. They come from a variety of industries and are both male and female.

My survey included two bottom-line questions. The first asked for their reaction to the following statement: "The current state of corporate governance, at least as it has manifested at my company, has made it more difficult to lead." More disagreed with that statement than agreed, but not by a huge margin. The second asked for reactions to another statement: "The current state of corporate governance, at least as it has manifested at my company, has made it more difficult for me to focus on the long term." The responses here were the reverse. More agreed than disagreed.

There was a series of subsidiary questions. Fortunately, only one CEO responded that he had declined to take a good idea to the board because he thought they would not go for it. Nearly all said that they, directly or indirectly had had to speak to a director about "stepping over the line into management matters." The CEOs were divided evenly on whether they had experienced directors "seeking information from members of management in a manner that is inconsistent with agreed-upon protocols."

The number of hours that CEOs spend on board matters ranged from one hundred to six hundred a year, with an average of more than two hundred hours per year. The group typically spent another one hundred hours a year on shareholder engagement. Some time on such matters is obviously to be expected. Whether three hundred aggregate hours on average (or about 10 percent of a really hardworking CEO's time) is excessive certainly depends on whether it is productive.

Finally, a few of the CEOs volunteered narrative comments. Negative comments included these:

- "The role of the board is going in the wrong direction which will in the majority of cases paralyze a CEO or frustrate a competent one."

- "The affection for process has become destructive."
- "The current reality makes public ownership relatively less attractive and deteriorating."

Positive comments were these:

- "Good governance helped me to be a better leader and CEO."
- "Good governance processes, combined with an aligned board, contribute to minimizing enterprise risk, which in turn frees up this CEO to lead and focus on long-term sustainability and success of the company."

Whether viewed as a theoretical matter or through the lens of experiences of actual CEOs, there is an appropriate concern that the New Era in Corporate Governance has created, or is at least trending toward creating, some serious impediments to CEO leadership and the ability to focus on the long term. In the next chapter, we consider what CEOs and boards can do to counteract those impediments.

13

Elements of a Solution

So, which steps should be taken to position a CEO to be an effective leader of a U.S. public company?

As a starting point, the CEO and the board should have a common and consistent understanding of the following:

- the purpose of governance, how the New Era in Corporate Governance has evolved (and which forces will contribute to further evolution), and their responsibilities to shareholders and other stakeholders (the subject of Part I of this book).
- the requirements and limitations of board centricity—as demonstrated in Part II, boards have plenty to do and plenty of reasons for wanting to do it well (directors who understand this and select the CEO with care will be less likely to become an impediment to that CEO's leadership; likewise, CEOs who invest appropriate time and energy into helping their boards fulfill their proper role will collect the reward of being freer to lead)
- how to be prepared for shareholder activism, why to accept activists' good ideas, but why to resist bad ideas and general shareholder-centric decision making (see Part III)

But both the CEO and the board must do more in order for the CEO to have the ability to succeed as a leader.

For the CEO

There is an old story about the young lawyer who approached a senior partner with the question, "How do I become a trusted advisor?" The reply was "start by being trustworthy."[1] Along the same lines, if the CEO asks, "How do I get the board to allow me to be a leader and support me in the pursuit of long term goals?" the answer may very well be "Show them that you are a leader, that you have long term goals for the company and a plan for achieving those goals." This means demonstrating all of the attributes of leadership described in chapter 12. CEOs should especially focus on those attributes that will be most visible to the board—think strategically; recruit and retain talented individuals and organize them as an effective team that looks to the CEO as a leader; communicate effectively both internally and externally; and convey "selfless ambition," with a focus on the success of the company, not personal success or compensation. This is a starting point.

In addition, the CEO must recognize his or her status as a public figure, whose personal behavior—at the company and in private life—reflects on the reputation of not just the company, but also the board. The CEO cannot give the board any legitimate cause for concern about character or integrity. In years past, there was a focus on financial shenanigans. In 2018 and into 2019, there has certainly been significant, important, and long-overdue attention to sexual misconduct.[2] But there are other categories of CEO personal misbehavior that have given boards pause,[3] including a rant at a neighbor.[4]

Moreover, a CEO who tolerates personal misconduct on the part of other executives or employees can, or should, be a source of concern to the board. At an extreme, unaddressed sexual harassment or acts of racism or religious intolerance in the workplace can expose the company to financial, reputational, and (even) criminal liability. Less extreme examples of "toxic" behavior can also be damaging. According to one study, it is more important to avoid a "toxic worker" than to find a "superstar."[5] Some CEOs might struggle with how to handle a superstar who has engaged in sexual misconduct. This should not be a struggle. For the good of the company (and the CEO's career), there should be a zero-tolerance policy. The only appropriate response to credible evidence of such behavior is to sever the relationship with the superstar.

Aside from personal attributes of leadership, character, and integrity, a CEO will have greater success in preventing a board from becoming an impediment if he or she clearly demonstrates an appreciation for his or her obligations to the board and the concerns of a board with reputational and (to a lesser extent) financial exposure. In significant measure, this involves transparency and timely conveyance of important information. One-on-one check-in calls with directors and written updates between meetings can be useful. A CEO should tell the board that he or she recognizes the duty of officers "to provide the board . . . with the information that [they] need to perform their [duties]."[6] Timeliness should factor in. Remember the "Godfather rule"—important news should travel fast; bad news, the fastest.

As a related matter, when it comes to decisions that properly involve the board, "don't get ahead of the board" should be the CEO's mantra (although the CEO needs to thread the needle between that and avoiding "leading from behind").

Most CEOs that I have observed over the years are well attuned to the requirement of not getting ahead of the board. They know how to broach sensitive and potentially controversial subjects. After appropriate consultation with the rest of the management team, the approach to the board sometimes starts with test marketing an idea with the LID, then moves to one-on-one conversations with other directors that start with "I was thinking . . ." It then evolves to further one-on-ones starting with "On that subject I raised with you, I have spoken to a number of board members and here is my current thinking." At that point, the subject may be ripe for discussion with the entire board, with excellent background materials to support a recommendation (which even at that point may be characterized as "preliminary"). This approach may sound like politics and time-consuming diplomacy, but it is also likely to elicit the best input from the board and enable a CEO to carry the day with a good idea that might otherwise get turned down.

I witnessed a great example of how *not* to do it. At a board meeting that I attended, the CEO for the first time broached with his directors the idea of exploring the sale of the company. He tried to hedge his proposal with a statement along the lines of "However, if you don't agree, I believe in the company and am fully prepared to continue to execute on our strategic plan. I simply think that a sale might yield the best outcome for the shareholders." The board discussed the proposal briefly and then asked for an executive session. The CEO, management team, and I went down the hall to another room. After a fairly long time, I was asked to come back into the room. I was told that the board concluded that the CEO had "given up" and decided to fire the CEO effective immediately and replace him on an interim basis with one of their members. They called me back in first, because they wanted guidance on the disclosure and other legal issues. It turns out that the board ultimately came to understand that the CEO's proposal had merit. They concluded that they would sell the company not too long after that fateful meeting. If the CEO had raised the proposal in a less jarring fashion, he might have been the one who carried it out.

A more common example of how CEOs can get ahead of the board relates to firing senior executives. Interestingly, in the *Disney* case involving Michael Ovitz, the Delaware Supreme Court indicated that, despite the fact that a board elects an officer, the CEO can (depending on the facts) have the legal authority to fire that person.[7] Just because the CEO has the authority, it is still a good idea to consult with the board, especially if the officer has significant contacts with the board or one of its committees.

Another example arises when a CEO gets a call from a peer at a competitor who wants to discuss "combining our two great companies" or from a representative of a private equity firm who wants to get together for an undisclosed (but predictably M&A purpose). The best path is to consult with the full board before taking the meeting. There may be a temptation to clear taking such a meeting only with the nonexecutive board chair or the LID, but that can be perilous. In one instance that I observed, when the CEO reported on the meeting (after the fact) to the full board, a number of directors were upset about not being consulted. One of them memorably thundered, "There

is no junior varsity on this board!" There were adverse consequences for both the CEO and the board chair (as well as the
lawyer—not me!—who didn't recommend speaking to the full
board in advance).

There are aspects of board operations that can help a CEO keep the
board from being an impediment to his or her leadership. The CEO
should, as a matter of routine, come to an agreement with the board
about which matters need to come to the board for decision and which
matters the CEO has standing authority to execute on (and perhaps
simply report about after the fact). As another technique, the agendas
of the board meetings should be constructed (in consultation with a
separate chair or the LID) in a fashion to keep the board from "getting
into the weeds." Further, the CEO should enlist the chair or LID as an
ally in keeping discussions on track.

Boards that are treated as a real strategic resource by a CEO will
rise to that task.

One company whose board I observed for years had a CEO
who was the biggest stockholder, was a superb leader, was supremely self-confident, and had a forceful personality. The board
of very accomplished directors was largely handpicked by the
CEO. In truth, he could have done just about anything he wanted.
Nevertheless, he really wanted to hear from his board and to benefit from the interaction of ideas through full board deliberations.
He made this clear to the board by running his meetings like
a law school professor with the Socratic method. Directors who
did not volunteer a view were called on.

Another board, in its self-evaluation process, suggested that
the CEO should start every meeting with this: "This is the issue
that is weighing on me right now, and what I am really wanting your input on today." That approach might run against the
instincts of CEOs who feel that they need to have all the answers to be "strong and masterful," but it demonstrates that, at

least that board, wanted to serve as real consultants on important issues.

Rather than reaching out to their own boards for advice, I have observed younger CEOs consulting with close friends or even fellow members of the YPO (formerly Young Presidents' Organization). This should be done with considerable caution, as seeking advice will sometimes require revealing confidential information about the company. I was deeply disturbed when a person not associated with a client revealed to me that he was aware of a sensitive issue involving preliminary, undisclosed CEO succession discussions at the client. My shocked look (I am not a good poker player) elicited the response from that person: "It's OK; he [the CEO] raised it for discussion at our YPO Forum." In fact, it was not OK at all!

Finally, if the CEO wants the board to stand up to activist ideas that do not have merit, the board needs to be exquisitely prepared to do so (see chapter 7).

For the Board

The starting point for having a CEO who succeeds as a leader is for the board to choose carefully and then help the person selected to transition to the new role. Choosing carefully entails the succession planning and thoughtful execution described in chapters 7 and 8, respectively. Top among the criteria for selection should be leadership ability.

Assisting in the transition is especially important when the new CEO comes from the outside, but it is also important when the successor is a public company CEO for the first time. The job of a public company CEO is dramatically different from being the CEO of a private company. The job of CEO is dramatically different from the role of any other member of a C-suite, even of a public company. The members of the board who are or have been public company CEOs can provide extremely helpful coaching and should undertake to do so. The board may also wish to encourage the successor to get third-party coaching.

On a couple of occasions, I have had a general counsel ask me to provide coaching to a new, first-time public company CEO. (More frequently, I have provided coaching to a first-time GC of a public company who came from a litigation background.) In one instance, I turned my notes of topics to cover with one CEO into an article.[8] One of the points in that article was that the skills and experience that helped the individual get the CEO job may not be enough to help him or her keep the job. That point was particularly relevant to another CEO whom I was asked to coach. His company was a consumer products company, and he was a remarkable marketer. Unfortunately, even with coaching he simply did not fully appreciate the need to spend sufficient time dealing with his board. When that blind spot was coupled with some disappointing operating performance, his tenure was cut short.

The board can help the new CEO get off to a good start in a couple of other ways. First, if the predecessor CEO is going to remain involved in the company for more than a short transitional period, the board needs to encourage the predecessor to help but to stay out of the way of the successor. This can be difficult structurally if the predecessor becomes the board chair or simply remains as a director. It can be exacerbated if the predecessor maintains an office at the company's headquarters. Staying out of the way can be difficult emotionally for the predecessor if the successor seeks to make changes that could imply criticism of how things were run in the past. Among the most difficult changes for some predecessors to accept are changes in strategy or in the senior management team. Nevertheless, it is important that the successor be given reasonably free rein to develop strategy (in consultation with the board) and to build his or her own team.

Second, the board should be attuned to the problems created for any CEO (and especially a newly appointed successor) if the board includes any CEO wannabe. After the CEO of GE was suddenly fired after fourteen months and succeeded by a relatively young former CEO on the GE board, it was reported that some other large company CEOs were wondering "whether they would be better off seeking out long-retired executives as directors because they might represent less competition."[9] If the board already includes a disruptive wannabe, that person likely cannot be removed by board action,[10] but also need not be reslated if he or she cannot contain ambition even after coaching. Such a person should clearly not be made nonexecutive chairman or chair of the compensation committee—or perhaps any other committee.

Once the new CEO has settled into the role, there are other things that the board can do to increase his or her chances of success as a leader:

- After there has been agreement on where to draw the line between management and the board, adhere to that agreement unless and until circumstances warrant an adjustment.
- In a similar fashion, when there has been an agreement on the protocol for board members seeking information, stick with that, too.
- Be careful about demands that directors make on the time of the CEO for anything that could be characterized as "care-and-feeding" of the board. (In fact, the board should be a bit suspicious if a CEO is voluntarily too concerned with such matters, thinking about reports of how Ross Johnson dealt with the RJR Nabisco board of directors.[11]) There will be some of that, to be sure, but that should be the job of the corporate secretary.
- Provide useful feedback in an effective and constructive manner. This often requires providing comments out of the earshot of the rest of the management team.
- When judging the quality of the CEO, resist overweighting superficial aspects of how well the board meetings run.

The ability of a CEO to be an effective leader focused on the long-term requires a board that has the will to stand up to financially oriented activists when their ideas or demands are likely to yield only short-term benefits.

There is one last thing that directors should do to make sure their company is run by a CEO who is a leader. If, despite careful selection, good transitional coaching, excellent feedback, and all the other things that will help the individual succeed as a leader, the CEO continues to fall short of what is needed, the board should make a change. Leaving in place an ineffective leader as CEO is bad for the company and probably bad for the individual. Any conclusion along those lines should be reached carefully and after displaying an appropriate degree of patience.

Of course, in the event of a proven or highly credible allegation of misconduct by the CEO of the type that violates the code of conduct or brings the company into disrepute, prompt and decisive action will be required of the board. This is regardless of the otherwise positive performance of the CEO and regardless of the personal relationship between members of the board and the CEO. A failure to act can subject the board to legal and reputational exposure. A public expression of regret by a board in having to terminate the CEO who clearly engaged in misconduct is a serious mistake. And, as the board of Alphabet (the parent of Google) learned in 2018 when thousands of its employees staged a walkout, it can be a mistake to make significant severance payments when terminating a senior employee following credible allegations of sexual misconduct.[12]

Attitude as Part of the Solution

In many ways, in addition to the factors described earlier, the success of the CEO as a leader is a matter of attitude. The board should define the role of the CEO in terms of leadership and its own role in terms of helping the CEO lead the management team toward achieving long-term goals. The CEO should look to the board as a collaborative resource, and not as something that regrettably goes with the territory of a public company. They both should respect and engage with all shareholders as owners but recognize that not all shareholders are motivated by what is in the best long-term interests of their fellow shareholders. They both should recognize that a positive corporate culture—including respect for colleagues and an embrace of diversity and inclusion—and corporate social responsibility can be important sources of sustainable competitive advantage and, thus, can redound to the benefit of the shareholders.

When the right individual is in the corner office and he or she is receiving and accepting the right level of support and oversight from the board, there should be no hesitation in answering the question, "Who's in charge?" It is imperative that the answer is "The CEO, of course."

Acknowledgments

In the early 1990s, the dean of the law school from which I graduated nearly two decades earlier invited me to lunch. It was a fairly typical "development" outreach. Because I had always had a bit of an academic itch in need of scratching and because I was planning far in advance for what I might do after retiring from full-time practice as a public company M&A lawyer, I posed the following question to him: "What do you think of adjunct professors?" His response was swift and definitive: "A terrible idea. They are not scholars. Frequently they cannot teach well. They are often alums who give money and work for free. You cannot get rid of them." So much for that idea.

The next year at lunch with the same dean for the same purpose—I buy lunch, and he asks for money—he startled me with the following question: "Would you ever consider teaching a seminar at the law school?" I immediately agreed to do so, before he remembered what a terrible idea that was.

My thoughts then turned to selecting the course. While it would have been the path of least resistance, and least preparation, to teach an M&A course, I was intrigued by the thought of developing a seminar on corporate governance. I say "developing," because at that time there was not nearly the attention being given to the subject as there came to be only a few years after that. This was well before corporate governance had become the industry that it is today. Indeed, in the early 1990s very few courses on corporate governance were then offered in law schools or business schools.

Beyond the opportunity to plow new ground, I was influenced by my sense that corporate governance would provide more to chew on in an academic setting than M&A. Moreover, it is such a dynamic subject that I envisioned starting each meeting of my seminar with current events.

In acknowledging those who influenced my thinking on this subject and helped me with this book, I obviously start with that law school dean who changed his mind and entrusted me with students at the University of Chicago Law School—Geoff Stone. Dean Stone went on to serve as the university's provost and then returned to teaching and writing. I also acknowledge Bob Zimmer, the president of the university who planted the seed of the idea for my seminar on leadership for undergrads in his college.

While I am solely responsible for the contents of this book, others contributed by reviewing early drafts and providing helpful input. Jack Jacobs, who served as a vice chancellor on the Delaware Chancery Court from 1985 to 2003 and as a justice on the Delaware Supreme Court from 2003 to 2014, provided especially important insights in his careful review of chapter 6. The others are Beth Berg, Alex Groden, Emily Cole Groden, John Kelsh, Tom Kim, Fred Lowinger, and Newton Minow. (While many of the reviewers and commentators are my colleagues at Sidley Austin LLP, the views expressed herein are exclusively mine and not necessarily those of my colleagues or of the firm. The discussion of legal matters in this book is current through March 31, 2019, and does not establish an attorney-client relationship with either Sidley or me.) Thanks, too, to Frank Oelerich (a veteran investment banker who helped with the primer on valuations appearing in appendix 4 and reviewed an early draft as well). I also thank the dozen or so current and former CEOs who responded anonymously to the confidential survey reported on in chapter 12. I should also thank the hundreds of students I have taught over the years for asking the hard questions and for writing the great papers that stimulated my thinking on this important subject.

And thanks to my editor, Jane Macdonald, who made me run through the publisher's rigorous review gauntlet and made this a better book than I would have written if left exclusively to my own devices. And, of course, thanks to my assistant Cathy Chow who helped me produce countless revisions of the manuscript.

Finally, special thanks to my wife, Connie, for all kinds of reasons, including encouraging me to take up teaching as an adjunct and to write this book when I did finally retire from the full-time practice of law at the end of 2016. This book is dedicated to her.

Appendix 1

Flowchart Illustrating Proxy Voting

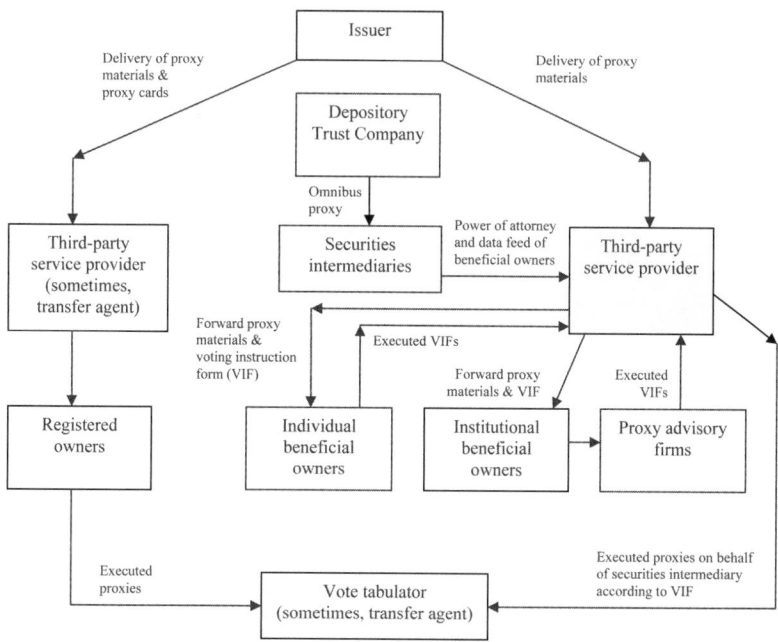

Appendix 2

Template for an Oral Board Self-Evaluation

Note: This is a template to be modified for a specific company—for example, modify as appropriate if there is a combined chair and CEO and use actual names of committees.

GENERAL APPROACH TO PROCESS
- Oral, not written, information gathering—that is, one-on-one conversations rather than questionnaires.
- Broad questions calling for free-form responses rather than granular inquiries. Use text below to facilitate the conversations; no need to cover all points in each conversation.
- Chatham House Rule—what was said, not who said it.

STARTING POINT ON BOARD EFFECTIVENESS
- How satisfied are you with the operation and effectiveness of the board?
- What is going well? What is not?
- How do you assess the following:
    information flow—timeliness, content, candor, and format
    agenda setting
    depth of board involvement
    relationship with CEO and senior management
    culture within the boardroom
    candor of discussions in board and executive sessions
    balance between presentation and discussion
    nonexecutive versus executive sessions (with and without nonindependent directors)

- More specifically, are you satisfied with board's engagement in
  business strategy?
  succession planning?
  competitive landscape and risk management?
  merger and acquisition discussions?
- Do you believe that you and the other board members are sufficiently current and conversant with trends and developments in the company's industry and related technologies?
- Has the dynamic changed in the last year? How?
- How do you rate the performance of the chairman, independent lead director, and CEO with respect to board effectiveness?
- What do you see as your role and/or unique contribution to the board's work?

STARTING POINT ON COMMITTEE EFFECTIVENESS

- How do you assess the following with respect to board committees?
  information flow—timeliness, content, and volume
  agenda setting
  allocation of work between board and committees
  frequency and depth of committee involvement
  relationship with pertinent officers and outside experts (e.g., for audit committee, CFO, and outside auditors)
  balance between presentation and discussion
- Specific questions to be tailored to the committee's role
- How would you evaluate the performance of the Committee Chairs?

GENERAL QUESTIONS

- Given present strategy, potential future developments and challenges and general considerations of best practices, does the board include members with the right skills, experience, and diversity? If not, what is missing?
- Is there sufficient clarity in the delegation of authority from the board to management?
- How would you compare the effectiveness of this board with other boards on which you currently serve or have served in the past?
- When you have been called on to make major decisions, have you been satisfied with the quality of information and analysis, the amount of time provided to reach a conclusion, and the involvement of "outside experts"?
- Do you have any comments about the performance of any specific director?

FOLLOW-UP ON PRIOR-YEAR EVALUATION

- Are you satisfied with the implementation of suggestions made during last year's evaluation, including the following:

    [List prior suggestions]

•   •   •

FORM OF REPORT BACK

- Oral to governance committee, then to full board
- Copy of board report outline to be retained by counsel
- Comments critical of any individual director to be shared only with the board chair, the chair of nominating committee, and the individual

Appendix 3

Template for M&A Agendas

Target Board Initial Meeting Agenda: Cash Deal[1]

1. Call to order; overview of agenda
2. Report on initial indication of interest and any subsequent communications from bidder; reminder about any recent past indications of interest from other third parties
3. Briefing by counsel on fiduciary duties, etc.
4. Report on due diligence on financial advisor conflicts of interest and proposed financial terms for engagement
5. Discussion about retention of financial advisor; action to authorize retention
   At This Point, Financial Advisors Enter the Meeting

6. Presentation by management:

   - Strategic and other considerations pertinent to responding to initial indication and exploring a possible transaction
   - Review of current projections, and acceptance (or confirmation by board of previous acceptance) of the projections

7. Presentation by financial advisors:

   - Preliminary valuation based on current projections
   - Review of other possible counterparties to a transaction of the type proposed by bidder, including assessment of ability to pay of both bidder and the other potential counterparties

8. Discussion and decision about whether to explore a possible transaction and, if so, the approach to follow to address *Revlon* obligations (in part in executive session, if requested)
9. Discussion and decision about response to bidder (in part in executive session, if requested)
10. Direction by board to management not to discuss personal arrangements with bidder unless and until authorized to do so by the board
11. Next steps, and tentative scheduling of follow-up meeting
12. Reminder by counsel regarding securities trading, confidentiality, and centralized response to any inquiries
13. Adjournment

Target Board Final Approval Meeting Agenda: Cash Deal

1. Call to order; overview of agenda
2. Update on events since previous meeting, including final price negotiation and summary of the course of negotiation of price (there will have been a number of meetings between the "initial" meeting and this "approval meeting" to get the input of the board on price and other critical issues during the course of the exploration and the negotiations).
3. Summary of previous briefings by counsel on fiduciary duties, etc.
4. Review by counsel of merger agreement and related documents (detailed summary of terms and course of negotiation and the actual documents supplied in advance); report by counsel on any antitrust or regulatory issues that could impact timing or feasibility of consummation
5. Confirmation by management of no change in projections; report on bidder's assessment of synergies and material issues, if any, raised by bidder during due diligence of target
6. Presentation by financial advisors:

   - Recap of prior due diligence report on conflicts (including any changes), and summary of financial terms of engagement
   - Valuation
   - Review of fairness opinion committee process; delivery of fairness opinion
   - Review of bidder's financing arrangements

7. Presentation by management:

   - Summary of management's personal financial interests
   - Recommendation with respect to the transaction

8. Review by counsel of resolutions to effect management recommendation
9. Review by counsel of history of board process and also discussion draft of factors that have been considered by the board over the course of this and prior meetings
10. Discussion (in part in executive session if requested)
11. Action on management recommendation
12. Review of communications program, including draft press release
13. Review of tentative timetable to closing
14. Reminder by counsel regarding "no shop" obligations, securities trading, confidentiality, and centralized responses to inquiries
15. Adjournment

Note

1. This is actually the second meeting following the receipt of an unsolicited indication of interest to acquire the target for cash. The first meeting would likely be a telephonic meeting promptly after the receipt of the indication and would be for purposes of (1) reporting on the fact of the receipt of the indication, (2) scheduling a special in-person meeting (or stating that there will be a discussion at a regular meeting that has been scheduled in the near term), and (3) seeking authorization for the retention of financial and legal advisors to help the board consider the indication at that subsequent meeting. This agenda covers a number of issues that might be spread out over several meetings. It should be reviewed in advance by counsel with the CEO and the chairman or LID. Modifications to the agenda will need to be made in the event that the initial indication contemplates consideration would be all or part stock.

The agenda is to be modified if, in the absence of an unsolicited indication of interest, management is proposing the exploration of a possible transaction. Again, this is likely to be the second meeting.

Appendix 4

Primer on Valuation Methodologies

Valuation Methodologies Used by M&A Bankers

- The "football field" in a typical banker's valuation presentation to a selling company board will be divided into a number of methodologies, including some or all of data provided for information, data that represents an analysis of value of the entire company in a change-in-control transaction, and other data.
- Data provided solely for information, related to the trading value of shares in a non-CIC context:
  - Fifty-two-week trading range
  - Analyst price targets
  - "Comparable companies" analysis—benchmarking based upon price-to-earnings (P/E) ratio or ratio of enterprise value to earnings before interest, taxes, depreciation, and amortization (EV/EBITDA), etc.
  - Sum-of-the-parts analysis—largely theoretical because of execution risk, transaction, costs and tax leakage, and used mostly if the company has disparate lines of business that would command different multiples on a stand-alone basis.
- Data that represents an analysis of value of the entire company:
  - Comparable deals—benchmarking against prices paid in other deals based on P/E, EV/EBITDA, etc.
  - DCF—arguably the most relevant assessment of intrinsic value, but potentially the most manipulable because it's subject to big swings depending on discount rate and terminal value; also is derived from projections (and extensions of management plans from five to ten years), which are inherently uncertain (e.g., success of new products, predicting cyclicality, secular changes in markets); to illustrate, opposing experts in Dell came up with DCFs of $28.61 per share and $12.68 per share.

- – Discounted future share price—in effect, values the successful execution of a business plan over two to four years.
- Other analyses:
  - – LBO—an ability-to-pay calculation that predicts the price that a private equity fund or sovereign wealth fund would be willing to pay based on projected cash flows, assumed targeted internal rate of return, debt levels and interest rates, and an "exit" in five years.
  - – Accretion/dilution analysis—another ability-to-pay analysis focused on strategic acquirers; dependent on an assumption of level of synergies, as well as projections for the target company.
  - – Premiums paid—another benchmarking item; arguably not relevant to intrinsic value but focused on by just about everyone; heavily influenced by time period selected and presence or absence of rumors during that period.
- Some or all of this gets rolled into the banker's judgment about whether a transaction is "fair from a financial point of view"—the formulation invariably used in rendering a fairness opinion.
- It is common to tell a board that a price can be "fair" without being "best" (in effect, the *Revlon* standard). Put another way, the banker's opinion is proof of fairness, but only process can prove best. Thus, a topping bid does not impeach a fairness opinion rendered at a lower price.

Appendix 5

Summary of Key Percentages

Ownership Triggers

5%	13D/13G; NOL (net operating loss) poison-pill trigger
10%	16(b); HSR "solely for investment" exemption
10%, 15%, 20%	Typical poison-pill triggers
15%	Delaware Section 203
20%	Equity accounting; 13G must go to 13D
33.3% (or possibly less)	"Negative control," if there is a two-thirds supermajority provision (see below)
50% (or possibly less)	Control (for *Revlon* and for shareholder with fiduciary duty); accounting consolidation
80%	Tax consolidation

Voting Requirements

50% of Votes Cast	Majority voting for directors; NYSE approval requirement for 20% issuances
50% of Outstanding Shares	Approval of mergers, of sale of all or substantially all assets, and of charter and/or bylaw amendments (unless supermajorities stipulated)

Voter Turnouts (according to *ProxyPulse* 2018, Broadridge + PwC)

91%	Institutional shares
28%	Retail shares
75–90%	Typical aggregate turnout at an annual meeting and at the higher end or even higher for a merger vote or in a proxy contest

Other Ownership Requirements

$2,000 for 1 Year	To submit a Rule 14a-8 shareholder proposal
3% for 3 Years	Typical proxy access requirement
$100 million of assets under management	Triggers requirement of 13F ownership reports by institutional investment managers; must be filed within 45 days following the end of a quarter.

Abbreviations in Notes

Note: The following abbreviations and acronyms are used in sources cited multiple times in these endnotes.

Bus. Law.	ABA's *The Business Lawyer*
DGCL	Delaware General Corporation Law
Dodd-Frank	Dodd-Frank Wall Street Reform and Consumer Protection Act of 2010
HLSCG	Harvard Law School Forum on Corporate Governance and Financial Regulation
IRC	Internal Revenue Code
ISS Guidelines	2018 Institutional Shareholder Services United States Proxy Voting Guidelines
NACD BRC	National Association of Corporate Directors Blue Ribbon Commission
NASDAQ Rules	NASDAQ Corporate Governance Requirements
NYSE Manual	New York Stock Exchange Listed Company Manual
SEC	United States Securities and Exchange Commission
SOX	Sarbanes-Oxley Act of 2002 (aka Public Company Accounting Reform and Investor Protection Act)

Notes

Introduction

1. Dan Neil, *2019 Volkswagen Jetta: Return of the Great Cheap Car*, WALL ST. J. (Aug. 10, 2018), https://www.wsj.com/articles/2019-volkswagen-jetta-return-of-the-great-cheap-car-1533921657.

2. Guhan Subramanian, *Corporate Governance 2.0*, HARV. BUS. REV. (Mar. 2015), https://hbr.org/2015/03/corporate-governance-2-0.

3. Jonathan R. Macey, *Corporate Governance: Promises Kept, Promises Broken* 9 (2008).

4. *Capitalism's Unlikely Heroes*, ECONOMIST (Feb. 5, 2015), https://www.economist.com/leaders/2015/02/05/capitalisms-unlikely-heroes; Walter Frick, *The Case for Activist Investors*, HARV. BUS. REV. (Mar. 2016), https://hbr.org/2016/03/the-case-for-activist-investors.

Chapter One

1. Michael C. Jensen & William H. Meckling, *Theory of the Firm: Managerial Behavior, Agency Costs, and Ownership Structure*, 3 J. FIN. ECON. 305, 308 (1976).

2. Adolf A. Berle Jr. & Gardiner C. Means, *The Modern Corporation and Private Property* (1933).

3. John C. Coffee Jr., *Liquidity Versus Control: The Institutional Investor as Corporate Monitor*, 91 COLUM. L. REV. 1277 (1991).

4. James McRitchie, *Corporate Governance Defined: Not So Easily*, CORP. GOVERNANCE (Aug. 1999), https://www.corpgov.net/library/corporate-governance-defined.

5. Andrei Shleifer & Robert W. Vishny, *A Survey of Corporate Governance*, 52 J. FIN. 737, 738 (1997), quoted in McRitchie, *supra* note 4.

6. Margaret M. Blair, *Ownership and Control: Rethinking Corporate Governance for the Twenty-First Century* (1995), quoted in McRitchie, *supra* note 4.

7. J. Robert Brown Jr. & Lisa L. Casey, *Corporate Governance: Cases and Materials* (2012), quoted in McRitchie, *supra* note 4.

8. Henrik Mathiesen, *Managerial Ownership and Financial Performance* (Samfund-slitteratur, PhD Ser. No. 2002-18, 2002), quoted in McRitchie, *supra* note 4.

9. Robert A.G. Monks & Nell Minow, *Corporate Governance* (1995), quoted in McRitchie, *supra* note 4.

10. Macey, *supra* introduction note 3, at 2.

11. Suneela Jain, Barbara Blackford, Donna Dabney, & James D. Small III, *What Is the Optimal Balance in the Relative Roles of Management, Directors, and Investors in the Governance of Public Corporations?* 1 (Conference Bd. Governance Ctr., White Paper, Mar. 13, 2014), https://ssrn.com/abstract=2407716.

12. Fin. Crisis Inquiry Comm'n, *The Financial Crisis Inquiry Report* xviii (2011).

13. Jeffrey M. Jones, *U.S. Stock Ownership Down Among All but Older, Higher-Income*, GALLUP (May 24, 2017), https://news.gallup.com/poll/211052/stock-ownership -down-among-older-higher-income.aspx.

14. Eric Morath, Opinion, *Stocks, Housing Lift Household Net Worth*, WALL ST. J., Sept. 22, 2017, at A2 fig.

15. Jason M. Thomas, *Where Have All the Public Companies Gone?* WALL ST. J., Nov. 17, 2017, at A15.

16. *Why the Decline in the Number of Listed American Firms Matters*, ECONOMIST: SCHUMPETER BLOG (Apr. 22, 2017), https://www.economist.com/business/2017/04/22 /why-the-decline-in-the-number-of-listed-american-firms-matters.

17. Michael Wursthorn & Gregory Zuckerman, *Number of Listed Companies Is Falling*, WALL ST. J., Jan. 5, 2018, at A8.

Chapter Two

1. Joseph L. Weiner, *The Berle-Dodd Dialogue on the Concept of the Corporation*, 64 COLUM. L. REV. 1458 (1964).

2. Milton Friedman, *The Social Responsibility of Business Is to Increase Its Profits*, N.Y. TIMES MAGAZINE, Sept. 13, 1970, at 173. An interesting contribution to the discussion about "for whose benefit" came in a somewhat offhanded way in a case decided a few days before the publication of Friedman's article. The case involved whether the attorney-client privilege can be asserted to protect communications between management and counsel to the corporation in a case brought by shareholders: "[I]t must be borne in mind that management does not manage for itself and that the beneficiaries of its action are the stockholders." Garner v. Wolfinbarger, 430 F.2d 1093, 1101 (5th Cir. 1970).

3. Lynn A. Stout, *The Shareholder Value Myth*, HLSCG (June 26, 2012), https://corpgov.law.harvard.edu/2012/06/26/the-shareholder-value-myth.

4. Joseph L. Bower & Lynn S. Paine, *The Error at the Heart of Corporate Leadership*, HARV. BUS. REV., May–June 2017, at 50.

5. *In re* Trados Inc. S'holder Litig., 73 A.3d 17, 40–42 (Del. Ch. 2013).

6. Revlon, Inc. v. MacAndrews & Forbes Holdings, Inc., 506 A.2d 173, 182 (Del. 1986).

7. *E.g.*, Ill. Bus. Corp. Act of 1983 § 8.85, 805 ILL. COMP. STAT. 5/8.85 (2018). The common formulation of the "other constituencies" can, oddly enough, be found in the decision in *Unocal Corp. v. Mesa Petroleum Co.*, 493 A.2d 946 (Del. 1985), issued by the Delaware Supreme Court in 1985. There the Court said that among the "concerns" a board can consider in adopting defenses to a hostile takeover is "the impact on 'constituencies' other than shareholders (i.e., creditors, customers, employees and perhaps even the community generally)." *Id.* at 955. The court went on to say, "While not a controlling factor, it also seems to us that a board may reasonably consider the basic stockholder interests at stake. . . ." *Id.* at 955–56. This formulation seems upside down when compared to how the law governing hostile takeovers has developed and should not be relied upon.

8. *E.g.*, *Articles of Incorporation*, PG&E CORP. (May 30, 2002), http://www.pgecorp .com/aboutus/corp_gov/pdfs/Corporation_ArticlesofIncorp.pdf.

9. See, e.g., Shenker v. Laureate Educ., 983 A.2d 408 (Md. 2009). *Compare In re* ShopKo Stores, Inc. S'holder Litig., No. 05-cv-677 (Brown Cnty. Cir. Ct. Sept. 2, 2005).

10. Dodge v. Ford Motor Co., 170 N.W. 668, 684 (Mich. 1919).

11. *Revlon*, 506 A.2d at 182.

12. William T. Allen, *Our Schizophrenic Conception of the Business Corporation*, 14 CARDOZO L. REV. 261 (1992).

13. Michelle Edkins, Managing Director, Global Head of Investment Stewardship, BlackRock, *Shareholder Activism: Good or Bad for the Economy?*, Remarks at the Economic Club of Chicago Forum (Apr. 5, 2017), https://www.youtube.com/watch?v =9AeJbANe1_Y, at 44:31.

14. Larry Fink, *Annual Letter to CEOs: A Sense of Purpose* (2018), and *Annual Letter to CEOs: Purpose and Profit (2019)*, BLACKROCK, https://www.blackrock.com /corporate/investor-relations/larry-fink-ceo-letter.

15. Andy Kessler, Opinion, *Stocks Weren't Made for Social Climbing*, WALL ST. J., Jan. 22, 2018, at A15.

16. Andrew Ross Sorkin, *New Goldman Sachs Fund Will Track Paul Tudor Jones's Feel-Good Companies*, N.Y. TIMES: DEALBOOK (June 11, 2018), https://www.nytimes .com/2018/06/11/business/dealbook/goldman-sachs-paul-tudor-jones.html.

17. *The JUST Capital Rankings on Corporate Tax Reform*, JUST CAPITAL (Feb. 28, 2018), https://justcapital.com/reports/the-just-capital-rankings-on-corporate-tax-reform.

18. James Mackintosh, *Social, Environmental Investment Scores Diverge*, WALL ST. J., Sept. 18, 2018, at B1.

19. James Mackintosh, *If You Want to Do Good, Expect to Do Badly*, WALL ST. J., June 19, 2018, at B1.

20. Vanessa Fuhrmans & Rachel Feintzeig, *CEOs Risk Speaking Up*, WALL ST. J., Mar. 2, 2018, at B3; April Hall, *A Social-Risk Tipping Point?*, DIRS. & BDS., 2d Quarter 2018, at 28; Sapna Maheshwari, *The Delicate Dance of a Progressive C.E.O. in the Trump Era*, N.Y. TIMES (Jan. 15, 2018), https://www.nytimes.com/2018/01/15/business /media/sonic-drive-in-clifford-hudson.html.

21. U.S. Dep't of Labor, Field Assistance Bulletin No. 2018-01 (Apr. 23, 2018), https://www.dol.gov/agencies/ebsa/employers-and-advisers/guidance/field -assistance-bulletins/2018-01.

22. Paul S. Atkins, Opinion, *California Public Employees Vote Against Pension-Fund Activism*, WALL ST. J., Oct. 19, 2018, at A17.

23. Richard Fausset, *Georgia Passes Bill That Stings Delta over N.R.A. Position*, N.Y. TIMES (Mar. 1, 2018), https://www.nytimes.com/2018/03/01/business/delta-nra -georgia.html.

24. Alan Rappeport, *Banks Tried to Curb Gun Sales: Now Republicans Are Trying to Stop Them*, N.Y. TIMES (May 25, 2018), https://www.nytimes.com/2018/05/25/us /politics/banks-gun-sales-republicans.html.

25. Sheera Frenkel, *Microsoft Employees Protest Work with ICE, as Tech Industry Mobilizes over Immigration*, N.Y. TIMES (June 19, 2018), https://www.nytimes.com /2018/06/19/technology/tech-companies-immigration-border.html; Michael Forsythe & Walt Bogdanich, *McKinsey Ends Work with ICE amid Furor over Immigration Policy*, N.Y. TIMES (July 9, 2018), https://www.nytimes.com/2018/07/09/business /mckinsey-ends-ice-contract.html.

26. Bus. Roundtable Letter to Sec'y, Dep't of Homeland Sec., on Immigr. Policies (Aug. 22, 2018), https://s3.amazonaws.com/brt.org/archive/letters/Immigration .Nielsen%20Letter%2008232018.pdf.

27. DGCL § 362.

28. *State by State Status of Legislation*, BENEFIT CORP., http://benefitcorp.net /policymakers/state-by-state-status.

29. For a discussion of the criteria B Lab considers in the certification process and the annual fee schedule, see *Certified B Corporation, Certification*, B LAB, https://bcorporation.net/certification.

30. Ronald Orol, *Strine: Big Investors Should Support B Corps Even When Activists Attack*, THE DEAL (Dec. 5, 2017), http://www.thedeal.com.

31. Elizabeth Warren, Opinion, *Companies Shouldn't Be Accountable Only to Shareholders*, WALL ST. J., Aug. 15, 2018, at A17. Richard Epstein wrote an interesting rebuttal to Warren's proposal in an op-ed: "One way to test the soundness of [her

proposal] is to ask whether it could be extended to noncorporate governing bodies," such as labor unions. Richard A. Epstein, Opinion, *Unions Have Stakeholders, Too*, WALL ST. J., Sept. 12, 2018, at A17.

32. Joseph E. Stiglitz, *Meet the "Change Agents" Who Are Enabling Inequality*, N.Y. TIMES, Aug. 20, 2018 (book review), https://www.nytimes.com/2018/08/20/books/review/winners-take-all-anand-giridharadas.html.

33. James O'Toole, *The Enlightened Capitalists: Cautionary Tales of Business Pioneers Who Tried to Do Well by Doing Good* 442 (2019).

34. *In re Trados*, 73 A.3d at 38.

Chapter Three

1. William L. Cary, *Federalism and Corporate Law: Reflections Upon Delaware*, 83 YALE L.J. 663 (1974).

2. Santa Fe Indus., Inc. v. Green, 430 U.S. 462 (1977).

3. Smith v. Van Gorkom, 488 A.2d 858 (Del. 1985).

4. *Unocal*, 493 A.2d at 952.

5. 15 PA. CONS. STAT. ANN. §§ 2541–48 (West 2018).

6. N.D. CENT. CODE §§ 10-35-01 to -33 (2018).

7. Oral Argument and the Court's Ruling at 14–15, *In re* Puda Coal, Inc. Stockholders Litig., C.A. No. 6476-CS (Del. Ch. Feb. 6, 2013), available at https://www.davispolk.com/files/uploads/Puda_Coal_Transcript_Ruling.pdf.

8. Letter from J. W. Van Gorkom to Newton Minow, Partner, Sidley & Austin, covering attached monograph, *The Trans Union Case* (May 5, 1987) (on file with author).

9. DGCL § 102(b)(7).

10. Graham v. Allis-Chalmers Mfg. Co., 188 A.2d 125 (Del. 1963).

11. *In re* Caremark Int'l Inc. Deriv. Litig., 698 A.2d 959 (Del. Ch. 1996).

12. Stone *ex rel.* S. Bancorporation v. Ritter, 911 A.2d 362 (Del. 2006).

13. *Unocal*, 493 A.2d 946.

14. Mercier v. Inter-Tel (Delaware), Inc., 929 A.2d 786 (Del. Ch. 2007).

15. Blasius Indus., Inc. v. Atlas Corp., 564 A.2d 651 (Del. Ch. 1988).

16. Boilermakers Local 154 Ret. Fund v. Chevron Corp., 73 A.3d 934 (Del. Ch. 2013).

17. City of Providence v. First Citizens Bancshares, Inc., 99 A.3d 229 (Del. Ch. 2014).

18. DGCL § 115.

19. Schoon v. Troy Corp., 948 A.2d 1157 (Del. Ch. 2008).

20. DGCL § 145(f).

21. DGCL § 109(b) (responding to ATP Tour, Inc. v. Deutscher Tennis Bund, 91 A.3d 554 (Del. 2014)).

22. CSX Corp. v. Children's Inv. Fund, 654 F.3d 276, 282 (2d Cir. 2011).

23. Melvin Aron Eisenberg, *An Overview of the Principles of Corporate Governance*, 48 Bus. Law. 1271, 1271 (1993).

24. The following table summarizes SOX by target group:

Target	SOX section	Section title and contents
Managements and boards	Title III	Corporate Responsibility (including clawbacks and D&O bar)
	Title IV	Enhanced Financial Disclosures (including Section 404 on management assessment of internal controls)
	Title VIII	Corporate and Criminal Fraud Accountability
	Title IX	White-Collar Crime Penalty Enhancements
Public accountants	Title I	Public Company Accounting Oversight Board
	Title II	Auditor Independence
Lawyers	Section 307 of Title III	Corporate Responsibility (Section 307 on rules of professional responsibility)
Analysts	Title V	Analyst Conflicts of Interest

The gatekeeper notion received a good bit of attention following the failure of Enron. See John C. Coffee Jr., *Gatekeepers: The Professions and Corporate Governance* (2006). See also Stephen Cutler, Director, Division of Enforcement, SEC, *The Themes of Sarbanes-Oxley as Reflected in the Commission's Enforcement Program*, Remarks at UCLA School of Law (Sept. 20, 2004), http://www.sec.gov/news/speech/spch092004smc.htm. Cutler described gatekeepers as the "sentries of the marketplace" and listed lawyers, analysts, and boards. In the *Rural Metro* case (one of the cases beginning in 2012 relating to financial advisors' conflicts of interest in M&A deals), the Delaware Court of Chancery characterized M&A financial advisors, in dicta, as gatekeepers. *In re* Rural Metro Corp. Stockholders Litig., 88 A.3d 54 (Del. Ch. 2014). SIFMA, the securities industry group, was so concerned about this characterization's potential implications for its members that it submitted an amicus brief on that single issue to the Delaware Supreme Court. In its opinion issued in the appeal of that case, the Court stated, "Adhering to the trial court's amorphous 'gatekeeper' language would inappropriately . . . suggest[] that any failure by a financial advisor to prevent directors from breaching their duty of care gives rise to an aiding and abetting claim against the advisor." RBC Capital Markets, LLC v. Jervis, 129 A.3d 816, 191 (Del. 2015).

25. *Sidley Best Practices Calendar for Corporate Boards and Committees*, Sidley Austin (2018), https://www.sidley.com/en/global/services/corporate-governance

-and-executive-compensation/sub-pages/the-sidley-best-practices-calendar-for
-corporate-boards-and-committees. The calendar is continuously updated.

26. The following table summarizes the Dodd-Frank governance provisions:

Section	Subject
951	Mandatory say-on-pay and golden-parachute votes
952	Compensation committees
953	Enhanced compensation disclosures, including pay-ratio disclosures
954	Enhanced clawback requirements
955	Disclosure of hedging by directors
971	Proxy access
972	Disclosure about combined chair and CEO provisions

27. Bernard S. Black, *Agents Watching Agents: The Promise of Institutional Investor Voice*, 39 UCLA L. Rev. 811 (1992).

28. Leo E. Strine Jr., *Can We Do Better by Ordinary Investors? A Pragmatic Reaction to the Dueling Ideological Mythologists of Corporate Law*, 114 Colum. L. Rev. 449, 449 (2014).

29. Burton G. Malkiel, *A Random Walk Down Wall Street: The Time-Tested Strategy for Successful Investing* (1973). Eleven editions have been released since the original publication, the latest in January 2019.

30. John C. Bogle, *The Little Book of Common Sense Investing* 74 (2010).

31. Justin Lahart, *The Case for Stock Picking*, Wall St. J., Aug. 18–19, 2018, at B12 fig.

32. John C. Bogle, *The Father of the Index Fund Sees a Reckoning Ahead*, Wall St. J., Dec. 1–2, 2018, at B1.

33. Letter from U.S. Dep't of Labor to Helmuth Fandl, Chairman of Ret. Bd., Avon Prods., Inc. (Avon Letter) (Feb. 23, 1988). Building on this letter, the DOL issued further guidance in Interpretive Bulletin (IB) 94-2 in 1994, 29 C.F.R. § 2509.94-2 (1994). It then issued IB 2008-02, 29 C.F.R. § 2509.08-2 (2008), in which it stated that a fiduciary may consider only economic interests when voting. It then issued IB 2016-01, 29 C.F.R § 2509.2016-01 (2016) (withdrawing IB 2008-02 and reinstating IB 94-2), stating its "longstanding position [first articulated in the Avon Letter] . . . that the fiduciary act of managing plan assets . . . includes decisions on the voting of proxies. . . ." IB 2016-01 also comments on involvement in ESG issues and shareholder engagement, including "active monitoring" of subjects such as "independence and expertise of candidates for the corporation's board" and "governance subjects and practices."

34. For a good summary of concerns about the influence of the proxy advisory firms, see U.S. Gov't Accountability Office, *Corporate Shareholder Meetings: Proxy Advisory Firms' Role in Voting and Corporate Governance Practices* (2016). The phrase "outsized influence" can be found in speeches and writings of SEC commissioners. In 2017 the U.S. House passed a bill called the Corporate Governance Reform and

Transparency Act, H.R. 4015, 115th Cong. (2017). The bill is designed to address "errors, misstatements of fact, and incomplete analysis," as well as conflicts of interest, on the part of advisory firms. The SEC held a roundtable for November 2018 on the proxy process to provide the staff "an opportunity to engage with market participants on topics including . . . the role of proxy advisory firms." In anticipation of the roundtable, the commission withdrew letters issued in 2004 to ISS and Egan-Jones that had been thought to be a basis for the advisory firms' outsized influence. On the day before the roundtable, the Corporate Governance Fairness Act was introduced with bipartisan support in the Senate. The act is designed to require proxy advisory firms to register as investment advisors under the Investment Advisors Act of 1940.

35. See Moody's, Rep. No. 78666, *Rating Methodology: U.S. and Canadian Corporate Governance Assessment* (Aug. 2003), https://www.moodys.com/sites/products /AboutMoodysRatingsAttachments/2002000000425793.pdf. The corporate governance assessment is one of "five areas of crucial importance to the credit worthiness evaluation of a company." See Moody's, Rep. No. 87539, *Research Methodology: Risk Management Assessments* (July 2004), https://www.moodys.com/sites/products /AboutMoodysRatingsAttachments/2002900000432768.pdf.

36. Robert M. Daines, Ian D. Gow, & David F. Larcker, *Rating the Ratings: How Good Are Commercial Governance Ratings?*, 98 J. Fin. Econ. 439, 440 (2010).

37. Michelle Celarier, *The Mysterious Private Company Controlling Corporate America*, Institutional Inv., Jan. 29, 2018, https://www.institutionalinvestor.com/article /b16pv90bf0zbj8/the-mysterious-private-company-controlling-corporate-america.

38. Mustafa A. Dah & Melissa B. Frye, *Is Board Compensation Excessive?*, HLSCG, June 26, 2017, https://corpgov.law.harvard.edu/2017/06/26/is-board-compensation -excessive.

39. Raymond J. Fisman, *Tax-Exempt Lobbying: Corporate Philanthropy as a Tool for Political Influence*, HLSCG, Apr. 16, 2018, https://corpgov.law.harvard.edu/2018 /04/16/tax-exempt-lobbying-corporate-philanthropy-as-a-tool-for-political-influence.

40. Martin Lipton, *No Long-Term Value from Activist Attacks*, HLSCG, Oct. 4, 2017, https://corpgov.law.harvard.edu/2018/10/04/no-long-term-value-from-activist-attacks.

41. Stephen M. Bainbridge & M. Todd Henderson, *Boards-R-Us: Reconceptualizing Corporate Boards*, 66 Stan. L. Rev. 1051, 1072 (2014). The authors expanded their law review article into a 2018 book titled *Outsourcing the Board: How Board Service Providers Can Improve Corporate Governance*. Bus. Law. devoted a substantial portion of its Spring 2019 issue to a symposium on this subject.

42. *Id.* at 1060–61.

43. *Id.* at 1062.

44. *Id.* at 1065.

45. *Id.*

46. *Id.* at 1066.

47. *Id.* at 1067.

48. *See Commonsense Corporate Governance Principles* (2016), http://www.gov
ernanceprinciples.org/wp-content/uploads/2018/10/2016-Open-Letter-Princi
ples.pdf.

49. *E.g., see* Steven Russolillo, *Activist Investors Flex Their Muscles in Asia*, WALL
ST. J. (May 8, 2018), https://www.wsj.com/articles/activist-investors-flex-muscle-in
-asia-1525756279.

50. Mark J. Roe, *Strong Managers, Weak Owners: The Political Roots of American
Corporate Finance* 22 (1996).

51. I.R.C. § 280G (2009); I.R.C. § 162(m) (2009), amended by the Tax Cuts and
Jobs Act of 2017 (TCJA), Pub. L. No. 115-97, § 13601, 131 Stat. 2054 (2017).

52. SOX § 304, 15 U.S.C. § 7243 (2017); Dodd-Frank, Pub. L. No. 111-203, § 954,
124 Stat. 1904, 1904 (2010).

53. See Vanessa Fuhrmans & Theo Francis, *Adding Numbers to Compensation Debate*, WALL ST. J., Feb. 2, 2018, at B5 (citing *CEO Pay Ratio Survey*, EQUILAR (2018),
https://marketing.equilar.com/31-2018-ceo-pay-ratio-survey).

54. See Cabinet Office, *Gender Pay Gap Reporting Guidance*, GOV.UK (Jan. 4,
2018), https://www.gov.uk/guidance/gender-pay-gap-reporting-guidance.

55. Dodd-Frank § 1502; Exchange Act Release No. 67,716, 77 Fed. Reg. 56,274
(Sept. 12, 2012) (to be codified at 17 C.F.R. pts. 240, 249 & 249b), adopting Rule 13p-1,
17 C.F.R. § 240.13p-1 (2018), and Form SD, 17 C.F.R. § 249b.400 (2018).

56. See Warren, *supra* note 31 in chap. 2.

57. Gabriel Rubin and Michael Wursthorn, *Democrats Take Aim at Stock Buybacks*,
WALL ST. J., Feb. 5, 2019, at A2.

Chapter Four

1. Klaassen v. Allegro Dev. Corp., C.A. No. 8626-VCL, 2013 WL 5967028, at *9
(Del. Ch. Nov. 7, 2013).

2. Steven Prokesch, *America's Imperial Chief Executive*, N.Y. TIMES: ARCHIVES
(Oct. 12, 1986), https://www.nytimes.com/1986/10/12/business/america-s-imperial
-chief-executive.html.

3. *See, e.g.*, Ram Charan, Dennis Carey, & Michael Useem, *Boards That Lead:
When to Take Charge, When to Partner, and When to Stay out of the Way* (2014);
NACD, *Key Agreed Principles to Strengthen Corporate Governance for U.S. Publicly
Traded Companies* (Aug. 31, 2011); Commonsense Principles of Corporate Gover-
nance 2.0, COLUM. L. SCH. IRA M. MILLSTEIN CTR. FOR GLOB. MKTS. & CORP.
OWNERSHIP (Oct. 18, 2018), https://millstein.law.columbia.edu/content/common
sense-principles-20; Bus. Roundtable, *Principles of Corporate Governance* (Aug. 2016),
https://s3.amazonaws.com/brt.org/Principles-of-Corporate-Governance-2016.pdf.

4. NYSE Manual §§ 303A.08 & 312.00 (2018), http://wallstreet.cch.com/LCM
/Sections; NASDAQ Rules 5635 & 5635-1 (2018), http://nasdaq.cchwallstreet.com.

5. ISS Guidelines §§ 3 & 5 (Jan. 4, 2018), https://www.issgovernance.com/file /policy/active/americas/US-Voting-Guidelines.pdf.

6. Paramount Commc'ns, Inc. v. Time, Inc., 571 A.2d 1140, 1154 (Del. 1989).

7. *Blasius*, 564 A.2d 651.

8. A shareholder rights plan (aka poison pill) was devised during the rise of the hostile takeover in the mid-1980s. There are two ways to describe its operation. Theoretically speaking, it allows all shareholders (other than the shareholder who "triggers" the pill by exceeding a specified percentage of stock without the consent of the board) to acquire shares in a company at half price. This would result in massive dilution of the value of the triggering shareholder's position in the company. Because of that theoretical operation, the practical operation of the pill is to deter any interested party from exceeding the specified percentage. The poison pill works well because it is implemented by the board without shareholder action and can be "dismantled" (i.e., redeemed) only by the board. The pill was first validated as a device by the Delaware Supreme Court in 1985. Moran v. Household Int'l, Inc., 500 A.2d 1346 (Del. 1985). In validating the exercise of the board's fiduciary duty in adoption of the pill in that case, the Court left for a later day whether the board could, in keeping with that duty, leave the pill in place. Later cases have addressed the validity of "upgrades" to the pill. The most important of those later cases related to a "dead hand" provision that impeded the ability of a subsequent board (elected, for example, by action of a hostile bidder) to redeem a pill. A variation on the dead hand was the "no hand" provision (a delayed-redemption provision preventing redemption for a period of months). Such provisions were struck down as "impermissibly depriv[ing] any newly elected board of . . . its statutory authority to manage." Quickturn Design Sys., Inc. v. Shapiro, 721 A.2d 1281, 1291 (Del. 1998); Carmody v. Toll Bros, Inc., 723 A.2d 1180 (Del. Ch. 1998).

9. Ivanhoe Partners v. Newmont Mining, 535 A.2d 1334 (Del. 1987).

Chapter Five

1. "Social loafing" is a term coined by psychologist Bibb Latane. It has appeared in a variety of dictionaries published by the Oxford University Press.

2. The SEC adopted a rule, required by Section 407 of SOX, mandating disclosure of whether its audit committee included at least one member who is a "financial expert" and if it does not, why. Exchange Act Release No. 47,235, 68 Fed. Reg. 5109 (Jan. 31, 2003) (to be codified at 17 C.F.R. pts. 228, 229 & 249). In that adopting release, the SEC stated that it did not intend that public identification as an expert would affect "such person's duties, obligations or liability." *Id.* at 5116. Compare the outcome in the Emerging Communications case discussed in chapter 6. In addition, under stock exchange rules, each member of the audit committee must be "financially literate." See NYSE Manual § 303A.07(a) cmt. and NASDAQ Rules 5605(c)(2).

3. Groupthink is a concept noted in an article by William H. Whyte Jr. in *Fortune* magazine in 1952. *Groupthink*, FORTUNE, Mar. 1952, at 114. It has been the subject of extensive research and writing in a variety of contexts, including business. See Marleen A. O'Connor, *The Enron Board: The Perils of Groupthink*, 71 U. CIN. L. REV. 1233 (2003).

4. For example, Catalyst, the organization promoting women in business and the professions, issued a 2004 report concluding that companies with a higher representation of woman directors performed better on the following metrics: return on equity, return on sales, and return on invested capital. *Companies with More Women Board Directors Experience Higher Financial Performance, According to Latest Catalyst Bottom Line Report*, CATALYST, https://www.catalyst.org/media/companies-more-women -board-directors-experience-higher-financial-performance-according-latest (last visited Dec. 26, 2018). However, the conclusions of such studies have been challenged. Katherine Klein, *Does Gender Diversity on Boards Really Boost Company Performance?*, KNOWLEDGE@WHARTON (May 18, 2017), http://knowledge.wharton.upenn.edu /article/will-gender-diversity-boards-really-boost-company-performance.

5. France and Norway require that 40 percent of public company board members are women. Vanessa Fuhrmans, *Pressure Tactics Diversify Boards*, WALL ST. J., Apr. 26, 2018, at B6. In September 2018 the California legislature adopted a bill (S.B. 826, 2018 Leg., 2017-18 Sess. (Cal. 2018)) mandating gender diversity on the boards of public companies "whose principal executive offices . . . are located in California," regardless of where they are incorporated (a feature that will subject it to constitutional challenge). Section 1 of the statute is a compendium of studies about the benefits of gender diversity in the boardroom. The lead editorial in the *Wall Street Journal* on September 11, 2018, declared it to be "a bill that will damage U.S. corporate governance." *California's Corporate Quotas*, WALL ST. J., at A16. The bill was signed into law on September 30, 2018.

6. A group called the Thirty Percent Coalition stated a goal that 30 percent of directors on S&P 500 boards be female by 2030. See the website 30PercentCoalition.org.

7. The New York State Common Retirement Fund announced that it would vote against all directors on boards that did not have a single woman director. Joann S. Lublin, *Pension Fund Opposes Boards Without Women*, WALL ST. J., Mar. 21, 2018, at B1.

8. Ben W. Heineman Jr., *The Inside Counsel Revolution: Resolving The Partner-Guardian Tension* (2016).

9. NYSE Manual § 303A.02; NASDAQ Rules 5605(2)(b).

10. These higher standards are mandated by Exchange Act section 10A-3(b)(1), 17 C.F.R. § 240.10A-3(b)(1) (2018).

11. See ISS Guidelines § 2, item 4.

12. Exchange Act Rule 16b-3(b)(3), 17 C.F.R. § 240.16b-3(b)(3) (2018) (defining nonemployee director).

13. Treas. Reg. § 1.162-27 (as amended in 1996) (defining outside director). To establish performance-based compensation, which prior to the TCJA was an exception to the $1 million ceiling, the performance goals had to be set by a compensation committee composed solely of two or more outside directors.

14. *In re* Oracle Corp. Deriv. Litig., 824 A.2d 917 (Del. Ch. 2003); but see Beam *ex rel.* Martha Stewart Living Omnimedia, Inc. v. Stewart, 845 A.2d 1040 (Del. 2004).

15. N.J. Carpenters Pension Fund v. infoGROUP, Inc., 2011 WL 4825888 (Del. Ch. Sept. 30, 2011).

16. Sterling Huang & Gilles Hilary, *Zombie Board: Board Tenure and Firm Performance*, 56 J. ACCT. RES. 1285 (2018), https://ink.library.smu.edu.sg/soa_research /1728; *Spencer Stuart Board Index 2015*, SPENCER STUART (2015), https://www .spencerstuart.com/~/media/pdf%20files/research%20and%20insight%20pdfs/ssbi -2015_110215-web.pdf.

17. The term "zombie directors" is also applied to those who fail to attain a majority vote but who remain on the board because their resignations have been rejected.

18. See Jacquelyn Lumb, *Boeing Is Unsuccessful in Attempts to Omit "Lap Dog" References from Shareholder Proposals*, SEC TODAY, Jan. 18, 2018, at 1.

19. DGCL § 141(d).

20. See Item 5.02(a)(1) of SEC Form 8-K (2018), https://www.sec.gov/files/form8 -k.pdf. The SEC brought an enforcement action against Hewlett-Packard for failure to make the required disclosure about the sudden resignation of a director in the midst of the investigation over boardroom leaks. The SEC stated: "The commission found [that] . . . the disagreement related to HP's corporate governance and HP's policies regarding the handling of sensitive information, and therefore was a disagreement related to HP's operations, policies or practices which was required to be disclosed." SEC Press Release No. 2007-103, SEC Settles Charges Against Hewlett-Packard for Misleading Disclosures Arising out of Company's Boardroom Leak Investigation (May 23, 2007), https://www.sec.gov/news/press/2007/2007-103.htm.

21. Section 8 of the Clayton Antitrust Act prohibits individuals from serving on the boards of two competing corporations, subject to exceptions based on overall size and amounts of competitive sales. 15 U.S.C. § 19 (2018).

22. ISS will regard any director as "overboarded" if he or she is the company's CEO and serves on the board of more than two public companies (other than his or her own) or he or she is any other director and serves on more than five public company boards in total. ISS Guidelines § 1, Board of Directors/Composition.

23. SEC Reg. S-K Item 407(b), 17 C.F.R § 229.407(b) (2018); *id.*

24. Bus. Roundtable v. SEC, 647 F.3d 1144 (D.C. Cir. 2011) (vacating Exchange Act Rule 14a-11, 76 Fed. Reg. 58,100 (Sept. 20, 2011)).

25. John Jenkins, *Proxy Access: Game Over?*, THECORPORATECOUNSEL.NET (Feb. 14, 2018), https://www.thecorporatecounsel.net/blog/2018/02/proxy-access-game-over.html.

26. Lyuba Goltser & Kaitlin Descovich, *ISS Board Practices Study Reflects Focus on Board Accountability*, GOVERNANCE & SEC. WATCH (Mar. 22, 2017), https:// governance.weil.com/whats-new/iss-board-practices-study-reflects-focus-on-board -accountability.

27. Lucian Bebchuk, John C. Coates IV, & Guhan Subramanian, *The Powerful Anti-takeover Force of Staggered Boards: Theory, Evidence, and Policy*, 54 STAN. L. REV. 887 (2002). See also the articles in response triggered by that article's conclusions.

28. See *In re* VAALCO Energy, Inc. Stockholder Litig., C.A. No. 11775-VCL (Del. Ch. Dec. 21, 2015) (interpreting DGCL § 141(k)). Some 175 Delaware corporations had interpreted section 141(k) incorrectly: they had annually elected boards but had invalid charter provisions that required "cause" for director removal. In a follow-up case, *Frechter v. Zier*, 2017 WL 345142 (Del. Ch. Jan. 24, 2017), a bylaw provision re-quiring a supermajority shareholder vote for removal was also held to be invalid. That supermajority requirement would have been upheld if it had been in the certificate of incorporation. Location matters!

29. Concept Release on the U.S. Proxy System, Exchange Act Release No. 62,495, 75 Fed. Reg. 42,982 (July 22, 2010) (to be codified at 17 C.F.R. pts. 240, 270, 274 & 275).

30. As but one example, see Robert J. Jackson Jr., Commissioner, SEC, *Perpetual Dual-Class Stock: The Case Against Corporate Royalty*, Address at UC Berkeley School of Law (Feb. 15, 2018), https://www.sec.gov/news/speech/perpetual-dual-class -stock-case-against-corporate-royalty. See also reference to Council of Institutional Investors in chapter 3.

31. See Press Release, S&P Dow Jones Indices, S&P Dow Jones Indices Announces Decision on Multi-Class Shares and Voting Rules (July 31, 2017), https://us.spindices .com, and *FTSE Russell Voting Rights Consultation Results*, FTSE RUSSELL (July 2017), https://www.ftse.com/products/downloads/FTSE_Russell_Voting_Rights_Consul tation_Results.pdf.

32. Williams v. Geier, 671 A.2d 1368 (Del. 1996).

33. David J. Berger, Steven Davidoff Solomon, & Aaron J. Benjamin, *Tenure Voting and the U.S. Public Company*, 72 BUS. LAW. 295 (2017).

34. EY Ctr. for Bd. Matters, *Corporate Governance by the Numbers*, Ernst & Young Global Ltd. (Nov. 30, 2018), https://www.ey.com/us/en/issues/governance-and -reporting/ey-corporate-governance-by-the-numbers.

35. ISS Guidelines, § 1, Board of Directors/Responsiveness.

36. Joann S. Lublin, *Boards Try Buddy System to Get Newcomers Up to Speed*, WALL ST. J., (Sept. 18, 2017), https://www.wsj.com/articles/boards-try-buddy-system-to -get-newcomers-up-to-speed-1505769025.

37. Jeffrey A. Sonnenfeld, *What Makes Boards Great*, HARV. BUS. REV. (Sept. 2002), https://hbr.org/2002/09/what-makes-great-boards-great.

Chapter Six

1. Guth v. Loft, Inc., 5 A.2d 503 (Del. 1939).

2. *In re* Walt Disney Co. Deriv. Litig. (Disney I), 907 A.2d 693, 697 (Del. Ch. 2005).

3. More specifically, the Model Act provides that directors "shall discharge their duties with the care that a person in a like position would reasonably believe appropriate under similar circumstances." MODEL BUS. CORP. ACT § 8.30(a)–(b) (AM. BAR ASS'N 2016).

4. Aronson v. Lewis, 473 A.2d 805, 812 (Del. 1984).

5. DGCL § 144(a).

6. *Ivanhoe*, 535 A.2d at 1345.

7. DGCL § 122(17).

8. Brophy v. Cities Serv. Co., 70 A.2d 5 (Del. Ch. 1949).

9. *In re Puda Coal*, Transcript of Oral Argument and the Court's Ruling (Feb. 6, 2013), at 23, www.delawarelitigation.com/files/2013/02/puda-case.pdf.

10. Malone v. Brincat, 722 A.2d 5, 10 (Del. 1998).

11. *In re* Walt Disney Co. Deriv. Litig. (*Disney II*), 906 A.2d 27 (Del. 2006) (quoting *Disney I*, 907 A.2d at 755).

12. *Stone v. Ritter*, 911 A.2d 362, 370 (Del. 2006).

13. *Graham*, 188 A.2d at 130.

14. *In re Caremark*, 698 A.2d at 970, 971.

15. *Stone*, 911 A.2d at 370.

16. *In re* Citigroup Inc. S'holder Deriv. Litig., 964 A.2d 106, 123, 124 (Del. Ch. 2009).

17. *Malone*, 722 A.2d at 14.

18. Arnold v. Soc'y for Sav. Bancorp, Inc., 650 A.2d 1270 (Del. 1994).

19. Chen v. Howard-Anderson, 87 A.3d 648 (Del. Ch. 2014).

20. Charles M. Nathan, *Maintaining Board Confidentiality*, HLSCG (Jan. 23, 2010), https://corpgov.law.harvard.edu/2010/01/23/maintaining-board-confidentiality.

21. J. Travis Laster & John Mark Zeberkiewicz, *The Rights and Duties of Blockholder Directors*, 70 BUS. LAW. 33, 47 (2014–15).

22. DGCL § 172.

23. Mendel v. Carroll, 651 A.2d 297, 306 (Del. Ch. 1994).

24. Benihana of Tokyo, Inc. v. Benihana, Inc., 906 A.2d 114, 122 (Del. 2006).

25. Controlled companies are exempted from NYSE governance requirements for a majority of independent directors and independent nominating and compensation committees. NYSE Manual § 303.A.00. There are similar exemptions from NASDAQ Rules 5615(c)(2) & IM-5615-5. The application of Revlon duties (discussed in chapter 8) in the context of a sale of a controlled company is addressed in *McMullin v. Beran*, 765 A.2d 910 (Del. 2000). For an interesting study of performance and other aspects of the controlled companies in the S&P 1500, see Edward Kamonjoh, *Controlled Compa-*

nies in the Standard & Poor's 1500: A Follow-Up Review of Performance & Risk, INV'R RESPONSIBILITY RESEARCH CTR. INST. (Mar. 2016), https://irrcinstitute.org/wp -content/uploads/2016/03/Controlled-Companies-IRRCI-2015-FINAL-3-16-16.pdf.

26. The requirement for up-the-ladder reporting by counsel has been around for a long time. *See* MODEL RULES OF PROF'L CONDUCT r. 1.13 (AM. BAR ASS'N 2018); and *In re* Carter & Johnson, Exchange Act Release No. 17597, [1981 Transfer Binder] Fed. Sec. L. Rep (CCH) ¶ 82,847 (Feb. 28, 1981). This requirement was emphasized as part of SOX and SEC Rules pt. 205.3, 17 C.F.R § 205.3 (2018).

27. Jedwab v. MGM Grand Hotels, Inc., 509 A.2d 584 (Del. Ch. 1986); *In re Trados*, 73 A.3d at 39–40.

28. Simons v. Cogan, 549 A.2d 300 (Del. 1988); Glinert v. Wickes Cos., 586 A.2d 1201 (Del. 1990).

29. Anadarko Petrol. Corp. v. Panhandle Eastern Corp., 545 A.2d 1171 (Del. 1988).

30. Bovay v. H. M. Byllesby & Co., 38 A.2d 808 (Del. 1944).

31. Credit Lyonnais Bank Nederland v. Pathe Commc'ns Corp., Civ. A. No. 12150, 1991 WL 277613, at *34 (Del. Ch. Dec. 30, 1991). This case is known to practitioners for its famous "Footnote 55."

32. Quadrant Structured Prods. Co. v. Vertin, 102 A.3d 155, 176 (Del. Ch. 2014), citing N. Am. Catholic Educ. Programming Found., Inc. v. Gheewalla, 930 A.2d 92 (Del. 2007).

33. Mills Acquisition Co. v. Macmillan, Inc., 559 A.2d 1261, 1283 (Del. 1988). See also Weinberger v. UOP, Inc., 457 A.2d 701 (Del. 1983), where two directors were faulted for not sharing a valuation report with their fellow directors.

34. Basic Inc. v. Levinson, 485 U.S. 224 (1988). See also the discussion at note 37 in chapter 6.

35. Reg. FD (for "fair disclosure"), 17 C.F.R. §§ 243.100–103 (2018), promulgated by the SEC in 2000, prohibits selective disclosure. More specifically, it requires that disclosures cannot be made selectively to any broker-dealer, investment advisor, investment company, or "holder of the issuer's securities, under circumstances in which it is reasonably foreseeable that the person will purchase or sell the issuer's securities on the basis of the information." However, there are circumstances when such disclosure can be made, including when the recipient "expressly agrees to maintain the disclosed information in confidence" with either an oral or written agreement. Regulation FD in effect codified prior case law. It is the reason for the practice of keeping earnings calls with analysts open to all comers. In the immediate aftermath of the adoption of Regulation FD, many companies stopped having one-on-ones with analysts. That practice has been reinstated, although it is a good idea to have either a witness to such a meeting or an immediate post-meeting debrief with counsel, or both. Some CEOs have used Regulation FD as an excuse not to speak with the press, even though literally it doesn't apply to such a communication.

36. Peter Lattman & Azam Ahmed, *Rajat Gupta Convicted of Insider Trading*, N.Y. Times: Dealbook (June 15, 2012), https://dealbook.nytimes.com/2012/06/15/rajat -gupta-convicted-of-insider-trading.

37. *Basic v. Levinson*, 485 U.S. 224, 263 n.17 (1988). Basic supports a "no comment" policy. Stock exchange rules (e.g., NYSE Manual § 202.03) do not. Most issuers stick with "no comment" even when pressed by their listing exchange. It is critical to recognize that "no corporate development" is not the same as "no comment." *In re* Carnation Co., [1984–1985 Transfer Binder] Fed. Sec. L. Rep. (CCH) ¶ 83,801 (July 8, 1985), Exchange Act Release No. 22214, 33 SEC Docket (CCH) 874 (July 8, 1985).

38. Stuart Gelfond & Arielle L. Katzman, *A Guide to Rule 10b5-1 Plans*, HLSCG (Mar. 24, 2016), https://corpgov.law.harvard.edu/2016/03/24/a-guide-to-rule-10b5-1 -plans.

39. Linda Chatman Thomsen, Director, Division of Enforcement, SEC, Remarks at the 2007 Corporate Counsel Institute (Mar. 8, 2007), https://www.sec.gov/news /speech/2007/spch030807lct2.htm (citing "recent academic studies [that] suggest that the Rule is being abused"). In addition, in 2019 a bipartisan bill was introduced in the House requiring the SEC to consider amending Rule 10b 5-1 to prevent abuse of plans (H.R. 624).

40. Feder v. Martin Marietta Corp., 406 F.2d 260 (2d Cir. 1969).

41. Securities Act Rule 144, 17 C.F.R. § 230.144 (2018), covers restricted and control securities. This imposes filing requirements on members of the board because control securities are defined as securities held by an affiliate, which in turn is defined to include persons "such as an executive officer, a director or large shareholder." SEC, Off. of Inv. Educ. & Advoc., Investor Publication, Rule 144: Selling Restricted and Control Securities (Jan. 16, 2013).

42. UniSuper Ltd. v. News Corp., 898 A.2d 344 (Del. Ch. 2006).

43. See Corporate Integrity Agreements imposed by the Office of Inspector General of Health and Human Services on any number of health-care companies; Jennifer Arlen & Marcel Kahan, *Corporate Governance Regulation Through Nonprosecution*, 84 U. Chi. L. Rev. 323 (2017). Note also that the SEC's settlement with Elon Musk over his Tesla-going-private tweet included a requirement that he step down as board chair, but not as CEO.

44. NACD's BRC Report Series is available at https://www.nacdonline.org/insights /blue_ribbon.cfm?itemnumber=61330.

45. *See, e.g.*, *Political Spending and Unintended Consequences*, Ctr. for Pol. Accountability, http://politicalaccountability.net/reports/political-spending-and -unintended-consequences. Political activity—both election spending and lobbying— is a subject of many shareholder proposals under Exchange Act Rule 14a-8, 17 C.F.R. § 240.14a-8 (2018). Retaining Michael Cohen for access to President Trump was a source of embarrassment and cost senior executives at Novartis and AT&T their jobs.

46. F. William McNabb III, Chairman & CEO, Vanguard, Open Letter to CEOs and Boards (Feb. 27, 2015), https://about.vanguard.com/vanguard-proxy-voting/CEO _Letter_03_02_ext.pdf.

47. SDX Protocol, http://www.sdxprotocol.com (last visited Dec. 25, 2018).

48. Del. Ch. Rule 23.1, https://courts.delaware.gov/rules/pdf/Chancery-Rule-Set _clean-9.10.2018.pdf.

49. *Aronson*, 473 A.2d 805.

50. Zapata Corp. v. Maldonado, 430 A.2d 779, 788–89 (Del. 1981).

51. Lewis v. Anderson, 477 A.2d 1040 (Del. 1984).

52. Gentile v. Rossette, 906 A.2d 91 (Del. 2006).

53. *In re* Trulia, Inc. Stockholder Litig., 129 A.3d 884 (Del. Ch. 2016).

54. DGCL § 262.

55. Jack B. Jacobs, Reappraising Appraisal: Some Judicial Reflections, Luncheon Remarks at Northwestern University School of Law, 15th Annual Garrett Corporate & Securities Law Institute (Apr. 27, 1995).

56. Jeffrey J. Rosen and William D. Regner, *Appraisal Rights: Navigating the Maze After DFC Global, Dell, and Aruba*, HLSCG (Apr. 17, 2018), https://corpgov.law.har vard.edu/2018/04/17/appraisal-rights-navigating-the-maze-after-dfc-global-dell-and -aruba.

57. Dell, Inc. v. Magnetar Glob. Event Driven Master Fund Ltd., 177 A.3d 1 (Del. 2017). *See also, e.g.*, DFC Glob. Corp. v. Muirfield Value Partners LP, 172 A.3d 346 (Del. 2017), and Verition Partners Master Fund Ltd. v. Aruba Networks, Inc., C.A. No. 11448-VCL, 2018 WL 922139 (Del. Ch. Feb. 15, 2018).

58. *Id.*

59. William T. Allen, Jack B. Jacobs, & Leo E. Strine Jr., *Realigning the Standard of Review of Director Due Care with Delaware Public Policy: A Critique of* Van Gorkom *and Its Progeny as a Standard of Review Problem*, 96 Nw. U. L. Rev. 449 (2002). See also, by the same three authors (all Delaware judges), *Function over Form: A Reassessment of Standards of Review in Delaware Corporation Law*, 56 Bus. Law. 1287 (2001).

60. Pell v. Kill, 135 A.3d 764, 784 (Del. Ch. 2016).

61. Cede & Co. v. Technicolor, Inc., 634 A.2d 345, 360 (Del. 1993) (quoting Citron v. Fairchild Camera & Instrument Corp., 569 A.2d 53, 64 (Del. 1989)).

62. *Aronson*, 473 A.2d at 813.

63. Calma *ex rel.* Citrix Sys., Inc. v. Templeton, 114 A.3d 563, 577 (Del. Ch. 2015).

64. *Cede*, 634 A.2d at 358.

65. *Disney II*, 906 A.2d at 73–74.

66. Paramount Commc'ns, Inc. v. QVC Network, Inc., 637 A.2d 34 (Del. 1994) (containing a concise articulation of the *Revlon* case).

67. *Unocal*, 493 A.2d 946.

68. *Aronson*, 473 A.2d 805.

69. *In re* Smurfit-Stone Container Corp. S'holder Litig., No. 6164-VCP, 2011 WL 2028076, at *24 (Del. Ch. May 20, 2011).

70. *Blasius*, 564 A.2d at 659–61.

71. Kahn v. Lynch Commc'n Sys., Inc., 638 A.2d 1110 (Del. 1994).

72. Corwin v. KKR Financial Holdings LLC, 125 A.3d 304 (Del. 2015).

73. *In re* Volcano Corp. Stockholder Litig., 143 A.3d 727 (Del. Ch. 2016).

74. Unitrin, Inc. v. American General Corp., 651 A.2d 1361, 1373 (Del. 1995).

75. Mercier v. Inter-Tel, 929 A.2d at 807.

76. *Id.* at 811.

77. *In re* MFW S'holders Litig., 67 A.3d 496 (Del. Ch. 2013).

78. *Cede*, 634 A.2d at 361.

79. DGCL § 102(b)(7).

80. DGCL § 141(e) (general reliance) and § 172 (relating to dividends and stock repurchases).

81. Smith v. Van Gorkom, 488 A.2d 858.

82. *In re* Emerging Commc'ns, Inc. S'holders Litig., No. Civ. A. 16415, 2004 WL 1305745, at *39 (Del. Ch. June 4, 2004).

83. DGCL § 141(e).

84. DGCL § 174.

85. Advanced Min. Systems, Inc. v. Fricke, 623 A.2d 82 (Del. Ch. 1992).

86. Annotated Model D&O Indemnification Agreement (Am. Bar Ass'n Bus. Law Sec., 2013).

87. For an excellent and thorough explanation of D&O insurance, see John Olson & Gillian McPhee, *Directors & Officers Insurance: A Primer*, NACD Report/Director Liability.

88. Gantler v. Stephens, 965 A.2d 695, 712–13 (Del. 2009).

89. *Rural Metro*, 88 A.3d 54.

90. *Corwin*, 125 A.3d at 311.

91. Louise Story & Eric Dash, *E-mail Shows Concerns over Merrill Deal*, N.Y. Times, Oct. 13, 2009, https://www.nytimes.com/2009/10/14/business/14bank.html.

92. Securities Enforcement Remedies and Penny Stock Reform Act of 1990 § 102, 15 U.S.C §78u(d)(2). The ban is viewed as a more proportional remedy than fines and criminal prosecution. In the original Act, the word "substantial" modified "unfitness"; it was removed with the enactment of SOX.

Chapter Seven

1. ISS Guidelines § 1, Board of Directors/Voting on Director Nominees in Uncontested Elections/Composition.

2. Sidley Best Practices Calendar, *supra* note 25 in chap. 3.

3. NYSE Manual §§ 303A.04 to .07. NASDAQ Rules 5605(c)–(e). NASDAQ provides that, as an alternative to an actual nominating committee, its listed companies may instead have nominees selected by "independent directors constituting a majority of the board's independent directors in a vote in which only independent directors participate."

4. *Id.*

5. In a securities class action against Goldman Sachs relating to the so-called Abacus transaction, the plaintiffs cited Goldman statements about its commitment to comply with the law. Goldman's Code of Business Conduct and Ethics (available at https://www.goldmansachs.com/investor-relations/corporate-governance /corporate-governance-documents/revise-code-of-conduct.pdf), for example, describes its "commitment to conduct our business . . . in compliance with all applicable laws, rules and regulations." It will be interesting to see whether language such as that will ultimately be correctly interpreted as an aspirational goal or somehow taken to be a representation to be relied upon by securities purchasers.

6. *The Nonexecutive Chairman: Offering New Solutions*, SPENCER STUART (2008), https://www.spencerstuart.com/~/media/pdf%20files/research%20and%20insight %20pdfs/cornerstone-of-the-board-the-nonexecutive-chairman_21jan2008.pdf.

7. DGCL § 220(d).

8. Amalgamated Bank v. Yahoo! Inc., 132 A.3d 752, 781 (Del. Ch. 2016).

9. *In re* Caterpillar, Inc., Exchange Act Release No. 30,532, Fed. Sec. L. Rep. (CCH) ¶ 73,830 (Mar. 31, 1992).

10. Financial Accounting Standards Board (FASB) ASC 280 establishes an "approach based on the way that management organizes the segments within the public entity for making operating decisions and assessing performance."

11. Calma *ex rel.* Citrix Sys., Inc. v. Templeton, 114 A.3d 563, 569 (Del. Ch. 2015). See also Williams v. Ji, C.A. No. 12729-VCMR, 2017 WL 2799156 (Del. Ch. Jun 28, 2017) (involving grants to directors of a parent company of options on subsidiary stock and applying an "entire fairness review") and *In re* Investors Bancorp, Inc. Stockholder Litigator, 177 A.3d 1208 (Del. 2017).

12. NYSE Manual § 303A.09. NASDAQ Rules do not have a similar requirement, although NASDAQ-listed companies typically engage in that practice.

13. Exchange Act Rule 10A-3, 17 C.F.R. § 240.10A-3 (2018) (adopting Exchange Act Release No. 47,654, 68 Fed. Reg. 18,788 (Apr. 16, 2003); NYSE Manual § 303A.07; NASDAQ Rules 5605(c).

14. NYSE Manual § 303A.07(b)(iii)(C) cmt.

15. Item 7 of SEC Schedule 14A, incorporating Item 407(d) of SEC Regulation S-K. See also Audit Committee Disclosure, Exchange Act Release No. 42,266, 64 Fed. Reg. 73,389.

16. TSC Indus., Inc. v. Northway, Inc., 426 U.S. 438, 449 (1976).

17. Rosenblatt v. Getty Oil Co., 493 A.2d 929 (Del. 1985).

18. SEC Staff Accounting Bulletin No. 99, 64 Fed. Reg. 45,150 (Aug. 19, 1999).

19. SOX § 303(a) and 17 C.F.R. § 240.13b2-2 (2018) (adopting Exchange Act Release No. 47,890 (May 20, 2003)).

20. SEC Litigation Release No. 18104, SEC v. Brian Adley, C.A. No. 03-10762 MEL (D. Mass 2003).

21. Michael E. Porter, *What Is Strategy?*, Harv. Bus. Rev. (Nov.–Dec. 1996), https://hbr.org/1996/11/what-is-strategy.

22. Report of the *NACD Blue Ribbon Commission on Strategy Development*, NACD (Oct. 12, 2014), https://www.nacdonline.org/insights/publications.cfm?itemnumber =12161.

23. *Paramount v. Time*, 571 A.2d at 1150. Time was seeking to acquire Warner. Paramount tried to acquire Time and brought suit to enjoin the Time-Warner deal. The court declined to issue the injunction. That decision was affirmed on appeal in an opinion stating that the Time board would have *Revlon* duties only when it "abandons its long-term strategy."

24. NYSE Manual § 303A.05; NASDAQ Rules 5605(d).

25. NYSE Manual § 303A.08; NASDAQ Rules 5635(c).

26. David F. Larcker & Brian Tayan, *CEO Compensation*, Stanford Graduate Sch. Bus. Corp. Governance Research Initiative (2015), https://www.gsb .stanford.edu/sites/gsb/files/publication-pdf/cgri-quick-guide-08-ceo-compensation .pdf. In addition to the clawbacks mandated in the event of financial restatements by SOX (*supra* note 24 in chapter 3) and Dodd-Frank (*supra* note 26 in chapter 3), there can be clawbacks based on other forms of misconduct, such as the kind of behavior covered by the #MeToo movement. Laurence Fletcher, *Big Investors Seek a #MeToo Clawback*, Wall St. J. (Sept. 23, 2018), https://www.wsj.com/articles/big -investors-seek-a-metoo-clawback-1537754820.

27. See, e.g., FASB, Statement of Financial Accounting Standards No. 123(R), relating to employee stock options.

28. See I.R.C. §§ 162(m) & 4999 (2018) ("excess parachute payments").

29. See Exchange Act Rule 16b-3, 17 C.F.R. § 240.16b-3 (2018), as well as proxy rule disclosure requirements under Item 7 of SEC Schedule 14A, incorporating Item 407(e) of SEC Regulation S-K.

30. Sarah Kent, *Shell Links Pay, Emissions*, Wall St. J., Dec. 4, 2018, at B2.

31. John R. Ellerman, Brian S. Scheiring & Keith Jesson, *Recent OSHA Ruling May Impact Ability to Use Safety as an Incentive Metric*, Pay Governance, Oct. 20, 2016.

32. ISS 2012–13 Policy Survey.

33. Dodd-Frank § 951.

34. ISS Guidelines Sec. 1, Board of Directors/Responsiveness.

35. ISS Guidelines Sec. 5, Compensation/Executive Pay Evaluation.

36. Charles M. Elson & Craig Ferrere, *Executive Superstars, Peer Groups and Over-compensation*, 38 J. Corp. L. 488 (2013).

37. In a paper titled *The Growth of Executive Pay*, Lucian Bebchuk and Yaniv Grinstein state that equity-based compensation, as a percentage of total CEO compensation grew from 41 percent (in 1993) to 78 percent (in 2000) at S&P 500 companies. Harv. Discussion Paper No. 510, Apr. 2005. The longest bull market in history (until recently) ran from 1990 to 2000, with a 400 percent increase in the S&P 500. Michael Wursthorn & Akane Otani, *U.S. Stocks Poised to Enter Longest-Ever Bull Market*, Wall St. J. (Aug. 21, 2018), https://www.wsj.com/articles/u-s-stocks-poised-to -enter-longest-ever-bull-market-1534843800.

38. Ingolf Dittman, Ernst Maug, & Oliver Spalt, *Indexing Executive Compensation Contracts*, HLSCG (Jan. 29, 2014), https://corpgov.law.harvard.edu/2014/01/29 /indexing-executive-compensation-contracts.

39. Steven N. Kaplan, *The Real Story Behind Executive Pay*, Foreign Affairs (May/June 2013), https://www.foreignaffairs.com/articles/2013-04-03/real-story -behind-executive-pay.

40. *Disney I*, 907 A.2d 693.

41. *Disney II*, 906 A.2d 27.

42. In 2009 the SEC issued new rules with respect to proxy statement disclosures, including a requirement for disclosures "that would help investors determine whether a company has incentivized excessive or inappropriate risk-taking by employees" but established a fairly high bar of "reasonably likely to have a material adverse effect on the registrant." *See* SEC Press Release No. 2009-268, SEC Approves Enhanced Disclosure about Risk, Compensation and Corporate Governance (Dec. 16, 2009), https:// www.sec.gov/news/press/2009/2009–268.htm, as well as SEC Rel. No. 33-9089, 74 Fed. Reg. 35,076 (July 10, 2009), and Reg. S-K Item 402(s).

43. Joann S. Lublin & Theo Francis, *Succession Planning Is Key to Smooth Transitions*, Wall St. J. (June 8, 2016), https://www.wsj.com/articles/succession-planning -is-key-to-smooth-transitions-1465410506 (describing the initiative for succession planning initiated one week before the new CEO of McCormick & Co. started his tenure as CEO).

44. Deborah Ball & Eric Sylvers, *Fiat Says It Didn't Know CEO Was Ill*, Wall St. J., July 26, 2018, at B1.

45. *Report of the NACD Blue Ribbon Commission on Talent Development*, NACD (Oct. 10, 2013), https://www.nacdonline.org/insights/publications.cfm?ItemNumber =7674.

46. Rick Wartzman & Lawrence Crosby, *A Company's Performance Depends First of All on Its People*, Wall St. J. (Aug. 13, 2018), https://www.wsj.com/articles/a-companys -performance-depends-first-of-all-on-its-people-1534125840.

47. See citations in note 42 in chap. 7.

48. Dep't of Justice, Justice Manual (f/k/a U.S. Attorneys' Manual), 9-28.000—Principles of Federal Prosecution of Business Organizations. Among the "factors to be considered" are "the adequacy and effectiveness of the corporation's compliance program at the time of the offense, as well as at the time of a charging decision." 9-28.300 (Nov. 2018). In this regard, "prosecutors may consider whether the corporation has established corporate governance mechanisms that can effectively detect and prevent misconduct" and "do the corporation's directors exercise independent review . . . rather than unquestioningly ratifying officers' recommendations." 9-28.800 cmt. (Nov. 2015).

49. U.S. Sentencing Comm'n, Organizational Guidelines, Overview of the Organizational Guidelines, https://www.ussc.gov/sites/default/files/pdf/training/organizational-guidelines/ORGOVERVIEW.pdf. The guidelines provide for "mitigating the potential fine range—in some cases up to 95 percent—if an organization can demonstrate that it had put in place an effective compliance program." Two of the criteria for an effective compliance program are "oversight by high-level personnel" and "effective communication to all levels of employees."

50. Daniel Diermeier, *Reputation Rules* (2011).

51. A dead-hand provision in a poison pill is one that prevents a board of directors elected by a dissident from being able to redeem the pill. As discussed *supra* note 8 in chapter 4, such a provision was invalidated in *Toll Brothers*. A dead-hand proxy put is a provision in a credit instrument that gives the creditors the right to put the debt back to the company at a premium if the board becomes comprised of a majority of directors elected by a dissident and the provision does not allow existing directors to approve the dissident slate prior to its election to eliminate the put right. See Sandridge Energy, 68 A.3d 242 (Del. Ch. 2013). See also the discussion at F. William Reindel, *"Dead Hand Proxy Puts"—What You Need to Know*, HLSCG (June 10, 2015), https://corpgov.law.harvard.edu/2015/06/10/dead-hand-proxy-puts-what-you-need-to-know.

52. NYSE Manual § 303A.03.

53. Leo E. Strine Jr., *Documenting the Deal*, 70 BUS. LAW. 679 (2015).

54. Among the best general conferences for directors are Northwestern's Kellogg School of Management Annual Corporate Governance Conference (held in May) and the Stanford Annual Directors College (held in June). KPMG has an excellent Audit Committee Institute, with sessions throughout the year in a number of cities.

Chapter Eight

1. For a great example of the progression of knowledge about a crisis over a short period of time, look at the press releases issued by BP in the weeks after the explosion of the Deepwater Horizon in April 2010.

2. Boris Groysberg, *Chasing Stars: The Myth of Talent and the Portability of Performance* (2012).

3. Fair Credit Reporting Act, 15 U.S.C. § 1681 (2017), which (despite its name) also covers background checks related to personnel decisions, including hiring, retention, and promotion.

4. Doris Kearns Goodwin, *Team of Rivals* (2005).

5. Jacquie McNish, *CSX Chief Hunter Harrison Has Died*, WALL ST. J. (Dec. 16, 2017), https://www.wsj.com/articles/csx-ceo-hunter-harrison-has-died-1513453754.

6. SEC Form 8-K Item 5.02(b).

7. SEC Form 8-K Item 5.02(c).

8. Joann S. Lublin, *Scandals Reshape CEO Searches*, N.Y. TIMES, Dec. 28, 2017, at B6.

9. In 2015 the SEC brought a cease-and-desist proceeding against KBR, Inc. effectively mandating an exception to confidentiality and anti-disparagement provisions in employment agreements to allow for whistle-blowing. *In re* KBR, Inc., Exchange Act Release No. 74,619, 111 SEC Docket 4 (Apr. 1, 2015).

10. Elena Lytkina Botelho, Kim Rosenkoetter Powell, Stephen Kincaid, & Dina Wang, *What Sets Successful CEOs Apart*, HARV. BUS. REV. (May–June 2017), https://hbr.org/2017/05/what-sets-successful-ceos-apart.

11. Steven N. Kaplan & Morten Sorensen, *Are CEOs Different? Characteristics of Top Managers* (Colum. Bus. Sch. Res. Paper No. 16-27, 2017), at 27.

12. Sue Shellenberger, *The Best Bosses Are Humble Bosses*, WALL ST. J., Oct. 10, 2018, at A11.

13. Thomas Gryta, *GE Digs Deeper into Use of Jets*, WALL ST. J., Dec. 13, 2017, at B1.

14. See Jon O. Shimabukuro, L. Paige Whitaker, & Emily E. Roberts, *Survey of Federal Whistleblower and Anti-Retaliation Laws*, CONG. RES. SERV. (Apr. 22, 2013). As of 2013, there were forty such laws. SOX §§ 806 and 1107 provide protections for whistle-blowers. Dodd-Frank § 922 relates to whistle-blowers who report to the SEC. For an example of the consequences of a CEO's trying to find out who blew the whistle, see Patrick Collinson, *Barclays CEO Jes Staley Faces Fine over Whistleblower Incident*, GUARDIAN (Apr. 20, 2018), https://www.theguardian.com/business/2018/apr/20/barclays-ceo-jes-staley-facing-fine-over-whistleblower-incident, and Nils Pratley, *Why Should Future Whistleblowers Believe They Will Be Safe?*, GUARDIAN (Apr. 20, 2018), https://www.theguardian.com/business/nils-pratley-on-finance/2018/apr/20/why-should-future-whistleblowers-believe-they-will-be-safe-barclays.

15. Upjohn Co. v. United States, 449 U.S. 383 (1981).

16. 18 U.S.C. § 1014 provides, "Whoever knowingly makes any false statement or report . . . for the purpose of influencing in any way the action of . . . any institution the accounts of which are insured by the [FDIC] . . . shall be fined not more than $1,000,000 or imprisoned not more than 30 years, or both."

17. SEC Form 8-K Item 5.05(b).

18. SEC Reg. S-K Item 303.

19. AU 341 ("going concern"); AU-C 706 ("emphasis of matter"), https//www.aicpa.org.

20. "Up the ladder" reporting requirements: ABA Model Rule 1.13; *In re* Carter & Johnson, Exchange Act Release No. 17,597; SEC Rules pt. 205.3.

21. *In re Smurfit-Stone*, 2011 WL 2028076.

22. *Paramount v. QVC*, 637 A.2d 34.

23. For example, *Shenker*, 983 A.2d 408. *But see In re ShopKo*, No. 05-cv-677.

24. Deal protections are provisions in a merger agreement that pertain to how the company being acquired behaves in the period between announcing the definitive agreement and when the shareholders vote or tender their shares—a period that can be as short as thirty days and as long as ninety. They typically include a "no shop" (with a "fiduciary out" to allow for conversations with unsolicited parties) and a "breakup fee" of 2 percent to 4 percent of the value of the deal (to be paid to the first bidder if it is "topped" and the deal goes to the "interloper"). Another typical provision is a "right to match" (meaning that the first bidder need not top the interloper to win. While the right to match might be thought to have a chilling effect (somewhat like a right of first refusal), in practice it does not seem to work that way. When a target company has significant shareholders, a bidder may request a "support agreement" of varying degrees of aggressiveness. There other forms of deal protections as well. The key is that the whole set cannot be deemed to be preclusive.

25. C & J Energy Servs., Inc. v. City of Miami, 107 A.3d 1049 (Del. 2014).

26. *Citron*, 569 A.2d at 66.

27. *In re* Dollar Thrifty S'holder Litig., 14 A.3d 573, 602 (Del. Ch. 2010).

28. *Basic v. Levinson*, 485 U.S. at 239.

29. *In re* Carnation Co., [1984–1985 Transfer Binder] Fed. Sec. L. Rep. (CCH) ¶ 83,801 (July 8, 1985), Exchange Act Release No. 22214, 33 SEC Docket (CCH) 874 (July 8, 1985).

30. *Arnold*, 650 A.2d at 1277, 1280.

31. See RBC Capital Markets v. Jervis, 129 A.3d 816 (the *Rural Metro* case).

32. *In re* Toys "R" Us, Inc. S'holder Litig., 877 A.2d 975, 1004 n.43 (Del. Ch. 2005).

33. Fox v. CDX Holdings, Inc., C.A. No. 8031-VCL, 2015 WL 4571398 (Del. Ch. July 28, 2015).

34. Items 4(c) and 4(d) of the Hart-Scott-Rodino premerger notification form (https://www.ftc.gov/enforcement/premerger-notification-program/form-instructions) requires the filing of "documents prepared by or for officers or directors used to evaluate or analyze the acquisition."

35. Joann S. Lublin, Dan Fitzpatrick, & Rebecca Smith, *Behind Duke's CEO-for-a-Day*, Wall St. J. (July 6, 2012), https://www.wsj.com/articles/SB1000142405270230 3684004577509223109488332.

36. Scott J. Davis, *Protecting Directors When Firms Fail Post-Merger*, HLSCG (Mar. 1, 2012), https://corpgov.law.harvard.edu/2012/03/01/protecting-directors -when-firms-fail-post-merger.

37. Cookie-jar reserves are overly generous accounting reserves established at the time of a merger or restructuring. They can be reversed in subsequent periods to bolster reported financial results. See Walter Schuetze, Chief Accountant, SEC Division of Enforcement, Remarks at Northwestern Law Garrett Institute (Apr. 22, 1999).

38. Gary Klein, *Performing a Project Premortem*, HARV. BUS. REV. (Sept. 2007), https://hbr.org/2007/09/performing-a-project-premortem.

Chapter Nine

1. Anupreeta Das, *Inside the Breakup of the Pritzker Empire*, WALL ST. J. (Nov. 26, 2013), https://www.wsj.com/articles/no-headline-available-1385421431.

2. DGCL § 122(17).

3. See Thomas, *supra* note 15 in chap. 1; *Why the Decline*, *supra* note 16 in chap. 1; Wursthorn & Zuckerman, *supra* note 17 in chap. 1.

4. *Expanding the On-Ramp: Recommendations to Help More Companies Go and Stay Public*, SIFMA (Apr. 26, 2018), https://www.sifma.org/resources/submissions/expanding-the-on-ramp-recommendations-to-help-more-companies-go-and-stay-public/.

5. Christopher Mims, *The Age of Tech Superheroes Must End*, WALL ST. J. (June 7, 2018), https://www.wsj.com/articles/the-age-of-tech-superheroes-must-end-1528387420.

6. Complaint & Demand for Jury Trial at ¶ 19, Elton v. Musk, No. 2018-0749 (Del. Ch. Oct. 17, 2018).

7. 805 Ill. Comp. Stat. 105/108.70(a) (2018).

8. Cindy M. Lott et al., *State Regulation and Enforcement in the Charitable Sector*, URBAN INST. (Sept. 2016), https://www.urban.org/sites/default/files/publication/84161/2000925-State-Regulation-and-Enforcement-in-the-Charitable-Sector.pdf.

9. Barbara Clemenson & R.D. Sellers, *Hull House: An Autopsy of Not-for-Profit Financial Accountability*, 31 J. ACCT. EDUC. 252 (2013).

10. Joseph E. Bachelder, *New York Courts Dismiss "Grasso" Compensation Case*, HLSCG (Aug. 28, 2008), https://corpgov.law.harvard.edu/2008/08/28/new-york-courts-dismiss-grasso-compensation-case.

11. I.R.C. §§ 4960 & 4999 (2017).

12. I.R.C. § 501(c) (2017).

13. *Governance and Related Topics—501(c)(3) Organizations*, INTERNAL REVENUE SERVICE (Feb. 4, 2008), https://www.irs.gov/pub/irs-tege/governance_practices.pdf. See also Sara Hall Ingram, Commissioner, Tax Exempt & Gov't Entities, Internal Revenue Service, Remarks at Georgetown University Law Center Continuing Legal Education Program: Nonprofit Governance—The View from the IRS (June 23, 2009).

14. John Woolfolk, *Silicon Valley Community Foundation Puts Founding CEO On Leave*, MERCURY NEWS (Apr. 26, 2018), https://www.mercurynews.com/2018/04/26/silicon-valley-community-foundation-puts-founding-ceo-on-leave.

15. Glenn Sulmasy, *Executive Power: The Last Thirty Years*, 30 U. PA. J. INT'L L. 1355 (2008–09); Curtis A. Bradley & Trevor W. Morrison, *Presidential Power, Historical Practice, and Legal Constraint*, 113 COLUM. L. REV. 1097 (2013).

Chapter Ten

1. Lindsay Fortado, *Why Activists Are Cheerleaders for Corporate Social Responsibility*, FIN. TIMES (Dec. 26, 2017), https://www.ft.com/content/6f9dc2cc-e512–11e7–97e2–916d4fbac0da.

2. The Center for Political Accountability, with the Zicklin Center for Business Ethics Research at the Wharton School, University of Pennsylvania, publishes the annual CPA-Zicklin Index, which benchmarks S&P 500 companies for "transparency and accountability practices," noting that "board oversight is a vital component of accountability."

3. Exchange Act Rule 14a-8, 17 C.F.R. § 240.14a-8 (2018).

4. On December 1, 2014, the SEC granted no-action relief to Whole Foods, effectively allowing the company to exclude a shareholder proposal. That decision was reversed on January 16, 2015. At issue was the provision that allows exclusion of shareholder proposals that directly conflict with a management proposal.

5. ISS Guidelines § 1, Board of Directors/Responsiveness. Under that guideline, ISS may recommend against individual directors or the entire board if "the board failed to act on a shareholder proposal that received the support of a majority of the shares cast in the previous year."

6. For example, Keith Meister started Corvex after leaving Icahn and Mick McGuire started Marcato after leaving Ackman's Pershing Square.

7. Ronald Orol, *It's Over: Icahn Beats Ackman in Battle Over Herbalife*, THESTREET (Feb. 28, 2018), https://www.thestreet.com/story/14505289/1/it-s-over-icahn-beats-ackman-in-battle-over-herbalife.html.

8. A "wolf pack" is the term used when a number of hedge funds with activist tendencies appear on a company's shareholder list. They try to avoid the kind of formal agreement among themselves that would constitute the formation of a "group" for SEC purposes—in which case, they would be required to file a joint 13D and their shares would be aggregated for purposes of determining whether a poison pill had been triggered. Drafting a poison pill to be triggered by, and thus deter, something short of a "group" runs a risk of being held to be ineffective because of vagueness. Some have tried "acting in concert," which is at least more definitive than "conscious

parallelism." Perhaps the first time the term "wolf pack" was used by a judge in an opinion was the Sotheby's poison-pill case. Third Point LLC v. Ruprecht, C.A. No. 9469-VCP, 2014 WL 1922029 (Del. Ch. May 2, 2014). The company became aware that three funds—Trian, Marcato, and Third Point—had taken positions in its stock, with Third Point taking the lead in interactions with the company. Among the factors the board considered in adopting the pill, and identified by the Court, was that "it was not uncommon for activist hedge funds to form a . . . 'wolfpack.'"

9. In 2016, ValueAct paid a record fine of $11 million. It claimed to be a passive investor relying on the "solely for investment" exemption while at the same time trying to influence the proposed merger of Halliburton and Baker Hughes. See Press Release, Dep't of Justice, Justice Department Obtains Record Fine and Injunctive Relief against Activist Investor for Violating Premerger Notification Requirements (July 12, 2016), https://www.justice.gov/opa/pr/justice-department-obtains-record-fine-and -injunctive-relief-against-activist-investor.

10. SEC Press Release No. 2015-47, Corporate Insiders Charged for Failing to Update Disclosures Involving "Going Private" Transactions (Mar. 13, 2015), https://www.sec.gov/news/pressrelease/2015–47.html (relating to orders in three enforcement proceedings).

11. In a proxy contest mounted by Ader Investment Management against International Game Technologies in 2013, one of Ader's candidates was a former CEO of IGT. *IGT: Former CEO Who Wants Board Seat Enjoyed "Old School" Perks*, REUTERS, Feb. 1, 2013.

12. In 2014 Starboard Value, with an 8.8 percent stake, succeeded in ousting the entire board of Darden Restaurants, the owner of Olive Garden. That unusual victory was attributed to a failure by the board to agree to take a shareholder vote on a proposed sale of another restaurant chain, Red Lobster. Christopher Boyd & Lisa Baertlein, *Darden Activist Ousts Olive Garden Owner's Full Board*, REUTERS, Oct. 10, 2014. In 2018 Starboard took aim at the entire Newell Brands board. Siddharth Cavale, *Newell, Starboard End Proxy Fight with Icahn's Backing*, REUTERS (Apr. 23, 2018), https://www.reuters.com/article/us-newell-brands-inc-starboard/newell-starboard -end-proxy-fight-with-icahns-backing-idUSKBN1HU1MP.

13. See the ISS report on the Ader Investment Management proxy contest with IGT.

14. A universal proxy is a proxy card in which all candidates (regardless of whether nominated by the board or a dissident) are listed. A rule to institute universal prices was proposed by the SEC in 2016. Exchange Act Release No. 79,164, 81 Fed. Reg. 79,122 (Nov. 10, 2016) (to be codified at 17 C.F.R. pt. 240).

15. DGCL § 211(c).

16. In late 2014, BONY Mellon settled with Trian, Nelson Peltz's activist fund, and gave a board seat to one of the fund's founding partners. In 2015 Marcato took a

position and campaigned for changes (including of the CEO). Trian disagreed and the CEO remained in place for two more years.

17. *In re* Icahn Partners LP v. Amylin Pharmaceuticals, Inc., C.A. No. 7404-VCN, 2012 WL 1526814 (Del. Ch. Apr. 20, 2012).

18. In 2018 Elaine Wynn, the largest single shareholder of Wynn Resorts, engaged in a successful withhold campaign against one of the directors who was closely associated with the disgraced former CEO, Steve Wynn, who was forced out of the company for sexual misconduct. She succeeded in obtaining the support of the three main proxy advisory firms, and the targeted director withdrew as a candidate two days before the annual meeting. At the same time, another of the Steve Wynn legacy directors, who was not targeted because the Wynn board was still staggered and he was not up for election, nevertheless resigned. My firm represented Ms. Wynn.

Chapter Eleven

1. Steven Davidoff Solomon, *With Fewer Barbarians at the Gate, Companies Face a New Pressure*, N.Y. Times: Dealbook (July 30, 2013), https://dealbook.nytimes .com/2013/07/30/with-fewer-barbarians-at-the-gate-companies-face-new-pressure /?mtrref=www.google.com&gwh=51B99CB5574E7588ECA7C1D5FED55C66& gwt=pay.

2. Air Prods. & Chems., Inc. v. Airgas, Inc., 16 A.3d 48 (Del. Ch. 2011).

3. Frick, *supra* note 4 in the introduction.

4. *Capitalism's Unlikely Heroes*, *supra* note 4 in the introduction.

5. Jeff Gramm, *Dear Chairman: Boardroom Battles and the Rise of Shareholder Activism* xv (2015).

6. Steven Davidoff Solomon, *General Motors' Stock Buyback Follows a Worrying Trend*, N.Y. Times: Dealbook (Mar. 17, 2015), https://www.nytimes.com/2015 /03/18/business/dealbook/general-motors-stock-buyback-follows-a-worrying-trend .html.

7. *In re* KKR Fin. Holdings LLC S'holder Litig., 101 A.3d 980 (Del. Ch. 2014).

8. Leo E. Strine Jr., *One Fundamental Corporate Governance Question We Face: Can Corporations Be Managed for the Long Term Unless Their Powerful Electorates Also Act and Think Long Term?*, 66 Bus. Law. 1, 8–9 (2010).

9. Peter F. Drucker, *Concept of the Corporation* (1946), quoted in Louis Hyman, *Temp: How American Work, American Business, and the American Dream Became Temporary* 49 (2018).

10. Dominic Barton et al., *Measuring the Economic Impact of Short-Termism*, McKinsey Global Institute (Feb. 2017).

11. Dominic Barton, *Capitalism for the Long Term*, Harv. Bus. Rev. (July 1, 2014), https://hbr.org/2014/07/capitalism-for-the-long-term; Press Release, Aspen Inst.

Am. Prosperity Project, A Framework for Fixing Our System of Long-Term Investment: Business Leaders Advance American Prosperity Project (Dec. 19, 2016), https://www.aspeninstitute.org/news/press-release/framework-fixing-system-long -term-investment-business-leaders-advance-american-prosperity-project/.

12. Malcolm S. Salter, *How Short-Termism Invites Corruption . . . and What to Do about It* (Harv. Bus. Sch. Working Paper No. 12-094, 2012).

13. SEC Press Release No. 2013-121, SEC Announces Enforcement Initiatives to Combat Financial Reporting and Microcap Fraud and Enhance Risk Analysis (July 2, 2013), https://www.sec.gov/news/press-release/2013-2013-121htm.

14. John C. Coffee Jr. & Darius Palia, *The Wolf at the Door: The Impact of Hedge Fund Activism on Corporate Governance*, 1 ANNALS OF CORP. GOVERNANCE 1, 57–58 (2016).

15. Strine, *supra* note 8 in chapter 11, at 10, 12.

16. Jamie Dimon & Warren E. Buffett, Opinion, *Short-Termism Is Harming the Economy*, WALL ST. J., June 7, 2018, at A17.

17. Mark J. Roe, *Corporate Short-Termism—In the Boardroom and in the Courtroom*, 68 BUS. LAW. 977 (2013).

18. Martin Lipton & Jay W. Lorsch, *A Modest Proposal for Improved Corporate Governance*, 48 BUS. LAW. 59 (1992), calling for "quinquenniel" (every five years) elections of directors.

19. Roe, *supra* note 17 in chap. 11.

20. Crown Emak Partners, LLC v. Kurz, 992 A.2d 377 (Del. 2010).

21. Henry T. C. Hu & Bernard Black, *The New Vote Buying: Empty Voting and Hidden (Morphable) Ownership*, 79 S. CAL. L. REV. 811 (2006).

22. Concept Release on the U.S. Proxy System, 75 Fed. Reg. 42,982.

23. *Basic v. Levinson*, 485 U.S. 224.

24. The chief investment officer of Fidelity, Peter Lynch, was a director of Morrison Knudsen from 1988 to the time the company filed for bankruptcy in 1996. The failure of the company has been blamed on a strategic expansion of its rail business beginning in 1990, while Lynch was a director. See Diana B. Henriques, *A Wizard Caught in Two Storms*, N.Y. TIMES (Mar. 10, 1995), https://www.nytimes.com/1995/03/10 /business/a-wizard-caught-in-two-storms.html, and John Greenwald, *The Wreck of Morrison Knudsen*, TIME, Apr. 3, 1995, at 52. The hedge fund Och-Ziff struggled in executing its CEO succession. See Gregory Zuckerman & Rob Copeland, *Founder and Protégé Clash at Hedge Fund Giant*, WALL ST. J., Jan. 24, 2018, at A1.

Chapter Twelve

1. John W. Gardner, *On Leadership* 2 (1st paperback ed. 1990).

2. *Id.* at 4.

3. *Id.* at 51.

4. Daniel Goleman, *Leadership That Gets Results*, HARV. BUS. REV. (Mar.–Apr. 2000), https://hbr.org/2000/03/leadership-that-gets-results.

5. A quip by my friend and Pulitzer Prize–winning journalist, the late Jack Fuller.

6. John D. Stoll, *Why CEOs Shouldn't Hang Around Too Long*, WALL ST. J., Oct. 6–7, 2018, at B6.

7. Report by Equilar, cited in John D. Stoll, *Pepsi's Indra Nooyi Proved the Power of Stability*, WALL ST. J. (Aug. 9, 2018), https://www.wsj.com/articles/how-should -pepsis-indra-nooyi-be-graded-1533819601.

8. The regular column in the *New York Times* titled "Corner Office" makes for interesting and occasionally illuminating reading. A compilation of those columns can be found in Adam Bryant, *The Corner Office: Indispensable and Unexpected Lessons from CEOs on How to Lead and Succeed* (2012).

9. Gardner, *supra* note 1 in chap. 12, at 23.

10. Gillian Tett, *Silos and Silences: Why So Few People Spotted the Problems in Complex Credit and What That Implies for the Future*, 14 FIN. STABILITY REV. 121 (2010).

11. Robert M. Gates, *A Passion for Leadership: Lessons on Change and Reform from Fifty Years of Public Service* (2016).

12. Christina Ingersoll, Richard M. Locke, & Cate Reavis, *BP and the Deepwater Horizon Disaster of 2010* (MIT Sloan Mgmt., Case Study No. 10-110, 2012).

13. Matt Murphy, *The Man Who Fixed Microsoft*, WALL ST. J., Feb. 2–3, 2019, at B4.

14. Dwight D. Eisenhower, quoted in David Brooks, *The Road to Character* (2015).

15. John Simons, *Activists Erode CEOs' Power*, WALL ST. J., Dec. 19, 2017, at 12.

Chapter Thirteen

1. See Gardner, *supra* note 1 in chap. 12, at 33.

2. The saga of Harvey Weinstein is well known, but (sadly) far from the only example. One source (Vox) has counted "more than 250 powerful people [including CEOs] who have been the subject of . . . misconduct allegations" as of October 8, 2018, https://www.vox.com/a/sexual-harassment-assault-allegations-list.

3. John D. Stoll, *The Lesson from Intel: It's a New Era for CEOs*, WALL ST. J., June 23–24, 2018, at B1. In 2018, "more CEOs were dismissed for ethical lapses than for financial performance or board struggles." Karlsson et al., PwC CEO Success study, May 15, 2019, strategy-business.com.

4. Michael Sheetz, *KB Home Cuts CEO's Bonus as Punishment for His Profanity-Laced Rant at Neighbor Kathy Griffin*, CNBC (Sept. 21, 2017), https://www.cnbc .com/2017/09/21/kb-home-cuts-ceo-mezgers-bonus-for-rant-at-neighbor-kathy -griffin.html.

5. Michael Housman & Dylan Minor, *Toxic Workers* (Harv. Bus. Sch. Working Paper 16-057, 2015).

6. *Amalgamated Bank*, 132 A.3d at 781.

7. *Disney II*, 906 A.2d at 69–70.

8. Thomas A. Cole, *Advice for a First-Time Public Company CEO*, NACD DIREC-TORSHIP, Sept./Oct. 2015, at 58.

9. Chip Cutter, *A New CEO Might Be Lurking on the Board*, WALL ST. J., Oct. 9, 2018, at B5.

10. See discussion in chapter 5 section "Electing Candidates."

11. "His first move[] after getting [in] charge at . . . [any company] was to ingratiate himself with the board of directors." Andrew Beattie, *Corporate Kleptocracy at RJR Nabisco*, INVESTOPEDIA (Jan. 17, 2018), https://www.investopedia.com/articles /stocks/09/corporate-kleptocracy-rjr-nabisco.asp. See also Bryan Burrough & John Helyar, *Barbarians at the Gate: The Fall of RJR Nabisco* (1989).

12. Daisuke Wakabayashi et al., *Google Walkout: Employees Stage Protest over Handling of Sexual Harassment*, N.Y. TIMES (Nov. 1, 2018), https://www.nytimes .com/2018/11/01/technology/google-walkout-sexual-harassment.html.

Index

ABA. *See* American Bar Association (ABA)

Abacus transaction, 237n5

ability-to-pay analysis, 214

A/B structure. *See* dual-class structures

Accountable Capitalism Act, 14, 31–32

Ackman, Bill, 164, 244n6

acronyms, 217

activism, shareholder, xii, xiii; board and, 165, 168 (*see also* board of directors; *and specific types, topics*); buybacks and, 175; CEO and, 189 (*see also* chief executive officer [CEO]); CSR and (*see* corporate social responsibility [CSR]); disclosure and (*see* disclosure); effects of, 174; ESG activism, 12, 13, 162 (*see also* environmental, social, and governance [ESG]); expertise and, 178 (*see also specific types, topics*); financial activism, 165–72, 175; first call, 111; follow-on attacks, 170; governance activism, 161; hedge funds and, 27, 28, 30, 77, 161 (*see also* hedge funds); index funds and, 26, 161; information gap and, 178; mock attacks, 111; monitoring for, 110; personality types, 171; poison pills and (*see* poison pills); proxy contest, 167–71 (*see also* proxy access); RFA and, 27, 165; shareholders and, 159–78 (*see also* shareholders); short slate, xix, 168; short-termism, 176, 177; success rates, 172; takeovers, xii, 109–13, 166, 167 (*see also* takeovers); types of, 161; white paper, 111; wolf pack, 110. *See also specific types, topics*

ADA. *See* Americans with Disabilities Act (ADA)

Ader Investment Management, 245n11, 245n13

advance notice bylaws, 110, 170, 172

advisors. *See* expert opinion

agency costs, 3, 7

Air Products/Airgas case, 145, 173–74

Allen, William T., 10, 14, 16, 59, 69, 176

American Bar Association (ABA), 56, 232n3

American Law Institute (ALI), x, 23, 224

Americans with Disabilities Act (ADA), xv, 8

Amylin case, 172

Antitakeover Statute, 18–19, 166

appraisal cases, 72

arbitrage, 16, 24, 174

About the Author

THOMAS A. COLE is Senior Counsel and Chair Emeritus of the Executive Committee of Sidley Austin LLP. He joined the firm upon graduation from the University of Chicago Law School in 1975 and became a partner in 1981. He retired from the full-time practice of law at the end of 2016, but he continues to consult with colleagues and clients. As a partner, he served as Vice President—Law of Northwest Industries Inc. from 1981 to 1985. For fifteen years, until April 2013, he served as chair of the firm's Executive Committee, which exercises general authority over the affairs of the firm. Throughout his tenure in firm leadership (and afterward), he maintained a robust practice on behalf of clients.

Mr. Cole focuses his practice on public company mergers and acquisitions and corporate governance. He is consistently recognized by Chambers USA and Chambers Global, including in their most recent editions. In 2001, Mr. Cole was recognized by Chambers Global as one of the 26 U.S. lawyers included in its list "Global 100 Lawyers"— "lawyers who stand out from their colleagues and are recognized internationally." He was designated an M&A "Dealmaker of the Year" for 2007 by the *American Lawyer*. He was selected for BTI Consulting's "Client Service All-Star" team in 2008, 2011, and 2014. In 2010 and 2013, he was named to "The Directorship 100," the NACD's list of "the most influential people in the boardroom community." In 2015, he was named an "M&A and Antitrust Trailblazer" by the *National Law Journal*.

Mr. Cole's corporate governance assignments have included advising public company boards and their standing and special committees on a variety of subjects, including internal investigations, CEO succession, shareholder activism, and proxy contests. From 1993 to 1998, and beginning again in 2013, he has taught the seminar on corporate governance at the University of Chicago Law School. Mr. Cole taught the same seminar at Harvard Law School during the spring semester of 2015.

He has been involved in approximately sixty announced public company mergers, spinoffs, and takeover defenses.

Mr. Cole has been active in many civic, charitable, and professional organizations. He is currently a member of the Board of Trustees of the University of Chicago. He served as Chairman of the Boards of Northwestern Memorial Healthcare and Hospital. He is a former co-chair of the Tulane Corporate Law Institute and former chair of Northwestern's Garrett Corporate and Securities Law Institute. In recognition of his initiatives in promoting diversity in the legal profession, he received the inaugural Thurgood Marshall Legacy Award in 2015.

Mr. Cole and his wife, Constance, live in suburban Chicago. They are immensely proud of their four daughters, four sons-in-law, and six grandchildren.